Networked Information Technologies, Elections, and Politics

Networked Information Technologies, Elections, and Politics

Korea and the United States

by Jongwoo Han

LEXINGTON BOOKS

Lanham • Boulder • New York • Toronto • Plymouth, UK

Published by Lexington Books
A wholly owned subsidiary of The Rowman & Littlefield Publishing Group, Inc.
4501 Forbes Boulevard, Suite 200, Lanham, Maryland 20706
www.lexingtonbooks.com

Estover Road, Plymouth PL6 7PY, United Kingdom

British Library Cataloguing in Publication Information Available

Library of Congress Cataloging-in-Publication Data
Han, Jongwoo, 1962-
  Networked information technologies, elections, and politics : Korea and the United
States / by Jongwoo Han.
    p. cm.
  Includes bibliographical references and index.
  ISBN 978-0-7391-4628-6 (cloth) — ISBN 978-0-7391-4630-9 (electronic) ISBN
978-14985-6404-5 (pbk)
  1. Political participation—Technological innovations—Case studies. 2. Internet
in political campaigns—Case studies. 3. Youth—Political activity—Technological
innovations—Case studies. 4. Information technology—Political aspects—Case
studies. 5. Political participation—Technological innovations—Korea (South)
6. Political participation--Technological innovations--United States. 7. Internet in
political campaigns—Korea (South) 8. Internet in political campaigns—United States.
9. Youth—Political activity—Technological innovations—Korea (South) 10. Youth--
Political activity—Technological innovations—United States. I. Title.
  JF799.H35 2012
  323'.04202854678—dc23   2011039762

Contents

Acknowledgments

Two main schools of thoughts in studying political science diverge in their emphases either on changes of power or the relative stability of the existing system. This book is a product of the author's decade-long observations on the changes that have been occurring in both Korea's and the United States' elections, politics, and democratic movements that result from the paradigm shift in political discourse from industrial age mass media-based public sphere to new networked information technologies (NNITs)-based networked cyber sphere. Witnessing and comparing Korea's presidential election in 2002 and the United States' 2008 presidential wlection allowed me to think about the impact of NNITs in electoral politics and how previously apolitical young generations have interacted with their use of NNITs. Korea's beef crisis and President Obama's legislation battle to reform the U.S. health care system have also provided an unprecedented opportunity to observe one of a few major changes occurring in political system in the Information Age. This idea of writing a book on this topic originated from courses such as Politics in the Cyberage, Contemporary Issues in the Information Age, and Cyberactivism and Democracy in Asia that the author has taught since the early 21st century.

I have to mention my walking trails where I have been blessed with many insights on the consolidation of this book project. Walking and thinking along the beautiful Old Erie Canal Track and Green Lakes in Syracuse have helped shape specific contours of this book. My wife, Kyunghee Lee, a college classmate and lifetime companion and two beautiful daughters, Hyemin and Jeongyoon, were with me all the time along these trails. I can't imagine the completion of this book without these family rituals.

I have had to rely on numerous debates, data, edits, and other supporting materials to demonstrate the main topics of this book, which came from my colleagues, friends and experts in the related fields, especially the following: Seonmi Na, Hyumi Kim, Jean Koh, Jongseong Hwang, Sungju Cho, Stuart Thorson, Ryan McKean, Hyunjoon Chun, Eric Berlin, Nancy Downes, Youngseek Kim, and Sean Miskell. I also want to thank Joseph Parry for his initial interest in this book prospect and Lenore Lautigar for her follow-through for a final publication. Two prestigious journals, the *Journal of Information Technology & Politics* and the *Australian Journal of International Affairs* graciously granted me to develop on two published articles on Korean presidential election and Korea's beef crisis for the second and third chapters of this book, respectively.

However, this book could have been impossible without my mother Sungja Cho whose life-long prayer and dedication of her love and support for what I am now. No word can describe my thankfulness toward her and I want to dedicate this book to my mom.

Jongwoo Han
August 2011

List of Tables, Figures, and Diagrams

Tables

Figures

Diagrams

Chapter 1

New Experimentation

Cyberspace, the Networked Public Sphere and the Youth in the United States and South Korea

A NEW EXPERIMENTATION

Never have changes in macro-political systems and structures come overnight—they have arisen gradually out of a long history of human interactions. The evolution of human society is divided into five stages, in Karl Marx's theory on historical materialism (1977), each with its own mode of production characterized by unique productive forces (economic base) and relations of production (e.g., the legal and political systems, institutions, and ideologies that support the major class system): primitive community, slave state, feudalism, capitalism, and communism via socialism.[1] Although each stage evolves out of the stage before, the transition from stage to stage is not understood in terms of evolutionary trajectories; rather, it is viewed as a paradigmatic shift that brings unique new productive forces (economy) and relations of production (political system). According to Marx, these transitions cannot be achieved within a short timeframe, but have always started with some new type of experimentation in terms of new productive forces that have brought about changes in the relations of production. According to this materialistic view of such historical changes in human society, the contemporary political institution of Industrial Age democracy is rooted in a production system that, though new, is based on the Industrial Revolution (1760–1840). In the mid-nineteenth century, the voluntary civic engagement of people from all classes, which the French philosopher Tocqueville observed in local communities throughout the United States, was part of a political experimentation based on capitalism. At the core of that experimentation was face-to-face interaction.

In our times, a century later, a prominent computer scientist is claiming that another new experimentation has begun, and this time it is being caused

1

by new information processing (computer) and transmission (network) technologies. Speaking of the impact of the Internet on human interaction, Murray Turoff (1997, 39), one of the architects of the Advanced Research Project Agency Network (ARPANET), which later became the Internet, argues that "We may now create, experiment, and use social systems that are potentially very different from those of the past. And we may do so rather quickly." Not fully agreeing with Turoff's claim for quick changes in our society and politics out of the Internet, I recognize the changes and impacts that these new computing and network technologies are gradually bringing into our lives. It is the aim of this book to explain the ways in which the use of new networked information technologies (NNITs)[2] has changed in the twenty-first century politics and society; to examine the nature of the impacts of NNIT-based experimentation upon the Industrial Age political system of democracy; and to gain insight into the implications of this new experimentation for democracy in the Information Age.

THE OLD EXPERIMENTATION IN AMERICA

In the mid-nineteenth century, when the French historian and philosopher Alexis Tocqueville visited America, he found that Americans were experimenting with a new type of political community wherein citizens actively participated in community affairs by forming and taking part in various volunteer associations. To Tocqueville, who was coming from a Europe still strongly influenced by the legacy of the Ancient Regime, such a phenomenon, which later came to be known as "local grass-roots democracy," seemed "exceptional" (Lipset 1996, 18) and represented a new social and political type of experimentation. This experimentation was also exceptional in that America was a blank canvas, with least traces of the old European system, ready to be painted with new tones from the palette of associational grass-roots local democracy.

The most important byproduct of the experimentation was social capital, a critical factor to the success of democracy and economic development (Fukuyama 1995; Putnam 2000; Baron, et al. 2000). Social capital can be defined as "multiple human resources networks, whether actual or potential, with certain characteristics of shared norms, values, attitudes, and trust built through prior collective action that can be utilized for future social and political mobilization" (Han 2007, 59). In the nineteenth and twentieth centuries, face-to-face local volunteerism and social capital became the backdrop of this new political experimentation in American democracy that centered on five credos: liberty, egalitarianism, individualism, populism, and *laissez-faire* (Lipset 1996; Putnam 2000).

Another important factor effecting democracy during the Industrial Age was the mass-media-based public sphere. Despite its contribution to expanding the scope of public discourse beyond that of the feudal era, the public sphere of the Industrial Age was lopsided in terms of communication; public discourse was subject to manipulation by gatekeepers in the mass media. Public discourse in this mass media-based public sphere, together with the thick social capital that arose from such abundant face-to-face interaction, constituted the backbone of democracy in the early Industrial Age.

It was a century ago that this experiment of creating volunteer-based new political communities through many new associations, such as 4-H and Rotary Clubs, first became firmly rooted in America; and today, a new kind of socio/political experimentation is on its way toward full realization. By comparing these two political experiments, separated by a century, we can notice many significant differences and similarities. One of the most striking contrasts between the local, face-to-face communities of nineteenth- and twentieth-century America and the global, virtual community of twenty-first century America stems from the way in which individuals interact and build community. Whereas the social capital and public sphere that this American experimentation started in the late nineteenth century was based on a one-way mass media and a form of trust accumulated through face-to-face interactions in local communities, contemporary society is now experiencing a new mode of networked public sphere (NPS) and online interactions in the cyber community that also entails conventional offline contact.

But the question remains as to whether NNIT-based, virtual interactions can unite community members as cohesively as the face-to-face American social capital that played such an instrumental role in creating grass-roots democracy. Does this NNIT-based new experimentation of the networked public sphere differ substantially from that of the Industrial Age mass media? Such cohesive political community is commonly purported to be *real* and genuine in the sense that members of a local community mostly know each other in a physical sense, whereas interactions in the cyber community are *virtual* and do not rely upon physical acquaintance (Woolgar 2002). Whereas, in the old American experimentation, a limited number of people participated within the limited geographical boundaries of their local community, nowadays, in the new experimentation, cyber communities can be formed without such spatial and temporal limitations. Thus, this new technology raises a series of significant questions. Can trust and social capital be built through virtual interaction in cyberspace? Are there certain aspects of virtual interaction that are real? Is virtual interaction sustainable? Who are the new players in the networked public sphere? How do they build political consciousness? And is it accurate to consider face-to-face interaction more real than virtual interaction?

THE NEW EXPERIMENTATION: CYBERSPACE, THE NETWORKED PUBLIC SPHERE, SOCIAL CAPITAL, AND THE YOUTH

Revolutionary developments of digital information technologies have resulted in the creation of cyberspace, which is defined by a suite of protocols—comprised of both hardware and software—that are open and nonproprietary (Lessig 1999, 27). Therefore, in order to comprehend how cyberspace works, we must understand how code (i.e., computing and networking software and hardware, Transmission Control Protocol and Internet Protocol (TCP/IP), and other rules in the cyber communities) regulates the flow of information. The code is the law by which cyberspace operates (Lessig 1999, 12) and which protects cyberspace from the established power of gatekeepers; this is also what makes it so attractive to new players. Hiltz and Turoff (1978: 473) foretold the impact of this new computer network system upon our society. Their vision was contrary to that of conventional computer and network scientists emphasizing the changes in social and human dimensions in our social and political systems:

> A CCS [Computer Conferencing System] as a computer-linked human network becomes an organic, growing thing, almost with a life and vitality of its own. Its current users feel that they cannot foresee its ultimate shape and capabilities; that the current stems are indeed just the embryo, the promise of growth and diversification to come. These systems can be seen as social systems, formed and shaped by their members, with the resultant structure subsequently influencing the human relationships within it; or as an instance of people-computer symbiosis that grows and changes as its members find new ways to use it to enable them to work together across space and time.

Before cyberspace had fully penetrated into our daily lives, many were agitated about the unknown nature of this newly emerging space in virtuality. As its adoption became increasingly widespread, many questions arose. Will cyberspace promise privacy and universal access? Will it preserve a space for free speech? Will it facilitate free and open trade? Will it strengthen social capital or reduce face-to-face interactions among network users? Will it affect politics and elections? And, ultimately, will it contribute to democracy or have negative impacts?

Answering these questions will require us to understand the nature of a new experimentation occurring in cyberspace by analyzing who will be the main players in this new networked public sphere, how these new actors will interact with others, and what actions they will take. In theory, the cyberspace made up of "code" could be neutral to any social actor. However, when this cyberspace is occupied and activated, it will most certainly shift the conventional power structure and dynamics because the new experimentation will ultimately generate new social and human relationships among social and political actors and organizations, and institutions. Hiltz and Turoff (1978: 481–482) argue that "computerized conferencing can serve to substitute electronic mobility for physical mobility, and permit a person to exchange communications on a fairly deep and meaningful level with many different interest-oriented groups. At the same time, there is likely to be considerable connectedness among the various groups, with many overlapping memberships" by forming "the common social interaction or work space for bringing persons together, wherever they are. At the same time, the cross-cutting nature of memberships in groups on a CC network would tend to prevent the isolation and segmentation that occur in modern societies when extreme specialization becomes the basis for the organization of work and play."

Less than two decades have passed since the World Wide Web began entering our lives in 1995, and although it has not been long enough to generalize any conclusions about the impacts of NNITs, some of these questions are already being answered. Now that so many people have daily access to the Net for information searching and sharing, communications, economic transactions and political discourse, enough data has begun to accumulate to offer some possible answers. The central objective of this book is to identify and explain the significant changes that interactions in cyberspace are currently bringing to the power structure that was originally built through old modes of human interactions through the mass media of the Industrial Age. More specifically, this book raises the question of whether cyberactivism is affecting the political institutions and established power structure in the public sphere as well as the dominant political forces.

One of the most important answers, this book claims, can be found in the emergence of the networked public sphere. The NPS, composed of a seamless web of analog and digital, wired and wireless technologies, has enabled NNIT-users to transcend the temporal and spatial limitations of the old American experimentation of the Industrial Age public sphere. This is mainly because information technology, which enables "a form of spontaneous order created through the interactions of decentralized actors" (Fukuyama 1995, 197), challenges traditional forms of political and corporate governance and alters conventional relationships among individuals, organizations and states. Following Daniel Bell's groundbreaking 1976 work, *The Coming of Post-Industrial Society*, scholars such as Webster (1995), Castells (1996, 1997), Trippi (2004) and Benkler (2006) predicted not only the rise of the network society, originating from the information technology revolution, but also the resulting fundamental transformation of the political structure.[3]

Benkler (2006) argues that this expanded NPS creates a unique space for discourse among peers, enabling them to bypass the gate-keeping forces of established mass media, build consensus for a national agenda, and mobilize forces to support agendas of their own. Examples of expanded NPS abound. Social network sites (SNSs) such as Facebook, MySpace and YouTube, and micro-blogging mediums like Twitter, among new online social media, are defined as Web-based services that enable users to "construct a public or semi-public profile," "articulate a list of other users," and/or "view and traverse their list of connections and those made by others within the system" (Boyd and Ellison 2007, 2). Through features such as these, new online social media is extending the trusted sources of news and information beyond the limits of established news and media as was clearly illustrated in the success of Barack Obama's presidential campaign: "With new media, people were more likely to learn about the Obama campaign from people they knew and trusted, who, theory informs us, are more influential in shaping beliefs, attitudes, and behavior" (Abroms and Lefebvre, 2009, p.419).

One example of a virtual political community was a cyber community called "My Barack Obama" (MyBO). This password-protected website allowed people to form a community as registered members and engage in support of their candidate of choice, Barack Obama. Through MyBO, supporters communicated with fellow members, planned supporting events, shared information and emotions, raised contributions and mobilized neighbors. By the end of the 2008 presidential election, MyBO had 1.5 million registered Web volunteers who had organized over 100,000 events (Abroms and Lefebvre 2009, 416). As John Guare's 1990 play *Six Degrees of Separation* aptly illustrates, people are more interconnected than they realize, both physically and virtually, which differs astoundingly from the Middle Ages, when the dialect spoken in one community was all but incomprehensible fifty miles away: "A group of fourteenth-century London merchants shipwrecked on the north coast of England were jailed as foreign spies" (Crowley 1999, 71). And similarly, in the fifteenth century, Crowley describes how "it took eighteen months for the news of Joan of Arc's death to reach Constantinople" (1999, 73). The convergence of digital social networks empowers those who were once isolated—young American Internet users—and enhances their potential to interconnect in cyberspace, as well as face-to-face, and become involved in elections and politics in general. Kleinberg (2008, 66) aptly describes the dynamics of cyber interactions: "At the scales of tens of millions of individuals and minute-by-minute time granularity, we can replay and watch the ways in which people seek out connections and form friendships on a site like Facebook or how they coordinate with each other and engage in creative expression on sites like Wikipedia and Flickr." A few unexpected links in one of these new online social media that act like shortcuts through the network can open up vast opportunities to connect previously disparate individuals. Since the symbolic affiliations and identity pointed out by Minkoff and Smith are currently growing in the virtual cyber community, the limited nature of imagined loyalty can be complemented by shrinking degrees of separation in the Information Age.

Hiltz and Turoff (1978: 482) predicted the arrival of a community like "My Barack Obama," in the 1970s, as well as John Guare's *Six Degrees of Separation* and community-based web portals in the following foresight:

> Such a scenario for the emergence of new forms of social and occupational and economic relationships depends on the assumption that the written word as it appears on one's terminal can indeed become the basis for forming and maintaining "electronic group life." That it is possible for people to "get to know one another" through their computer, to develop emotional and social ties, and to develop norms and rituals, has been illustrated in Chapters. Of course, groups formed and sustained by a CCSA need not use only that means of communication; there could be telephone calls, and face-to-face meetings or video conference or Picturephone call to supplement the computer-mediated ties.

It is also important to understand, before delving any deeper, who the major players are in this emerging NPS. Young generations in their twenties and thirties were born at a time when this cyberspace had a much stronger presence than ever before. For those born in the early- and mid-twentieth century, face-to-face contact had been the norm for socio-economic, cultural and political interactions; however, the SNSs and other online social networking mediums that are most popular among young generations have recently helped reverse the apolitical orientation of the youth and their general indifference toward politics, elections and public discourse (Han2010; Smith and Rainie 2008; Ellison, et al. 2007; Huysman and Wulf 2004; Min 2007; Prell 2003; Shklovski, et al. 2004; Williams 2006; Zhao 2006).

The Golden Age of the World War II generation's civic-mindedness began to wane by the time of the Baby Boomer generation, bringing about civic malaise and significant changes in voter turnout rates and levels of trust in neighbors (Putnam 2000, 25–6). This collapse of social capital and the waning of civic-mindedness, is attributed by Putnam to "generational" or "inter-cohort" change, as opposed to "individual change" (2000, 34); however, in his analysis of the capability of technology to incite generational change, Putnam wavers:

> Most social change involves both individual and generational processes. The use of new technology, like the telephone or the Internet, illustrates this sort of

mixture. When the innovation is introduced, many people try out the new phone or the new Web browser. As individuals change their behavior, virtually none of the early growth in usage is attributable to generational change. (2000, 34)

Analyzing the elections in 2008, Owen (2009, 9) concludes that the campaigns' application of NNITs, such as "websites, blogs, video-sharing sites, social networking sites, and podcasts" brought forth two significant changes: it enabled candidates to bypass the gatekeepers of the conventional media and contact voters directly; and it increased the popularity of user-generated content and media. The main user of these NNITs is the youth, who had previously been blamed for lower voter turnout rates and the overall decline of social capital in the United States and South Korea. Nowadays, though, they are unique in that they tend to directly engage far more actively than older generations in the campaign process by communicating with supporters; making, sharing and distributing their own campaign promotion materials in the NPS of new social media; planning events to promote their choice of candidates; fundraising; and mobilizing for votes (Smith & Rainie, 2008). This phenomenon distinguishes them from the older generations, who are accustomed to more traditional election campaign methods. Although a longitudinal attitude and behavior survey would be required in order to generalize the claim that young generations' interactions in the NPS increased their voter turnout rate, this book attempts—by examining the 2002 presidential election[4] in Korea and the 2008 presidential election in the United States—to conceptualize the transformation of the youth in two of the world's most wired countries from apolitical and insignificant to progressively more engaged and influential through network activities, both in cyberspace and face-to-face interactions. An important question on this topic will be whether NNIT-activated new experimentation by mainly young generations will be a fleeting method of mobilization in politics and elections or if this phenomenon will have an enduring impact upon bonding and bridging among citizens, social capital, and the transformation of a previously apolitical and disinterested constituency.

The case studies of this book cover the first decade of the twenty-first century with two presidential elections in two most NNIT-advanced and-activated countries. Due to a short time span, this study's ability to make an argument on the long-term enduring impact of a new experimentation on the formation and expansion of social capital and political mobilization may be limited. Within this limited time span, the U.S. case seems to indicate consistent increases in voter turnout since 1996 presidential election and the ever increasing use and influence of NNITs on national political agendas, reflected in the use of social media like Twitter and Facebook during President

Obama's health care reform legislation battle. In the Korean case, the presidential election in 2007 does seem to contradict the 2002 presidential election outcome because conservative party candidate won the poll with the largest margin of victory. However, a careful examination of the 2007 election will reveal the reasons for seemingly dwindled power of cyber election campaign and for the shift of power from liberal to conservative political forces.

Even though the 2007 election in South Korea was an inverse of the 2002 election, a series of candle light demonstrations that seriously challenged the Lee Administration within the first 100 days of his administration does illustrate the enduring impact of the social capital cultivated by the series of democratic movements against the military dictatorship from the 1960s to 1980s and the NNIT-galvanized social movements and electoral campaigns in the early twenty-first century. Accordingly, chapter 3 on Korea's beef crisis serves as an example of how the social and political forces activated during the 2002 election campaign had continued in the political movement against the conservative right-wing president in 2008. In addition, the election on April 27, 2011 has demonstrated the power of online social media in the most recent mobilization of liberal and opposition constituency, which resulted in the complete collapse of the conservative ruling party candidates for the National Assembly and local governments. Chapter 2 will provide a comparative analysis of what happened in the 2007 presidential election and 2011 election, which will highlight the enduring power of this new experimentation with two important points: (1) NNIT-oriented politics can be activated for causes and candidates that span the political spectrum, and (2) the impact of NNITs will depend upon the characters of each election and candidates. In other words, a popular Republican candidate in the United States and a ruling party candidate in Korea can win the poll using NNITs.

DEMONSTRATION EFFECT

Civic and political engagement among younger generations has been awakened by a series of events that demonstrated their power to bring about change, and as a result, skepticism over the positive impact of NNITs upon social capital seems to have dwindled. Back in 2000, Putnam, for one, had voiced doubt that the younger generations' civic engagement would ever return to the levels seen during the anti-war and Civil Rights movements of the 1960s and '70s, implying that NNITs were unlikely to revitalize the American youth's civic engagement (2000, 170–1). By 2008, however, Putnam (2008, 37) recognized that the "truly phenomenal turnout, often three or four times greater than ever before measured" during the 2008 primaries and caucuses, had been due in part to the widespread use of NNITs. The predominance of digital social networking technology is consistent with the results of recent surveys, such as the Pew Internet and American Life Project (Smith and Rainie 2008), which confirmed that youths were being galvanized into participation through their use of NNITs. Consistent with these findings, many scholars (Ellison, et al. 2007; Huysman and Wulf 2004; Min 2007; Prell 2003; Shklovski, et al. 2004; Williams 2006; Zhao 2006) now see a positive association among the use of NNITs, the bonding of voters, and the expansion of social capital.

Considering that the central players in cyberspace are the youth, a key issue in the new experimentation is to explain how these previously disparate, indifferent and apolitical young people became not only involved and activated but also a formidable force in major political discourse and elections. The concept of a "demonstration effect" seems to be the best conceptual tool for analyzing how they have been co-opted into becoming concerned stakeholders in the politics of the Information Age. A demonstration effect occurs when, as a byproduct of some successful mobilizations and protests, many separate individuals realize what great political potential they could wield as a group, and how a successful protest could be reproduced. Often, a group of people or organizations learn of their potential influence from the success of previous demonstrations. Analyzing a series of protests, Cornell and Cohn (1995) and Minkoff (1997) offer an explanation as to what makes a successful protest: a cycle of successful protests generates demonstration effects (Cornell and Cohn 1995; Minkoff 1997), which incite other constituencies to activism (Minkoff 1997, 779) by raising consciousness, defining occasions for action, and guiding protestors in regard to successful tactics (Cornell and Cohn 1995, 369). In this book, the demonstration effect is examined in relation to the 2002 and 2008 presidential elections of Korea and the United States. For a demonstration effect to succeed, it must be preceded by an intermediate phase where a generation mobilizes around salient events. Successful mobilizations then lead to demonstration effects, whereby younger generations learn to utilize NNITs as tools for political action, come to form generational consciousness, and begin to recognize their own power within the political arena.

For example, in the case of Korea, the mobilization of younger generations involved an intermediate phase of collective action around smaller political or non-political events, such as the Utah Winter Olympics, the World Cup Soccer Games, and the anti-American candlelight demonstration, all leading up to the 2002 presidential election in Korea. Before this series of test-run mobilizations, which were based around international sports games and instigated national sentiments of patriotism that evolved into anti-Americanism and were a lynchpin in the Presidential Election in December 2002, there was a negative campaign for the General Election in 2000 where former college students (the 386 Generation) used the Internet technology to defeat corrupt members of the National Assembly. This defeat movement was the first negative election campaign on a large scale in Korea (such campaigns were illegal at that time) and served as a demonstration effect for Korean constituents including the younger generation on how Internet technology can bypass conventional party politics and legal jurisdiction and aggregate opinions and demands of voices not reflected in the conventional public sphere and national political discourse. Hiltz and Turoff's prediction was realized in this voter revolution in Korea by combining the power of cyberspace with conventional civic organizations and social capital cultivated by 386 Generations. Hiltz and Turoff (1978: 473) said:

> The fundamental effect of computerized conferencing, we believe, will be to produce new kinds of and more numerous social networks than ever before possible. Along with this will come massive shifts in the nature of the values and institutions that characterize the society. Hence we next consider some fundamental social impacts that we expect as a result of this innovation, including changes in values, social structure, and economic institutions; changes in sex roles, transportation, and ultimately the shape of urban areas themselves; and dangers, such as potential infringements on privacy, surveillance, and the use/abuse of "social engineering" through the new computer-telecommunications technologies. ."

Civic activism fueled a hot debate in Korean politics following the unveiling of a blacklist of "unfit candidates" for the upcoming April 13th General Election for the National Assembly in 2000. The Citizens' Council for Economic Justice (CCEJ, *Kyung-shil-lyun* in Korean), the nation's largest civic organization, released a list of 164 politicians. It was joined by another civic organization, the Citizens' Commission for a Fair Election in motivating citizen participation. Several web sites such as www.ngokorea.org, www.naksun.co.kr, and www.emocracy.co.kr were created to defeat the named political figures based on evidence of crimes such as corruption or embezzlement related to past elections, efforts to draw attention to candidates' political records such as involvement in past authoritarian regimes, votes against reforms, changes of party affiliation, and personal defects such as unethical behavior and vulgar or discriminatory statements. This movement was the first of its kind in that country's history.

With the Citizens' Coalition for the 2000 General Election's home page (www.ngokorea.org) recording 50,000 visitors since its opening, the Internet already made its mark as the most influential medium in contemporary

Korean politics. The list, which singled out reform-resistant lawmakers, exploiters of regional antagonism, and 'low-quality' politicians, included 128 members of the National Assembly, 42 percent of the incumbents, out of a total of 299 seats. In the end, 68 percent of those incumbents listed in the defeat movement website failed to maintain the seat in the National Assembly as an outcome of the election.

Further, the Citizens' Coalition for Economic Justice intended to file complaints from potential candidates who would be excluded from parties' official nomination and file cases charging constitutional violations against party leaders. Conventionally, the party nomination process had been obscured in back-room deals between party leaders and candidates. The old practices of the selection of party candidates were based more on personal relationships with party leaders or on the scale of funds contributed to political parties than on objective evaluations of candidates' qualifications and electoral popularity.

In contrast to advanced democratic countries, where civic groups such as Americans for Democratic Action (http://adaction.org) legally rate the activities of their representatives and other elected officials, the current Korean election law prohibits all except individuals and labor unions from engaging in political campaigns supporting specific candidates and makes such activities punishable by law. Reflecting the interests of incumbents, the Constitutional Court and the Central Election Management Commission upheld the current law on the grounds that it keeps elections fair. Activists argued that this 'election defeat movement' is fair because it makes relevant information available to voters and helps them make reasonable choices. Reacting to the denunciation of political institutions and politicians, and supported by the public, civic organizations launched a national campaign to revise the election law. On January 19, the twentieth day after the release of the blacklist, the ruling and opposition parties bowed to citizen activism and respectively promised to "refer to" or "respect" the blacklist in the nominating process for the April general election. Also, they cautiously suggested that the current election law needs to be revised to allow rating activities by civic organizations.

Prior to the election, Korea had drastically expanded its investment in information technology and information infrastructure. According to Alexa statistics (www.alexa.com), in the early twenty-first century, Korean Yahoo ranked second among the world's Internet companies in terms of access time. One-fourth of the total population, around 40 million, enjoyed Internet access. Fifty percent of Koreans used cellular phones. The impatient national character of Koreans was even believed to help Korea become one of the leading countries in the Information Age. As citizens were empowered by the wide deployment of information technology, government information policy reversed the traditional superiority of the state and political institutions over civil society and citizens. It was the power of information technology that created a virtual cyberspace that facilitated the swift formation of the alliance of over 300 civic organizations and enabled them to establish a political dialogue or "strategic conversation" across diverse communities. The power of anonymity in virtual space allowed such a negative political campaign to unfold for the first time in Korean election campaign history. With a more transparent political system, information on each politician becomes available, making the party nominating process more objective, and dismantling the absolute power of a handful of party leaders. The information society, thus, is beginning to erode existing political systems and ideology, bringing about the devolution of traditional political authority.

Virtual space may increasingly allow citizens to avoid the nation-state's conventional jurisdiction over political activities. The national government has no established legal authority to restrict the flow of information if the web site is opened overseas. Such a site is not subject to Korean election laws. This Korean case clearly indicates that the dispersed availability of information and communications technologies can be far more relevant than levels of income for predicting a nation's degree of democratization and must have served as a demonstration effect of the role of the younger generation's political participation during the 2002 test-run mobilizations.

This study also identifies a series of national events or agendas in U.S. politics that illustrate the awakening of the American youth's awareness about a national agenda and their participation in political discourse about social and political agendas as well. For example, one such series—the 9/11 terrorist attack in 2001; the Iraq War in 2003; the Howard Dean phenomenon and U.S. presidential election in 2004; the mid-term election in 2006; and the U.S. primaries and caucuses—led up to the presidential election in 2008. This presidential election fell on the heels of yet another series of national events—the running of three democratic candidates (Clinton, Edwards, Obama) in October 2007; Obama's Iowa win in January 2008; Clinton's New Hampshire win in January 2008; Clinton's remark on the Kennedy assassination; the Pastor Wright controversy; and Obama's speech on race. Each series of events serves as a battery of test-run mobilizations, illustrating how a young generation that was connected through NNITs and SNSs contributed, first, to the formation of social capital among themselves and, second, to the galvanization of young generations into political participation (i.e., voter turnout). These collective actions, in the Korean and American cases, demonstrate efficacy and compel younger generations to recognize their potential political power as well as the rewards that their participation and engagement can bring.

In general, the demonstration effect comprises the following five stages: (1) accumulation of attention around salient, non-political events, such as sports; (2) deliberations in the networked public sphere (NPS) as an alternative channel to industrial mass media; (3) formation of awareness of their own power in the NPS as individual actions aggregate in online and offline spaces and through the existing mass media; (4) consolidation of their power through test-run mobilizations when those salient non-political events become political; and (5) construction of generational orientation and consensus on contemporary political issues. The realization of their power in the new networked public sphere is mostly articulated in the first three stages, resulting in the formation of a generation of individuals who share a common social and political orientation on national and global agendas. Due to the "ease of consensus discovery and development," as Hiltz and Turoff (1978: 471) predicted, involving "the size of the audience and/or how easily new ideas can be propagated throughout the society." Obviously conventional mass media such as television, as well as newspapers, magazines, books, and radio, and other communications outlets such as large public meetings, fax, telephone would be very high on this dimension, too generating a synergic effect with NNITs. " According to Skinner, the evolution of a society relates to the increase of a culture's sensitivity to the remote consequences of its acts. Television, in this context, has had dramatic impact on American society." (Hiltz and Turoff, 1978: 471). The test-run mobilizations can be quite unexpected and fortuitous; however, the self-awakened masses begin to see the opportunity to seize those accidental moments as opportunities for mobilization through intermediate stages, as Cornell and Cohn (1995) and Minkoff (1997) point out. In the case of Korea, it was through test-run mobilizations that the previously disparate and apolitical youth, who had grown up under the highly hierarchical ideology of Confucianism, began to recognize their power in the NPS and exert it in the major social and political mobilizations and elections (Han 2007). Ultimately, the concept and the operationalization of the demonstration effect will play a central role in explaining how, in both countries, the interdynamics of young generations' use of NNITs has affected electoral discourse and post-election politics. Chapter 3, on Korea's beef crisis and the Internet, and chapter 5, on the President Obama's use of Twitter in the healthcare reform (HCR) legislation battle, both provide examples of how the NNIT-mobilized demonstration effect that occurred before the presidential election was instrumental in facilitating massive (in the Korean case) and efficient (in the American case) mobilizations for political agendas.

THE NEW EXPERIMENTATION AND THE ESSENCE OF POLITICAL COMMUNITY

The last issue that this book raises is in regards to the relationship between the virtuality created by the use of NNITs and its impact upon the main characteristics of the political community that the old American experimentation produced. To answer this, we must ask two questions. What is the essential nature of a political community? Will interactions in cyberspace and the NPS ultimately change this political community?

These issues are closely related to questions about how political consciousness, identity, and community are formed, and ultimately lead us to question the nature of modern political community, the nation-state—how did a nation-state achieves sovereignty; where did that power originate; and how solid is the basis of that power? Even though the nineteenth-century American experimentation produced thick layers of social capital, the basis for that political identity as a sovereign state was fragile in the sense that such political solidarity was all "imagined." To explain the imagined nature of any political community that is based on nationalism, Anderson (1991, 6) says:

> It is imagined because the members of even the smallest nation will never know most of their fellow-members, meet them, or even hear of them, yet in the minds of each lives the image of their communion . . . In fact, all communities larger than primordial villages of face-to-face contact (and perhaps even these) are imagined. Communities are to be distinguished, not by their falsity/genuineness, but by the style in which they are imagined.

According to this view, even the smallest nation is established on a very limited basis of genuine acquaintance, and sovereignty is achieved through the imagination. In that primordial community, face-to-face interaction was the only way to build up trust and identity. The primordial community, accordingly, was limited in the sense that communities were not to be built on 100 percent genuine acquaintance among the members, which also holds true for communities in the contemporary world. That is why Anderson (1991, 6) argues that communities are to be distinguished by "the style in which they are imagined," not by the quality of the membership recognition, that is, whether it is false or genuine. The intrinsic nature of political community is the same in virtual communities. For example, the transformation from the "medieval dream of a single people under one emperor and one pope" to that of "subjects of a particular kingdom or citizens of a nation" (Gonzalez 1996, 60) was also achieved through the imagined notion of being a nation even though people had an extremely limited basis of genuine physical acquaintance. In fact, the development of information and communications technologies has enabled a plenitude of members, both near and far, to imagine that they belong to the same political community. Thus, the degree to which the sense of a political community was "imagined" in a nation-state might have been less than in feudal society when various nations were under a few dynasties in Europe; however, the "imagined" nature of the political community did not disappear—it remained strong, much stronger than average citizens in any nation-state would think. In other words, no nation-state—not even the smallest—is built on 100 percent acquaintance of mutual membership recognition, and even the strongest case of political solidarity and identity is, ultimately, virtual. Even though American grass-roots democracy in local communities was unprecedented in its cultivation of thick social capital through face-to-face voluntary associational activities (Putnam 2000), it was intrinsically partial, fragile, imagined and virtual because all of that local solidarity was projected towards the center as a nation.

Jean-Jacques Rousseau's notion of "general will" from his 1789 *Declaration of the Rights of Man and the Citizen* during the French Revolution is reminiscent of Anderson's point on the nature of nation-state community as "being imagined." As Anderson makes an issue of the incomplete nature of 'nation-ness' in that there is no way for each member to know most of their fellow-members in the even the smallest nation, Rousseau's notion of general will is also obscure and controversial in that Rousseau questions how a community can aggregate the common desire or interest of the community as a whole. Rousseau also applied the concept of general will to small and homogeneous states. The rule of law within a nation state simply reflects the ability of the state to enforce such laws within its territorial boundaries, and may not reflect the extent to which these laws derived from the general will or the character of the general will, i.e. whether community members engage in political debate and mobilization through one on one and face to face interactions. Both concepts of "general will" and "nation-state" or "nation-ness" are all imagined. Thus, the nature of such community concept is not real but virtual.

In light of the intrinsic limitations of political community in general, this book raises the question of what impact the NNIT-activated cyber interactions would have on the nature of the contemporary political community. Scholarly reactions to the new experimentation, especially virtual interaction in cyberspace, have been mainly pessimistic in their common claim that NNITs are inadequate, as a medium, to support social interaction, or that NNITs would take time away from face-to-face (i.e., "real") interactions (Katz and Rice 2002; Kraut and Kiesler 2003; Wellman and Haythornthwaite 2002; Watt, et al. 2002). According to this view, NNITs would dilute social capital and thereby endanger the foundations of democracy; however, NNITs, as a relationship technology that re-routes the ways in which we used to relate to one another, is constantly reproducing new sets of relationships in business, politics and our daily lives as well. For example, explosive increases in physical traffic (e.g., air travel, museum visits) in recent years are purported to be causally linked to increases in emails and other electronic communications (Woolgar 2002, 17–8).

This book argues that the virtual-ness of cyber activism is not essentially different from the imagined-ness of any form of political community in general. In addition, the more that people use NNITs for social interactions, the more that activities in cyberspace may contribute to the bonding and bridging of the social capital, as many scholarly articles have recently claimed (Boyd and Ellison 2007; Dutta-Bergman 2006; Ellison, et al. 2007; Huysman and Wulf 2004; Quan-Haase 2002; Williams 2006; Woolgar 2002; Zhao 2006). Woolgar (2002, 1–2) even suggests that NNITs may "replace face-to-face interactions" for more trusted interactions offline and that, "Given their potential radically to transform many fundamental and wide-ranging aspects of society, these new technologies requires us to rethink the very basis of the ways in which we related to one another." While the associational volunteer activity that Tocqueville observed in nineteenth-century America was exceptional in that it represented a clear break from the European Ancient Regime, and exemplified a new political experimentation in the accumulation of face-to-face social capital, the nature of that American experimentation was essentially no different from that of cyber interactions that take place through the use of NNITs.

Imagined, or virtual, togetherness was strengthened through the development of the public sphere, the notion of which was introduced by Jurgen Habermas (1992) in *The Structural Transformation of the Public Sphere*. The public sphere, according to Habermas (1992, 27), is a forum for the bourgeois class "to engage . . . in a debate over the general rules governing relations in the basically privatized but publicly relevant sphere of commodity exchange and social labor." During the feudal era, governance was mostly conducted through personal patron–clientele relationships among ruling classes, while the masses were excluded from the governing process. As the bourgeoisie emerged and began to challenge the privatized power of feudal aristocracy, they began to form their own sphere of discourse in the public—this was the "public sphere." With the development of information technologies (e.g., Gutenberg's movable type) and printed materials (e.g., pamphlets, newspapers, magazines, books), the public sphere began to play an instrumental role in the consolidation of the political identity of the rising classes and the emergence of a nation-state by articulating *imagined* togetherness and enhancing the limitedness of a political community based on *face-to-face* recognitions.

Whereas virtual togetherness can be viewed as thin, face-to-face interactions can be seen as thick social capital. Habermas' notion of the public sphere being based on the historical development of the bourgeois class and their challenging of the feudal private governing structure was later generally adopted by modern communications theory as "a place [or a forum] where community members could collectively form public opinion in an environment removed from the government or economy" (Westling 2007, 2). NNITs, in turn, have affected the style in which people engage in the public sphere. Altogether, both imagined and real togetherness play a necessary role in constructing national unity.

Since the 1960s, in the United States, as social movement organizations were nationalized, centralized and bureaucratized, the social capital of local face-to-face interactions became diluted and weakened. Such changes in social movement organizations resulted in the creation of various kinds of collective identity. Minkoff (2001, 189–90) drew a contrast between the thick social capital that was formed through local, face-to-face interactions and a "mediated form of collective identity" or "symbolic forms of affiliation and similar social-structural position." Minkoff (2001, 189) argues that this mediated form of collective identity "nonetheless provides a sense of integration into an abstract collectivity, which is a minimal requirement for further involvement on collective affairs." Smith (2001, 201) also points to the emergence of "symbolic affiliation and social integration" in transnational social movement organizations, which generally entail no physical interactions.

The fear of losing the original form of solidarity (i.e., social capital formed through close physical and regional-based interactions) is well reflected in many scholarly works on late twentieth-century American society. Even though face-to-face social capital has become much thinner and weaker than before, the social movements of the late twentieth century also produced "the initial self-concept and organization necessary for the further development of group ties" (Minkoff 2001, 190), which in turn strengthened the sense of "symbolic communities." Nowadays, the intensive use of NNITs in all aspects of our lives, combined with the rapidly increasing amount of social and political interactions in cyberspace, is accelerating the dilution of social capital while increasing the mediated form of collective identity. The nineteenth-century American experimentation that was based on associational volunteerism through face-to-face interactions is now encountering a new reality in which NNITs, as relationship technology (RT), are expanding the scope of human interactions beyond spatial and temporal limitations.

Although NNITs can detract from face-to-face interaction and weaken the density of social capital, NNITs can also serve as effective tools for bonding imagined togetherness and bridging diluted forms of symbolic identity, as Scott Heiferman, founder of Meetup.com, explained when describing his goal of "using the Internet to get people off of the Internet." A new computer-mediated experimentation that transcends spatial and temporal limitations is now adding new dimensions to the conventional offline face-to-face community. In this way, the community that was built through close physical contacts is now being overlaid by a virtual layer that often leads to further face-to-face contact—a cyber community. This book attempts to clarify the nature of this newly emerging space of cyber community and networked public sphere, to examine how different it is from the conventional space of face-to-face interactions, and to investigate what changes may arise from this new transformative experimentation.

VIRTUALITY IN POLITICAL COMMUNITY

The essential nature of the communications and information technologies that evolved into the infrastructure of the Internet era has been to facilitate the process of production, transmission, storage, and reprocessing of information and knowledge over great distances as a complement to face-to-face interactions. In that sense, information technologies always involve virtual interactions.

Generally, the adjective "virtual" can have two meanings: (1) that which is not real but may display the salient qualities of the real; and (2) that which is temporarily simulated or extended by computer software (Robbins 2009, 11–2; Harrison 2009). The former simply means "not real or genuine," but the latter exclusively refers to computer-created virtuality, which is "the property of a computer system with the potential for enabling a virtual system to become a real system by encouraging the real world to behave according to the template dictated by the virtual system" (Turoff 1997, 38). The core components of virtual reality are its persistence, its multiuser nature, the use of avatars, and the use of a Wide Area Network (WAN) (Robbins 2009, 11). What Robbins's definition lacks is recognition of the social functions that cyber communities aim to conduct through virtual reality. In this book, the term *virtuality* will be used to mean "a shared and persistent space for multiple users constructed by computer and network technologies, where given functions can perform what people want to socially achieve by linking wide areas of common human interests and value systems" (Robbins 2009, 11). Granted, virtual interaction is not identical to face-to-face interaction, but it does perform the basic functions that a community needs: communications, opinion aggregation and deliberation. And ultimately, cyber activism is just as real as face-to-face interaction as will be discussed below. Woolgar (2002, 17) argues that "Not only do new virtual activities sit alongside existing 'real' activities, but the introduction and use of new 'virtual' technologies can actually stimulate more of the corresponding 'real' activity." In effect, virtual reality becomes what we negotiate it to be; as Turoff (1997, 40) points out, "In a philosophical sense, virtuality is a process of 'negotiated reality' in which the uses of computer systems as groups or organizations negotiate an agreed-upon reality."

The idea of "negotiated reality" is not new to us. In fact, sovereign nation-states came to exist, according to Anderson (1991, 44–6), due to the development of printing technology and capitalism combined, by consolidating the symbolic unity that was based on the loyalty and patriotism of the citizens. Anderson (1991, 46, 44) concludes that "the convergence of capitalism and print technology on the fatal diversity of human language created the possibility of a new form of imagined community, which in its basic morphology set the stage for the modern nation" because it created "unified fields of exchange and communication below Latin and above the spoken vernaculars," which correspond to Turoff's notion of negotiated reality. As a result of these unified fields of exchanges and communication in vernaculars, a large cluster of new political entities emerged in Europe between 1776 and 1838 (Anderson 1991, 46). As discussed above, however, it is theoretically impossible to build political unity and community consciousness through face-to-face interactions alone. So, in essence, the virtual nature of the nation-state and the virtuality of the online cyber community are not radically different. Pointing to the imagined nature of the modern political community, this book argues that the emerging online community, which is often criticized as being merely "virtual" or not real, is not fundamentally different from the face-to-face modern political community.

Plato's Dialogue on Dreams and Zhuangzi's Dream of the Butterfly

How different are these spaces—the real and the virtual? The famous story of Zhuangzi's dream of becoming a butterfly offers a new perspective into this issue, asking us to consider whether the essential difference between waking and dreaming are analogous to the difference between face-to-face and virtual communities. The influential Chinese philosopher, Zhuangzi (370–301 BC), believed to be one of the founders of Chinese Taoism, raised the fundamental question of what is real in life. The story goes like this: "In his dream, he suddenly realized that he had become a butterfly, but he felt uncertain as to whether he had become a butterfly in his dream or whether a butterfly had become Zhuangzi in the butterfly's dream. Despite this confusion, one thing that is certain is that a difference exists between Zhuangzi and the butterfly."[5]

Despite Zhuangzi's uncertainty about whether he was a man or a butterfly in his dream, he concludes definitively that two distinct realms exist. In support of this view, Chong (2006, 381) and Moller (1999) add that these two realms are just as authentic as life and death. This study argues that, just as Zhuangzi's waking and dreaming are equally real, the virtual interactions in cyberspace are just as real as the face-to-face interactions that occur in what we commonly believe to be "real life"—they are only different in terms of the way in which they interact.

Similarly, Plato's *Theaetetus*,[6] which portrays Socrates's thoughts about ontological and epistemological questions, gives us a Western analog to Zhuangzi's musings on the existence of two equally real realms. Socrates discussed the distinction between dreaming and waking as follows:

Socrates: Do you see another question which can be raised about these phenomena, notably about dreaming and waking?

Theaetetus: What question?

Socrates: A question which I think that you must often have heard persons ask: How can you determine whether at this moment we are sleeping, and all our thoughts are a dream; or whether we are awake, and talking to one another in the waking state?

Theaetetus: Indeed, Socrates, I do not know how to prove the one any more than the other, for in both cases, the facts precisely correspond; and there is no difficulty in supposing that during all this discussion, we have been talking to one another in a dream; and when in a dream, we seem to be narrating dreams, the resemblance of the two states is quite astonishing.

Socrates: You see, then, that a doubt about the reality of sense is easily raised, since there may even be a doubt whether we are awake or in a dream. And as our time is equally divided between sleeping and waking, in either sphere of existence, the soul contends that the thoughts which are present to our minds at the time are true; and during one half of our lives, we affirm the truth of the one, and, during the other half, of the other; and are equally confident of both.

Theaetetus: Most true.

Close to the roots of Western civilization, this classic conversation confirms Zhuangzi's point that life, in the dreaming mode, is as real as life in the waking mode; and it is my claim that virtual activities in cyberspace correspond to the dreaming mode in both Zhuangzi's story and Plato's *Theaetetus*.

After almost two millennia, these two philosophical observations have become a reality—namely, through advancements in technology, virtual identity has become real. A short article published on Atlantic.com by Coates

(2009, December 16) points out how relationships forged in cyberspace can feel as real as offline reality. To demonstrate how people form relationships and attachments in cyberspace, the author describes a player of the massively multi-player online game World of Warcraft (WoW) who was mourning the death of an Internet game pal he had never met.

Last month, a little before Thanksgiving, I heard while we were playing that he was coughing rather loudly. I jokingly said he should consider taking up smoking if he was going to cough so much, and he admitted that he had pneumonia . . . After the raid was over, I wished him well and told him "no more coughing" in my best big brother voice. I logged in the next day, and his friend from college told me that he had died, presumably of a pneumonia-related pulmonary embolism. At first, I thought that the friend was playing a joke in very poor taste. Then, what an obnoxious irony to have my last words to him: "stop coughing." He never listened to me before. So after an initial shock, I then found myself crying over a person I had never met. I didn't even know what he looked like until I saw his obituary!

The article goes on to say "we aren't that far removed from the days when people fell in love, and sometimes married, through letters. WoW has taught me a lot about how the basic nature of humans is almost impossible to suppress." If we can agree that face-to-face and cyber communities are both equally real in the same way that waking and dreaming are equally real, then we can entertain the following assumptions about the impacts of networked public spheres upon contemporary societies:

- The new networked public spheres that are being created by NNITs are significantly re-intermediating conventional relationships among actors in society in much the same way as other Industrial Age information technologies such as the telegraph, Victorian Internet (Standage, 1998), phone, radio and TV fundamentally changed people's way of life and politics;
- The transformation brought forth by NPS is real and capable of generating social capital and serving the political community;
- The use of NNITs and activities in the cyber community can, in fact, complement the imagined loyalty in nation-states because NNITs and cyberactivism may strengthen the process of bonding and bridging the social capital among the members of the community;[7]
- Such an emerging trend is likely to affect the young generations and their political participation more than it will affect any other voting group since youths are the most active users of NNITs in the cyber community and have the lowest voter turnout;
- The 2002 Korean presidential election suggests that, while voter turnout generally declined among all generational groups, NNITs may play a

decisive role in shaping the political cohesiveness and voting patterns of younger generations in electoral politics;

- The 2002 Korean presidential election served as a demonstration effect to a series of candlelight protests against the current regime that had decided to resume importing American beef in 2008;
- The 2008 U.S. presidential election illustrates that the Democratic candidate Obama successfully tapped into the power of formerly apathetic young voters and created an influential "Long Tail"[8] of support, which might be capable of redefining political/electoral discourse, and which poses important questions for the future of elections and democracy; and
- Given the increasing use and influence of NNITs, social networking sites (e.g., Facebook) and microblogs (e.g., Twitter) have exerted some influence over the most controversial political agendas of the Obama administration—the health care reform legislation battle.

GLOBALIZATION, INFORMATIZATION, AND REINTERMEDIATION

The advent of new age always comes with the reconfigurations of the sets of relationships among the major stakeholders such as the state, public or private organizations including corporations, and individual in a form of citizenship (Friedman, 2000; Shapiro, 1999; Ong, 1999; Jameson and Miyoshi 1998). Now, with the wide deployment of information technology, such reconfiguration among these players is taking place disintermediating their roles and relationships and reintermediating new power relationships among them. "Bypassing editors, educators, and other gatekeepers who stand between us and whatever it is we seek,"[9] preexisting power configuration between writers and editors, teachers and students, politicians and voters are under serious challenge. Cleveland (1985: 60) points out five different hierarchies: hierarchies of power based on control, hierarchies of influence based on secrecy, hierarchies of class based on ownership, hierarchies of privilege based on early access to valuable resources, and hierarchies of politics based on geography. The democratization of technology and information disintegrate the bases of hierarchies in socio-economic system and demand institutionalizations of new rules of games.

Middlemen in commerce, publications, and governments are forced to transform themselves into new functions. In economic sector, traditional broker in the stock market has to cede their power to virtual daily trader and software program. The thriving emergence of Internet stores such as Amazon .com, eBay, and flooze.com begin to challenge industrial version of business system. Electronic government and cyber-democracy[10] come to erode current political middlemen system, representative democracy, demanding more power delegation from the center to periphery, decentralization. One-stop online systems in the area of Electronic Government project intercepts in the existing relationships between citizens and political appointed and career public officials and disintermediates citizens from multi-layers of bureaucratic job categories.

A wave of disintermediation and accompanying reintermediation logically leads us to a set of questions of, first, how we articulate new power relationships between public and private entities, states (government) and citizens, and so on. Based on an assumption that current information technology revolution will eventually affect the fundamental power relationships among major stakeholders in society, the next question to answer is on accountability of what public action is and whose accountability of such public action in a new power relationships.

Digital Social Networking Technology

The World Wide Web successfully launched in 1995 and began to link residents and organizations in the every part of the globe. In doing so, the internet fundamentally changed relationships among agents, organizations, and institutions in their scopes and scales of activities and interactions. These revolutionary changes result from technology that, despite its unchanging binary nature, originated from the technological shifts from analog circuit switching to digital packet switching. Due to digital packet switching and communications protocol technologies, people and organizations can transcend temporal and spatial limitations in their everyday life as well as transform the conventional working relationships with and among governments (e-Government), business (e-Commerce), community (e-Community), and individuals (social networking sites such as www.MySpace.com in 2003 and www.Facebook .com in 2004). Further development from wired to wireless, the spread of broadband infrastructure and cellular-messaging connections, and mobile networking technology creates a seamless web of human networks that can match even strangers with their time, place, and things to do.

The convergence of new networked information technologies and human social networks has begun to form digital social networks, which are generating fundamental changes in the process of conducting business in corporations, government, politics, elections, and personal relationships (Kleinberg, 2008). In the beginning, there were some doubts regarding the emergence of social networks, in that social networks might risk becoming impersonal and undesirable as they continue to grow in scale. Rather, theoretically unlimited networking capacity begins to form its own new rules of games. In other words, expanding digital social networks can strengthen the vital few but not rule out the challenging potential of trivial many in the networks. As John Guare's 1990 play *Six Degrees of Separation* aptly pointed out that "everybody on this planet is separated by only six other people," converging digital social networking power sheds light on the potential connectedness of individuals in the network and can connect and empower those who were once isolated. Further, Hiltz and Turoff (1978: 483) extend Guare's "six degrees of separation" emphasizing that "the number of persons an individual can maintain active and close communications with on a CCS (Computer Conferencing System) is between there and ten times that possible with current communications technology." Thus, those newly connected can do something that they were never able to do before. "At the scales of tens of millions of individuals and minute-by-minute time granularity, we can replay and watch the ways in which people seek out connections and form friendships on a site like Facebook or how they coordinate with each other and engage in creative expression on sites like Wikipedia and flickr" (Kleinberg, 2008: 66).

However, the emerging digital social network has its own structure that influences actors in the network. "Social network analysis conceptualizes social structure as a network with ties connecting members and channeling resources, focuses on the characteristics of ties rather than on the characteristics of the individual members, and views communities as 'personal communities,' that is, as networks of individual relations that people foster, maintain, and use in the course of their daily lives" (Wetherell, et al, 1994). Before the era of expanding network society, the way that we perceive the world was highly clustered, orderly, and structured. However, a few unexpected links can provide shortcuts throughout the network and open up the possibility of new connections among previously disparate individuals. As a result, those newly connected individuals can produce new results in their scope of activities. The potential to create new paths connecting strangers is unlimited because the network structures and communication protocols are decentralized.

Information Technology and Global Governance

The concept of globalization has many facets that have not been thoroughly examined. Based on their research on the openness of a world economic system, Hirst and Thompson (1996) argue that the level of globalization was higher in the era of Pax Britannica than that of Pax Americana and point out the problem of unsubstantiated arguments of globalization school. Being global denotes different contexts in different stages of history.

According to Anderson (1983: 12), "nation-ness is the most universally legitimate value in the political life of our times." Dynastic control and governance of medieval Europe across geographical boundaries, many different ethnic groups and vernaculars, and cultures[11] were all possible because documentary interchangeability was limited within the population who can read and write the only printable language, Latin. The wide use of vernaculars in print-capitalism accelerated the sense of community sharing regional news through documentary interchangeability. Publications of news and nobles in vernaculars reinforced human interchangeability in the regions and eventually formed a sense of community based on imagination. Anderson argues that nationalism and the idea of sovereignty arose from the successful print-capitalism.

The general population in medieval Europe was severely fragmented while a few dynasties shared a sense of being global in their governing structures and systems. The ruled were divided and many different nations happened to be under a dynastic control. The printing technology[12] awoke the nation-ness and dissolved European dynastic governance by making differences in ethnic background, languages and territorial distinctions independent of each other. The process of nation-building at this stage was to articulate a political space where differences in those areas could be distinguished from each other. Before the era of nation state, being global was sensed in the governing structure and shared rules, codes, and practices of a few royal families.

> But in the older imagining, where states were defined by centers, borders were porous and indistinct, and sovereignties faded imperfectly into one another. Hence, paradoxically enough, the ease with which pre-modern empires and kingdoms were able to sustain their rule over immensely heterogeneous, and often not even contiguous, populations for long periods of time. . . . Through the general principle of verticality, dynastic marriages brought together diverse populations under new auspice. Paradigmatic in this respect was the House of Habsburg. (Anderson, 1983: 26)

When they were dissolved, it was "imagined as sovereign because the concept was born in an age in which Enlightenment and Revolution were destroying the legitimacy of the divinely-ordained, hierarchical dynastic realm" (Anderson, 1983: 16).

In the era of nation state, differences in languages, ethnic backgrounds, and cultures has generally been maintained and competed in different containers. Sovereignty has drawn the lines for rule of games that sustained such differences. Being global was to internationalize the exchanges of resources within the boundaries of not affecting the basis of being difference. It was a survival game of containing and sustaining the differences. Government was in the center of sovereignty and accountability in this game.

Again, the same means, information technology, brings the era of nation state into different environments. "Some commentators see this decline in the salience of the nation state, the proliferation of plural and often competing loci of power, and the rise of forms of private power as analogous to the Middle Ages" (Pierre, 2000: 24) Globalization and informatization generate an environment where multiple sovereignties and national identities compete each other. The information age in many ways seems to be similar to the era of medieval Europe in terms of power relationships among major stakeholders.

Beginning with an analysis of the underlying technological trends that have facilitated the "virtual organization" as an efficient new organizational form, Mowshowitz goes on to speculate that structural changes comparable in their depth and scope to those that accompanied the transformation of feudalism to capitalism will accompany the new revolution. He points to trends already evident in traditional authority structures, particularly the family and the nation-state. In regard to the latter, he posits either its "decline" or its "end"; if the nation-state does not disappear, he seems to suggest, it will become virtually irrelevant (Whitaker, 1999: 160).

Whitaker argues that the current transformation brought by globalization and informatization in the political structure will go back to the era of feudalism in many ways. He claims that "with the decline of state resources and thus of state power, private centers of economic power will gradually assume political power. As in medieval feudalism, the basic functions of government will come to be exercised by private parties. . . . Private parties will exercise authority in their name, not in the name of a law that transcends their own power" (Whitaker, 1999: 161).

We can isolate the decentering of power and authority, the detachment of sovereignty from territory, the erosion of many of the traditional prerogatives of the nation-state and the blurring of lines between the public and private sectors, the transformation of work and the creation of an underclass of the apparently permanently unemployed and unemployable, growing disparities of wealth and poverty not only on a global scale but also within the so-called rich nations, the growth of private security and private justice. This could point in the direction of "feudalism" with dispersed centers of economic and political power and a hierarchy very steep at the bottom but somewhat flatter at the top as shifting congeries of powerful "barons" (corporations?) challenge the authority of relatively weak "kings" (state?). Whitaker elaborates:

> Virtual feudalism shares the political features of classical feudalism, but its economic base is abstract wealth, and the social system based upon it may be very fluid. The central institution of virtual feudalism will be the virtual fief,

rather than the manor or landed estate of European feudalism. Assets will be distributed on a global basis as "virtual resources," i.e., the particular form of abstract wealth may change from moment to moment depending on the institution's financial needs and market conditions. (Whitaker, 1999: 163)

In this era of virtual feudalism, agents and units that have been forced to be different from each other within the container of nation states are building alliances based on their interchangeable similarities. This constructs a basis for a web of global governance. Hirst and Thompson describe the roles of the nation-state in the future as follows:

1. Nation-states will play a significant role in economic governance at the level of both national and international processes
2. Nation-states will not function less as sovereign entities but more as the components of an international polity
3. Citizenship will continue to be important and nation-states will still retain their central role ensuring a large measure of territorial control-the regulation of populations
4. Nuclear competition and war will become less significant to both nation-states and citizens
5. New communication and information technologies will loosen state's exclusive of control of their territory, thus diminishing the state's capacity for cultural control and homogenization In time, these processes will threaten the idea of an exclusive and virtually self-sufficient national culture. As a result, the state will have to seek bases of citizen loyalty outside primitive cultural homogeneity
6. Sovereignty will be is alienable and divisible and serve as a source of legitimacy in transferring power or sanctioning new powers within new systems of international governance and structure. The art of international governance will increasingly center around distributing power.
7. NGOs will play a larger role in governance.

Governments and Accountability

Globalization and informatization challenge governments in the world to redefine its scope and to digitalize their conventional way to deliver public services to citizens. In a production system where all national economies are integrated into the logic of global capital and transnational corporations, on the question arises of how do we hold private entities accountable for their activities that may conflict with many important values and current resource allocation in various regions. Friedman (2000: 206) points out many examples including the danger of workers' rights under the global net of sweatshops. The scope of government refers to "both the range of government activity and the degree to which governments engage in activities which have an impact on people's daily lives."[13]

In the field of public administration, an approach that is called "the New Public Management" studies how public sectors have adopted market values and market mechanisms for maximizing efficiency and productivity. In a broad sense, such efforts are labeled as 'reinventing government.' When the digitalization in the reinventing process is emphasized, it is called 'electronic government.' In realizing electronic government, innovation is key. The delegation of government power and function to private entities has occurred extensively resulting in the new phenomena of "entrepreneurial government" (Osborn & Gaebler, 1992), the "hollow state" (Milward, 1996; 1993), "government by proxy" (Kettl, 1993; 1988), "shadow state" (Wolch, 1990), or "government by the market" (Self, 1993; 2000). An inroad of the market mechanism into public jurisdiction raises an issue of accountability: government responsibility of private delivering of services previously in the realms of public to citizens.

Retreat of Sovereignty and a Problem of Accountability

Globalization adds more complex dimensions to the problem of the impaired accountability[14] of the nation states to their citizens. Overall retreats of state and governments and encroachments of global capital, "transnational practices"[15] (Sklair,1991; Drucker, 1997) the "stateless corporation" (*Business Week*, 14 May, 1990), and powerful emergence of non-governmental organizations in international affairs have highlighted the new kinds of citizenship. Such transnationality creates safe havens for individuals and private companies whose identities and scope of activities refuse to belong to an ultimate power of a country. An example is a detached-family in which a father makes money in A country and his wife and children are in B country for a better education. They own multiple citizenships. As a result, the concept of "flexible citizenship"[16] better explains blurred concepts of sovereignty and the citizenship established during the industrial age. Ong (1999) argues that the absolute power of a nation state needs to be revised to be able to reflect the changes taking place in globalized world and suggests a concept of "graduate sovereignty"[17] and "flexible citizenship."

The concept of sovereignty and citizenship that has described power relations between states and citizens need to be redefined. The idea of sovereignty was to disintegrate the ancient regimes and arbitrary power of old dynastic control and to form a new power relationship between public and private entities, which has provided the most critical power base for the nation states. It has two clear dimensions: geographical and political.

Geographical sovereignty clearly confines the physical boundary where the power a nation state can be extended. Ohmae (1990), however, argues that the intensification of the global economy detaches regional economic zones from sovereign state and incorporates them into a part of global economy, 'region state.' Now, the development of growth triangles[18] or the Multimedia Super Corridor (MSC)[19] create multinational zones of sovereignty in both international and domestic settings. The growth triangle is a zone where multiple nationalities coexist to form a industrial complex bringing the best resources from each country to attract global capital, technology, and extended market. Examples are concentrated in South Asian regions. Sijori is a representative of growth triangles where Indonesia, Malaysia, and Singapore form a triangle zone of cheap labor, abundant resources, capital and technology. Another is Brunei-Indonesia-Malaysia-Philippines. The Multimedia Super Corridor is a project that Malaysian government initiated in order to establish a "springboard to serve the regional and world markets for multimedia products and services." In it, competing sovereignties intermix in the forms of codes, rules, and practices of labor relations, taxations, visa status, security, and cultures. These two illustrations support the argument that the retreat of sovereignty generates the problem of accountability domestically and internationally.

The political dimension of sovereignty outlines the relationships between political community and its members as a set of citizens' rights and obligations toward public authorities and political institutions. The Internet creates a loophole of political sovereignty where the legal jurisdiction of a country physically cannot control the political activities of citizens. According to Lessig (1999: 27), the architecture of the Internet is defined by "a suite of protocols that are open and nonproprietary and that require no personal identification to be accessed and used." It creates a cyberspace that is quite different from public sphere in the era of nation state. Constitutional values and the enforcement of such values in the cyberspace become harder and harder. A series of codes, software, hardware, and networks generates anonymous space for individuals and groups. By going online, both private and public entities can bypass government regulation and declare a sanctuary where sovereignty of nation state cannot reach. Governments cannot enforce their laws on the Web servers for anti-government organizations, gambling, and pornography located offshore. The Internet also empowers and enables citizens and non-government organizations to challenge the power of political leaders and conventional institutions.

Global trends of transnational practices, especially in economic and cultural-ideological realms, produce a new dimension of the problem in accountability of a nation state: social sovereignty. The concept of social sovereignty has rarely recognized in social science literature. Putnam (1993: 29) defines the social capital as the "existence of norms of reciprocity and networks of civic engagement, a dense interlocking web of horizontal associations." Such social capital has overall remained within the boundary of national territory forming national identities as a community. However, transnational practices and the globalized economy have eroded social sovereignty and have begun to implant foreign rules, codes, and practices in society. The Rodeo Street of Apkoojeong in Seoul, South Korea is a place where American fast food chains and fashion stores are densely crowded. Here, codes of conducts and behavior patterns are far apart from traditional Confucian codes of conducts. The populations of growth triangles and Special Economic Zones (SEZs) are subject to different codes, rules, and practices of value and enjoy different kinds of rights, discipline, caring, and security. (Ong, 1999: 217)

In this context, the issue of accountability has different implications. Transnational practices erode national identity and social cohesiveness and facilitate the import of global trends into domestic soil and the outflow of population and resources to foreign countries. The erosion of social sovereignty goes unnoticed and intensifies the retreat in political and geographical sovereignty. Weakened social sovereignty does not pose an immediate threat to public authority and institutions. Accordingly, there seems to be no overt problem of accountability. Rather, ever weakening social sovereignty accelerates the homogenizing power of globalization and domesticates population to foreign identities. Therefore, rather than posing a direct issue of accountability, it obscures an issue of accountability and puts conventional authorities and institutions in a defensive stance.

Citizenships and Accountability

The counterpart of the concept of sovereignty is a citizenship. Retreat in national sovereignty loosens control over citizens. In a world "where lines of authority are increasingly more informal than formal, where legitimacy is increasingly marked by ambiguity, citizens are increasingly capable of holding their own by knowing when, where, and how to engage in collective action." (Rosenau, 1992: 291) A classical notion of citizenship divides into three subcategories: civil, political and social rights (Marshall, 1950) According to Marshall, 'civil' citizenship refers to the rights necessary for individual freedom while political rights comprises franchised rights in participating in the elections or candidacy for public positions. The social rights of citizenship embrace broader range of issues from social welfare to cultural identity of that society. The first two concepts are firmly established at least in the legal sense. However, the social sense of citizenship varies over time and depends upon the social and cultural atmosphere that the society creates and is directed.

Ong's notion of variegated citizenship[20] (1999: 217) explains how citizens becomes independent of a single national identity and jurisdiction in a globalized world. Citizens have a variety of choices to make in their selection of residence, business operations, educations, and so on. Empowered citizens by the democratization of technology and information can form extensive coalitions and challenge government and existing political institutions. The issue of accountability rises when strengthened power of citizen itself deeply involves the political processes. The Supreme Court of the Republic of Korea ruled on January 26, 2001 that citizen coalition movement during the general election for the National Assembly in Korea in April, 2000, which defeated corrupt politicians, was illegal[21] on the ground that it violated the current election law. If civic coalition had constructed its Web site to publish the list of corrupt, thereby unfit, politicians offshore and if they had not waged physical negative campaigns in the streets, then could the Supreme Court still rule that it was illegal against the current election law? The augmented power of citizens and civic groups by the revolution of information technology put these citizens into the trap of making their actions and voices illegitimate. At the same time, the cunning use of Internet for a political purpose can bypass the government jurisdiction of legal power. The flexible citizenship that allows multiple national identities and visas also produces a loophole of government authority. For example, Marc Rich, who fled from the jurisdiction of the federal government of the United States to Switzerland to avoid the punishment for his tax evasion threatens the justice system and social cohesiveness of American society.

Governance versus Government

Here, we need to clarify the confusing notions of 'government' and 'governance,' and unsystematic usage of both terms in the practice of social science as a whole. Despite the difficulties to delineate the historical origins of the term *government*, it has a historical context. The Industrial Revolution had a great impact upon the rise of modern concept of government. "Governments are industrial-age organizations, based on the same command-and-control model of the enterprise that was created for the industrial economy. Bureaucracy and the industrial economy rose hand in hand." (Tapscott, 1996: 161). Hirst (2000: 28) also points out that the "modern institutions of representative government were mostly designed in the nineteenth century to superintend states with much more limited functions than today, and it is no wonder that they do not work well today as sources of accountability." Widely accepted usage of the term government has specifically been employed to describe a constitutional institution that has legitimate source of coercive power and authority within the sovereign territorial national boundary, that is, nation-state (Rosenau, 1992; Czempiel, 1992; Rose, 1993). The government controls and regulates natural and social resources and directs citizen activities, thus insuring the implementation of duly constituted national policies. In short, the usage of the term government is mainly restricted to the administrative domains and central discretion of the nation-state. Also, the traditional liberal democratic model of the state and government was based on "a sustained separation of state and society."[22] This model can't accommodate the increased power of citizens and non-governmental organization in the contemporary society.

On the other hand, the term *governance* has been applied in very loose and broad sense. Governance is about how to maintain the steering role of political institutions despite the internal and external challenges to the state. It is also, presumably, more palatable than government, which has become a slightly pejorative concept. (Pierre, 2000: 4) Although it is not clear how far back can trace the term to its original usage, governance refers to a more encompassing concept of the governing process including not just the province of the state but also varieties of activities in civil society.[23]

According to Pierre (2000: 3), governance has dual meanings: the state's ability to adapt to its external environment and the theoretical representation of coordination of social systems and the role of the state in that process. Thus, the term *governance* expands the level of analysis into the levels of individual, communal, national, and international identities. It also embraces diverse units of analysis bringing the dimensions of public and private, state (government) and non-state (non-governmental), and politics and economy together into the object of inquiry.[24]

Indeed, Foucault's interpretation of the liberal notion of "government" discerns theoretical assumption of the conceptual differences of contemporary use of the terms *government* and *governance*. Foucault's study of Anglo-Scottish liberalism presents a novel interpretation of the term *government*. He defines the term *government* as "the conduct of conduct" in diverse realms of society. In his definition, government is understood as a "way of doing things," and he does not confine the act of "doing something" in the political institution, government. According to him, government can refer "to the government of oneself, to the government of souls and lives, to the government of household, and to the government of the state by a prince." (Burchell, 1993: 266) Thus, the scope of government in his scheme is expanded from the micro-level agents to macro political actions. His definition gives clear grasp of the totality and its interconnectedness of the complex dimensionality of the different forms of government.

Also, "the coexistence of parallel, competing and overlapping authorities"[25] in the society is automatically brought to the fore of significant research objects. Rose (1993: 289) indicates that Foucault's concept of governmentality does not presuppose the compulsory power base. Government as a political institution is to be faced with the dilemma that it is not capable of intervening in the every forms of government as a way of doing. "The objects, instruments, and tasks of rule must be reformulated with reference to these domains of market, civil society, and citizenship, with the aim of ensuring that they function to the benefit of the state as a whole" (Rose, 1993: 289). Rather, Foucault appears to be concerned about how the aggregation of such diverse sources of actions in the society as a whole can be democratically achieved.

Rose (1993: 296) argues that strategies of pluralization and autonomization "embody a wish for a kind of "de-governmentalization of the state"—a detaching of the center from the various regulatory technologies that it sought, over the twentieth century, to assemble into a single functioning network, and the adoption instead of a form of government through shaping the powers and wills of autonomous entities." This is a new kind of socio-political arena that the Informational Revolution is creating. New voices and actions of micro-level agents in the society, which are either newly created or re-empowered by the revolution in the telecommunication technology, requires different forms of government in the public and private discourse. Especially, citizens get more and more competent and are able to "see the aggregation of micro actions into macro outcomes"[26] as they are equipped with new technological tools making their voices reflected in the public sphere more efficiently. This poses a serious challenge to the conventional state and government. The basis of government power based on the citizen loyalty may be more easily exposed to uncertainty.

On the other hand, citizens are on their own in the new environment "where governance is increasingly operative without government, where lines of authority are increasingly more informal than formal, where legitimacy is increasingly marked by ambiguity."[27] This raises an important question of what will drive and motivate the citizen in the world where opposite trends contradict each other, represented as bifurcation of global system: centralization vs. decentralization and integration vs. fragmentation.

Governance and Accountability

Quite contrary to arguments made by scholars in the school of the New Public Management, Hirst (2000: 21) argues that "the state is not so much reduced in scale and scope, nor hollowed out: rather it is fragmented and merged with non-state or non-public bodies." The current model of state and government that is based on clear dichotomy of state and society structurally does not have political and institutional capacity to steer increasing power and demands from empowered citizens and civic organizations. It becomes a burden to contain such fragmentations within the scope of government activities and authority. In order to adapt itself to changes in external and internal power configurations and to coordinate their demands, state (government) has to delegate their power, functions, and institutions. When a government delegates power and functions, it shares accountability. When core political institutions delegate decision-making power to citizens and non-governmental organizations, the risk of lost accountability can be avoided while state and government can maintain their ultimate source of legitimacy and sovereignty.

The establishment of such a governance system entails a new institutional arrangement reflecting changed power configurations between the state and society. Hirst (2000: 28) suggests the "associative democratic model, which involves developing as many of the functions of the state as possible to society and democratizing as many as possible of the organizations in civil society." Associative self-governance would establish basic democratic legitimacy for organizations, thereby reducing the need for external governance to protect those affected and reducing the need to provide formal external rules for every contingency, according to Hirst (2000: 29)

Public policy juries can serve as an example of associative democratic model. Rosell (1999: 102) proposes a model of public policy juries: "Citizens would be selected to serve for a week on a public-policy jury, to which different levels of government could present policy issues. In the legal system juries are made up of people from a wide range of backgrounds who engage with each other to make decisions that have real consequences. These people are not technical experts but they make the critical decisions within that system. Given that the jury system (selection by lot) was the basis of Athenian democracy, it is interesting to think about who such a system might be adapted to address public issues." In reality, such model was adopted in the selection process of 'unfit politicians' in the year 2000 April general election of Korea. The 100 Voters Committee was composed of representatives from civic organizations and general citizens in the ratio of 6:4.[28] They examined total 329 candidates for the member of the National Assembly by adopting seven criteria including corruption, illegal records, and reform-minded attitudes. In a global context, such associative democratic model can be found in active movements of non-governmental organizations against international regimes such as World Bank, World Economic Forum, and IMF.

CONCEPTUALIZING THE OBAMA PHENOMENON:
BLUE OCEAN OF LONG TAIL
OF NNIT-ACTIVATED YOUNG CONSTITUENCY

Putnam (2000, 25–6) posits that the civic-mindedness of the World War II generation—who were the main beneficiaries of America's old experimentation—began to wane by the time of the Baby Boomer generation, bringing about civic malaise and significant changes in voter turnout and levels of trust in neighbors. In this way, the generational social capital that had been established through volunteer associational activities, such as the Rotary Club and 4-H Clubs, and energetic participation in local politics (i.e., the old experimentation that Tocqueville had observed in nineteenth-century America) gradually lost steam. As mentioned earlier, Putnam attributes this collapse of social capital and the waning of civic-mindedness to "generational" or "intercohort" change, as opposed to "individual change" (2000, 34).

Putnam's view neglects to consider the power that NNIT use by previously apolitical and disparate young generations could cultivate. In other words, *Bowling Alone*, the book he published in 2000, overlooked the impact of NNITs on social capital and civic-mindedness. But now, a full decade into the new experimentation of the twenty-first century, the situation has changed because the use of NNITs, especially by the youth, has affected the way in which people interact in specific political contexts. Analyzing the elections in 2008, Owen (2009, 9) concludes that the campaigns' application of digital technology brought forth two significant changes: it enabled candidates to bypass the conventional media gatekeepers, thereby contacting voters directly; and it enabled user-generated content and media to become increasingly popular, which Owen (2009, 9) attributes specifically to the emergence of NNITs such as "websites, blogs, video-sharing sites, social networking sites, and podcasts." This study argues that, although a longitudinal attitude and behavior survey would be required to generalize the following claim, it appears to be a sign of a generational change that NNIT-oriented young voters are participating in public campaign discourse by creating and sharing digital campaign contents in cyberspace for the candidates they support.

When Putnam published *Bowling Alone* in 2000, it was much too early to assess the long-term social effects of the Internet and online social media upon social connectedness and civic engagement; however, two presidential elections have since been completed, accompanied by phenomenal growth in the use of the Internet and other NNITs, especially in Korea and the United States. Although the old experimentation in face-to-face civic-mindedness was waning, what has really reversed that trend is the fact that the main users of these NNITs is the youth—the same young people who had previously been blamed for lower voting turnout rates and the decline of social capital in general. Now they are unique in that they tend to engage directly, far more actively than older generations, in the campaign process by communicating with supporters; making, sharing and distributing their own campaign promotion materials in new social media (e.g., Facebook, YouTube, Twitter); planning events to promote their choice of candidates; fundraising; and mobilizing for votes. This phenomenon distinguishes them from older generations that are accustomed to the traditional, analog methods of election campaigns. Based on the argument that such a generational phenomenon in the 2008 presidential election, with its increased amount of youth votes, gravitated more toward Senator Obama, this section attempts to conceptualize the transformation of young generations from disparate and apolitical to cohesive and increasingly engaged through network activities, both in cyberspace and face-to-face interaction, in the Obama phenomenon (Jones and Fox 2009).

As mentioned above, the term "long tail" was originally used in the field of statistics to describe a major portion of a particular frequency distribution. More specifically, Patton and Gressens (1926), as well as Viner (1929), used the concept of a "long tail" to describe relatively insignificant portions in a frequency distribution and, later, when applied by others to marketing, an uninfluential majority of consumers in a given market. In their effort to study the representative current ratio of the public utility industry, for example, Patton and Gressens (1926, 313) referred to a "long tail [that] considerably increased the arithmetic labor . . . and [had little influence on] the characteristics of the distributions." This concept calls to mind the earlier Pareto Principle, formulated in 1906 by economist Vilfredo Pareto, who observed that 20 percent of the Italian population of the day—the "vital few"—owned 80 percent of the national wealth, and that the remaining 80 percent of the population—whom he described as the "trivial many"—had little influence on the economy. This uninfluential "trivial many" of 80 percent, in the works of both Viner (1929) and Patton and Gressens (1926), corresponds to the notion of a long tail comprised of a majority with "little influence on the characteristics of the distributions." Here, "long tail" denotes the formerly apolitical majority of the youth whose votes had been wasted due to their indifference toward electoral politics.

More recently, the distinction between a "vital few" and a "trivial many" (i.e., long tail) continues to be seen as important in certain fields—as in the entertainment industry, for example, where executives have routinely targeted marketing efforts toward the top 20 percent of "hits" (i.e., "the vital few") in any product line (e.g., movies, books, CDs, DVDs) and toward the customers who buy them. In the last ten years, however, many online businesses, including Amazon.com, Rhapsody, and Netflix, have started focusing their marketing on the formerly "trivial many" of 80 percent. Recently, despite a conventional emphasis on pleasing the vital few, information technology has enhanced marketers' ability to match the 80 percent of less popular product lines with the previously trivial many of the customer base. Amazon. com's recommendation list, which suggests additional book titles after each purchase, exemplifies the way in which marketing targets this long tail—by focusing on the needs and desires of the trivial many and using its database software to find new markets for less popular titles, thereby increasing the influence of both previously uninfluential customers and products.

This is the basis of the changes that the new experimentation is bringing about—first, in the non-political realms of young generations' everyday life, and then transferred to more socially and politically sensitive issues. Such was the case in Korea, where the young generations noticed their cohesiveness first in areas of their individual interests, such as sporting events and entertainment, and then later began to wield that power in the realm of politics.

Similar to this previously uninfluential majority of customers (i.e., the long tail, Pareto's 80 percent, the trivial many), which has become increasingly influential due to the power of NNITs to find customers for unpopular items, the majority of previously apolitical younger citizens are now becoming increasingly engaged in political discourse through their use of NNITs.

Commenting on the use of this marketing strategy, Anderson claimed that a largely insignificant "long tail" becomes a newly empowered and increasingly influential "Long Tail," which helps us to conceptualize how previously indifferent, disparate and uninfluential young voters are now becoming increasingly influential and formidable in electoral politics and political discourse in general. The transformation of the long tail into the Long Tail is a new phenomenon that cyberactivism is bringing about as part of the new experimentation. By using NNITs, the trivial many have gained great influence in the electoral market, and the outcome of this conversion process is captured in the notion of the Long Tail.[29] Describing the Long Tail, as "customer demographics that buy the hard-to-find or non-hit items," Anderson (2004) noted that this group's power had increased within the market to the extent that "more than half of Amazon's book sales [came] from *outside* its top 13,000 titles." Similarly, movies that are not in the top 3,000 account for one-fifth of Netflix's total rentals, and the majority of songs streamed by Rhapsody fall outside of its top 10,000. Through widespread use of NNITs, this rich but previously overlooked market that lies beyond the reach of physical retailers is steadily growing. In regard to this rising trend identified by Anderson (2004), Brynjolfsson et al. (2006) point out that the widespread availability of NNIT markets has lowered the cost of matching customers with products (many of which are obscure items) and this new pattern has resulted in an increase in the market share by traditionally insignificant customers. In his view, widespread use of this Internet channel most likely modifies the traditional ratio of 80/20 to 72/28, producing a highly significant 8 percent shift in margin.

Already established within the fields of economics and marketing, the significance of the Long Tail can now be applied, for the purposes of this study, to the field of electoral politics. First noted in 2004, and now growing in numbers and influence, younger voters, who were formerly apolitical and insignificant but who are now equipped with NNITs and allied through off-line political activities, became a fervid force in the presidential primaries and caucuses in 2008. Politically awakened by a series of pressing national issues, these young voters have—through the use of the Internet, cell phones, and networked public spheres, such as new social media—formed distinctive generational features of engaging in cyberspace (Jones and Fox 2009, 5) and become the influential Long Tail of young voters who, in the 2008 presidential election, happened to gravitate toward Democratic candidate Obama.

The unfurling of this Long Tail has, in turn, contributed to the rise of a 'Blue Ocean' in American electoral politics, an original concept coined by Kim and Mauborgne (2005) to describe a newly emerging market. Here, the concept of a "Blue Ocean" can be applied to describe the way in which the Obama campaign captured an unexplored electoral market comprised of a previously apolitical but increasingly influential Long Tail, thereby seizing the opportunity to set new rules of the game in electoral campaigns. This Blue Ocean was characterized by a sudden influx of massive numbers of new young voters who, despite their previous lack of involvement, became highly political once they possessed the ability to communicate and mobilize electronically through an "expanded networked public sphere" (Benkler 2006, 212–72).

Unlike a "Red Ocean," which refers to an existing market with long-defined and well-accepted industry boundaries and rules of play, a so-called "Blue Ocean" is a previously unknown or newly rising market with seemingly endless opportunities and relatively undefined rules (Kim and Mauborgne 2005). While a Red Ocean's potential for growth has already been exhausted, a Blue Ocean's potential for growth may well be unlimited. More specifically, the Red Ocean, in terms of electoral politics, represents the older age groups with the higher voter turnout and conventional media and campaign measures, whereas the Blue Ocean represents the Long Tail of young voters whose involvement was activated by the use of NNITs, which are creating new games with new rules in electoral campaigns. To the constituency, the entry of more young voters into the electoral market represents the transformation of the "trivial many" that constituted a long tail into a newly empowered force to reckon with—the Long Tail. To candidates, this emergence of the Long Tail is also a Blue Ocean in electoral politics, serving as a new opportunity to explore NNIT-oriented strategies of appealing to young generations and their particular political preferences.

IT AS RELATIONSHIP TECHNOLOGY AND THE EMERGING INFLUENCE OF YOUNG GENERATIONS

Humans have developed information technologies to describe and shape their world since pre-history, and even the newest devices are merely contemporary versions of earlier technologies. For example, today's binary code, the *sine qua non* of digital communication, is based on the ancient binary numbering system. Pre-historic mural painting was the predecessor of blogging, and signal fires, ancient Egyptian hieroglyphics, carrier pigeons, and the optical telegraph served as early mechanisms for communicating at a distance. Gutenberg's fifteenth century movable type made possible Martin Luther's radical "Ninety-five Point Thesis" that challenged the authority of the Catholic Church in the sixteenth century Protestant Reformation. In 1791, three years after the French Revolution, Claude Chapped invented the *telegrapher*, or "far writer" (originally, called the "tachygraphe,"—Greek for "fast writer") (Standage, 1998: 9). By Victorian times, there existed a rudimentary analog "Internet"—a patchwork of telegraph networks, submarine cables, pneumatic tube systems, and messengers" (Standage, 1998: 101), which functioned as the first efficient global communication network. In 1984, the French government established the Minitel, its own version of an electronic communication system. Today the Internet, like these earlier technologies, serves as both tool and creator of an ever-expanding series of trans-global hubs such as YouTube.com, Myspace.com, and Facebook.com that realize the human desire for social networking on a global scale.

One has only to consider how a technology such as the cell phone improves or harms human relations to see that, in a very real sense, information technology is relationship technology, (IT = RT). IT as RT, at least initially, disrupts the conventional power relationship and engenders a new power relationship in which NNIT-equipped network participants dominate. This process is nourished by constant feedback from the technical dis/re-intermediations occurring in every realm of our society. Although technology is not uniformly a democratizing force, (e.g., surveillance tapping techniques), generally speaking, IT decenters the conventional power of highly visible "Big Brother" and creates many invisible "little sisters" everywhere (Whitaker, 1999).

The mediating role of the political party—aggregating public opinion, policymaking, political socialization, financing, and managing elections—is now being assumed, to a large degree, through new NNITs. For example, the technical tools on the website of the Obama campaign, www.Barackobama. com, assist in serving numerous important campaign-related functions: registering new voters, starting an affinity group, joining and creating a listserv for friends, downloading an Obama news widget, selecting "Make Calls" to receive a list of supporters' phone numbers and help disseminate news, signing up to receive text-messages, choosing twelve Obama ring tones for a supporter's cell phone, and providing easy fund-raising tools (Green, 2008). The basic goal of this approach is to equip supporters with digital tools that they can use independent of the formal campaign, thus gradually substituting for the many functions of the old industrial model analog political party.

It is inevitable that the political party as we know it would start to devolve as society became rapidly networked. Following Daniel Bell's pioneering 1976 work, *The Coming of Post-Industrial Society*, scholars[30] such as Webster (1995), Castells (1996, 1997), Trippi (2004), and Benkler (2006) predicted not only the rise of the network society originating from the information technology revolution, but also the resulting fundamental transformation of the political structure. This is mainly because information technology, which enables "a form of spontaneous order created through the interactions of decentralized actors" (Fukuyama, 1999: 197), challenges traditional hierarchical forms of political and corporate governance and alters conventional relationships among individuals, organizations, and states.

The current unprecedented Long Tail of Obama's Blue Ocean is an outcome of IT's re-intermediating effect. First of all, as was noted earlier, the Long Tail of Obama supporters consists primarily of previously apolitical, younger generations whose great potential in real politics was awakened by 9/11 and its aftermath. More likely to engage in political action that was also social, they were able to share the experience of supporting a new kind of candidate who matched their political taste. Four years before, they had realized their potential power within electoral politics when Howard Dean galvanized their predecessors. In 2008, better organized and more technologically savvy, the supporters who comprise this Blue Ocean now own their own networked public sphere in cyber space and are shaping political discourse to an unprecedented degree. They possess the most powerful tools—NNITs—and use them adeptly for acquiring, sharing, communicating information, mobilizing voter turnout, and raising unparalleled numbers of campaign donations for the candidate of their choice. They possess and control their own networks of databases, such as MySpace, Facebook, and LinkedIn and have their own means of broadcasting, such as YouTube, thus controlling both social/political content and networks.

This characterization of Obama's Long Tail of Blue Ocean corresponds to Han's (2007: 59) definition of social capital: "multiple human resources networks, either actual or potential, with certain characteristics of shared norms, values, attitudes, and trust built through prior collective action that can be utilized for future social and political mobilization." Similarly, Fukuyama points that "[i]f networks are to be truly productive of order, they necessarily depend on informal norms taking the place of formal organization—in other words, on social capital." In the current presidential campaign, Obama's Long Tail, comprised of a diverse and activated constituency, has, by favoring him over Clinton or McCain, acted as important social capital. To the primarily young voters, the "trivial many" for most of the past 40 years, Obama's constant call for "change" evokes trust. Barackobama.com has been the first truly successful attempt to tap into these young generations' trust, their networking database infrastructure, and their political networks. In 2004, Howard Dean's meetup.com page initiated the large-scale transformation of the political landscape through the use of technologies but ultimately failed to convert the energies of his young supporters into the nomination in the primaries and caucuses (PBS, 2008: 3).

One of the major keys to Obama's success was in his early understanding of the changing battle conditions in electoral politics. The Republican Party, likewise, also recognized the potential of NNITs-derived campaign resources and launched the "voter vault," a database of likely GOP supporters for fundraising and votes as did Clinton supporter Harold Ickes, who created the campaign's "Catalyst," (Lasky, 2008). However, one major difference between these tools and those of the Obama campaign is that while the Clinton and Republican databases were proprietary, Obama's was open-source. Chris Hughes, the 24-year-old co-founder of Facebook, which has more than 70 million active users, most under the age of thirty, constructed Obama's database. In this regard, for Obama supporters, "Barackobama.com capitalize[d] on 'viral growth'" (Lasky, 2008). Simply put, once Obama's message goes out, it is immediately—and at no cost to the campaign—sent to as many as 70 million active users of Facebook, or all $(N^{31}-1)!$, who further disseminate it. These and other generally young technophiles comprise electronic herds—a network army that serves as the vanguards of the Obama campaign.

The recent presidential candidates did not create this new Blue Ocean; rather, the technology revolution and the central players of those advancements in technology did. The candidates tapped into it. Computer and network-savvy young volunteers for the Obama campaign maximize software power when organizing campaign operations in the fields. According to Isaac Garcia, CEO of Central Desktop, the precinct captains in Obama's campaign volunteered to use Central Desktop's social software, a wiki-based or Web-based collaboration platform[32], for the Texas primary and caucus that includes "254 counties and over 8,000 voting precincts, and a population falling into all different ethnic, economic and age demographics" (Catone, 2008, March 4). The young digital supporters of the Obama campaign have outrun conventional soldiers equipped with older analog strategies.

WHY SOUTH KOREA AND THE UNITED STATES?

Much in the same way that America's freedom from the legacy of Europe's Ancient Regime gave rise to the old experimentation of volunteer associational activities in nineteenth-century America, the extensive deployment of NNITs is giving rise to a new experimentation in the cyberspace of the Information Age. The blossoming of the new experimentation that this book characterizes as a phenomenon of the Information Age, as well the impact of this new experimentation upon contemporary politics, is most evident in the cases of Korea and the United States for three reasons:

* First, the rapid and extensive deployment of NNITs;
* Second, the highest concentration and actual usage of NNITs among previously apolitical young voters; and
* Third, countries with either seismic political crises or a series of NNIT-induced, test-run mobilizations around non-political events salient to younger generations.

By far, the most important condition that must be met by any country included in a study of this sort is that their society be wired and equipped with basic information technologies; however, the availability of NNITs alone is not enough for the full realization of the new experimentation. The intensive and extensive use of NNITs in every aspect of individuals' lives and every realm of a society has to reach such a degree that activities in the virtual space represent significant propitiations in the overall political discourse and deliberation as well as social settings in a society. In an effort to understand the level of informatization in a society, researchers have tried to measure societies' level of deployment and actual usage of NNITs.

It is easier to measure the deployment level than the actual usage, though, especially in political and social contexts. The International Telecommunication Union has developed more sophisticated indices measuring the level of Information and Communication Technology (ICT) infrastructure and access, the level of use and intensity of ICT, and the level of capacity to use ICT effectively (ITU 2009 a, 21). Access level is measured by the following

indicators: fixed telephone lines per 100 inhabitants, mobile cellular telephone subscriptions per 100 inhabitants, international Internet bandwidth
(bits/s) per Internet user, proportion of households with a computer, and
proportion of households with Internet access at home (ITU 2009 a, 33).
Usage level is measured by the following indicators: Internet users per 100
inhabitants, fixed broadband Internet subscribers per 100 inhabitants, and
mobile broadband subscriptions per 100 inhabitants (ITU 2009 a, 33). Level
of skill is measured by adult literacy rate, secondary gross enrollment ratio,
and tertiary gross enrollment ratio (ITU 2009 a, 33). These three main indices
are called ITU's Information and Communication Technology Development
Index (IDI) and were presented to the World Summit on the Information
Society in March 2009, which was intended to benchmark information society developments on an international level. In this IDI, South Korea ranked
first in two major categories (i.e., actual usage and skills) in both 2002 and
2007, and ranked fourth in the access category in 2007 within Asia and the
Pacific region (ITU 2009 a, 41–3). In IDI's overall ranking, South Korea was
first in both 2002 and 2007 (ITU 2009 a, p. 22). Considering that Asia and the
Pacific region have emerged as a world leader with 42 percent of the world's
mobile cellular subscriptions (the highest), 47 percent of the world's fixed
telephone lines, 39 percent of the world's Internet users, 36 percent of the
world's fixed broadband subscribers, and 42 percent of the world's mobile
broadband subscriptions at the end of 2007 (ITU 2009 a, 1), South Korea's
informatization and substantial usage of that NNIT infrastructure can serve
as a model for the rest of the world, especially for countries with developing
economies and democracies.

According to Table 1.1, Major Information Technology Indicators,
Republic of Korea and G-7 Countries, which I compiled from ITU's World
Telecommunication/ICT Indicators Database Online in 2009, Korea and the
United States are leading the world's informatization even among the most
industrialized and democratic countries in the world. In the three major cat-
egories of ICT access, usage, and capacity to use the infrastructure, these
two countries are at the top; South Korea, with the second smallest popula-
tion, surpassed the United States, Canada, France, Germany, and the United
Kingdom.[33]South Korea ranked first in the categories of Percent of Digital
Main Lines, Fixed Broadband Internet Subscribers, Internet Users per 100
Inhabitants, Proportion of Households with a Computer and its Usage, and
Proportion of Households with Internet Access and its Usage. It is quite phenomenal that South Korea, with the lowest GDP among these countries, is
leading all these nations in ITU's ICT.

The United States, despite lagging behind other European G-7 countries in terms of NNIT infrastructure, also leads in the category of actual

Table 1.1. Major Information Technology Indicators, R.O.K. and G-7 Countries, 2003

Indicators	R.O.K.	U.S.	Canada	France	Germany	Italy	Japan	U.K.
Population (thousands)	47,463	292,617	31,636	60,008	82,583	57,961	127,736	59,282
Digital Main Phone Line (%)	100.0	98.3	99.8	100.0	100.0	99.9	100.0	100.0
Cellular Subscribers per 100 Inhabitants	70.77	54.90	42.01	69.5	78.47	97.95	67.84	91.52
Fixed Broadband Internet Subscribers (thousands)	11,178 (0.023%)	27,744 (0.009%)	4,513 (0.014%)	3,569 (0.005%)	4,470 (0.005%)	2,250 (0.003%)	14,917 (0.011%)	3,114 (0.005%)
Internet users per 100 Inhabitants	65.50	62.61	64.0	36.27	54.00	39.48	48.26	61
Prop. of Households with a Computer	78	62	67	46	65	48	78	63
Prop. of Individuals Who Used a Computer	69	64	65 (2000)	N/A	64	39	45	73 (2004)
Prop. of Households with Internet Access	69	55	57	31	54	32	54	55
Prop. Of Individuals Who Used Internet	66	60	64	49 (2002)	56	29	68	65

Source: World Telecommunication/ICT Indicators Database Online, International Telecommunication Union (ITU), 2009

usage: Internet Users per 100 Inhabitants and Proportion of Individuals Who Used a Computer and the Internet, as Table 1.2 clearly shows. However, the more important aspect of informatization in terms of a new experimentation lies in the current status of democracy, civic organizations and the overall power of civil society relative to the power of state in a society. Although the trust that was accumulated through the face-to-face, local, voluntary interactions of nineteenth- and twentieth-century America has been diluted by bureaucratization, centralization and nationalization, the tradition of civic disobedience that began in the 1960s and '70s through a series of social movements remains strong in American society today.

Interestingly, the technological foundations of the new experimentation also originated in the United States, including the ARPANET in the 1960s, as well as other major innovations that made the Internet possible, such as the modem, TCP/IP, and the establishment of an international organization for the management of the Internet, the Internet Corporation for Assigned Names and Numbers (ICANN). As chapters 4 and 5 will demonstrate, American society also leads the world in terms of the actual usage of those advanced NNITs in the recent major context of electoral politics and political discourses on major national agendas. Due to the strong civil society and IT industries in the United States, U.S. adoption and infusion of NNITs in the political realm has been smooth and has set an example for the rest of the world. As Diani (1997; 2001) noted, social capital grows out of a series of social movements. Accordingly, the successful adoption and use of NNITs for political activation and participation require not only the NNIT infrastructure but vibrant civil society and civic activities as well. There are many countries with a high level of mobile cellular phone subscriptions, for example, that still maintain strong authoritarian regimes; however, the widespread use of technology alone does not explain the full realization of this new experimentation.

South Korea's story is slightly different. Korea's political culture and institutions originated from strong Confucianism and endured twenty-five years of militarism under Japanese colonial control. After being liberated from Japan, Korea experienced a civil dictatorship under the founding president, Rhee Seung-man (1948–1960), and then chaotic instability under the regime of Jang Myun in 1960, after the political revolution of April 19. Until the June 10 Resistance in 1987, Koreans lived under military dictatorship with strong influence of authoritarian Confucian political culture. A strong tradition of civil disobedience has become a defining trait of the modern political history of Korea. The success of General Park Chung-hee, who seized power through a military coup in 1961, in a miraculous economic development, repressed political freedom and produced a long series of opposition movements from universities and labor unions.

Table 1.2. Comparison of the Republic of Korea and the United States: The New Experimentation

	R.O.K.	U.S.
Information and Communication Technology Development Index (IDI)	World's leading edge	One of the most advanced
Original Political System	Confucian Yi Dynasty with a tradition of strong state and weak civil society, Japanese militarism, civil and military dictatorship	Model of democracy: the 19th century experimentation of face-to-face, voluntary, civic participation
Status of Democracy in the 20th Century	One of the most substantial democracies in Asia achieved in the late 1990s as a by-product of a series of militant democratic anti-dictatorship movements (1960s–1987); recently activated civil society and civic organizations with social capital that is the strongest in Korea's political history since 1990s	Waning of American civic-mindedness and social capital accumulated during the 19th century face-to-face, voluntary associational participation in the local community, due to nationalization, centralization, and bureaucratization of civic organizations and activities
Young Generations in Elections and Politics	The '386 Generation' led the overthrow of the military regime in 1987; the '2030 Generation' recognized their power in cyberspace through a series of test-run mobilizations and exerted decisive influence in the 2002 presidential election; teenagers mobilized candlelight demonstrations against President Lee for his decision to resume beef import from the U.S.	Generation Y or Millennials aged 18–32, used to be apolitical, now active in cyberspace, conceptualized as President Obama's Blue Ocean of "Long Tail", exerted formidable influence in the 2008 presidential election and mobilized in President Obama's healthcare reform process, using new online social media (e.g., Twitter)
Demonstration Effects and Test-mobilizations	386 Generation's defeat movement in 2000; 2030 Generation's international sports games (Utah Winter Olympics, World Cup) and anti-American candlelight protest and presidential election in 2002 served as demonstration effects for 2008 candlelight vigil on beef imports by teens	9/11 terrorist attack as a generational awakening milestone, Iraq War in 2003, 2004 presidential election, 2006 mid-term election, primaries and caucuses, and presidential election in 2008 served as demonstration effects for President Obama's HCR legislation

As will be explored in chapter 2, after a series of demonstrations led by university students finally brought democracy to South Korea in 1987, those militant anti-government democratic forces in Korean society began to focus on non-political issues, such as environmental protection, social welfare and other aspects of socio-economic equality. Contrary to the American experience of voluntary associational activities in the local community, though, Korean society was able to establish itself as a strong civil society through a long political opposition movement against a repressive political regime. This fact provides important insight into how a formerly authoritarian political regime with a Confucian tradition of strong state and weak society became the most vibrant democracy in Asia and in the world (Han 1997), leading the way in the new experimentation with NNIT use in political discourse and electoral politics. The presence and activities of strong civic organizations in the late 1990s coincided with the extensive deployment of NNITs. In the 1990s, civil society and NNIT infrastructure experienced explosive growth simultaneously, and as a result, democratic forces in Korea strengthened geometrically (Han 2007). These democratic forces began to use NNITs to make their voices heard in the political discourse and to exert their influence in political contexts.

This is how the Korean version of a new experimentation started in a culture where no trace of a strong civil society had previously existed. The concept of the demonstration effect aptly explains how such an undemocratic society, through a series of anti-government movements, was capable of being transformed into a society that is now considered to be experiencing a new experimentation in cyberspace through the extensive deployment of NNITs. Information technology, as relationship technology, is capable of reinforcing the existing power structure; however, the use of NNITs can also activate a complacent majority or empower the ruled or oppressed. Despite being democratized in the late twentieth century, the Korean political system still has several unsolved problems: the political parties still depend heavily on the charisma of their leaders; the National Assembly has not carried out its own mission to legislate; the executive power still overwhelms both the legislative and judiciary branches; and politics are divided along the lines of East–West regionalism and conservative–liberal ideology. In these contexts, the use of NNITs might shift the power balance and empower the voices that have not been reflected in the political discourse. For this reason, this book focuses on the rising power of young generations in both South Korea and the United States.

Before 1987, the youth in South Korea was not a factor in politics, and they still have the lowest voting rate among all age groups. In the United States, the youth's voter turnout rate has waned since the 1960s, and they are the age group with the lowest voting rate. Thus, young generations in both countries have the biggest potential to be cultivated when their eyes are opened to their potential in cyberspace.

Until Korea underwent American military occupation and began adopting American capitalism and liberal democracy directly after being liberated from Japanese colonial control in 1945, no commonality in socio-economic and political system could be found between the United States and Korea. The United States was established over two centuries ago by European settlers, Pilgrim fathers, and Puritans who had migrated to the continent to escape the rigid class system of the European Ancient Regime. Due to the process of acquiring independence from European forces, the characteristics of the American political system were unique and unprecedented, compared to Western and European standards.

The political culture of South Korea, on the other hand, as summarized in Table 2, was strongly influenced by Confucianism, a very rigid hierarchical class system, the superiority of state over society (economy) and executive power over legislative and judiciary powers (governing structure), seniority over juniority, and collectivism over individualism. Since, in Confucian culture, a person is not considered an adult until married, young unmarried people within traditional Korean society had no voice in family or public affairs. Interestingly, the exception was the young Confucian university students who were considered the guardians of the Royal Shrine of Confucius in the *Seongkyunkwan*[34] during the Yi Dynasty (1392–1910).They were among the few elites given the right to appeal and demonstrate against the king and government. Ironically, this tradition has continued in modern Korea—the overthrow of the military dictatorship in 1987 was the outcome of a series of protests led by university students in the early 1960s.These university students were the ardent supporters of liberal democracy and the most militant democratic forces in modern Korea. In a society with a long tradition of Confucian and military authoritarian regime, the social capital needed for liberal democracy was accumulated over almost half a century among university students, intelligentsia and the labor union through anti-dictatorship movements. Combined with the social capital generated and transferred through a series of democratic movements, the young generations in Korea's networked public sphere exerted unprecedented influence in the 2002 presidential election, which later seriously challenged the legitimacy of the Lee regime, which took office in 2008.Korea's democratization can be juxtaposed with America's old experimentation of face-to-face, local grass-roots democratization; they are currently leading this new experimentation that originated from the active participation of NNIT-induced young generations in electoral politics and general political discourse.

SUMMARY OF CHAPTERS

Exactly how does the use of NNITs impact political community? Based on the way in which these revolutionary changes have co-opted young generations, how do they affect the formation of social capital and the new experimentation? While exploring these issues, this book will examine cases in Korea and the United States that demonstrate the specific impacts of NNITs in major political discourse and elections.

Despite high expectations about NNITs' potential to influence democratic outcomes, few studies have provided clear evidence that NNITs have actually changed political discourse or election outcomes. With this in mind, chapter 2, "From Indifference to Making the Difference" examines how young, politically indifferent, Korean NNIT users involved themselves in mainstream Korean political discourse and became the linchpin in the election of President Roh Moo-hyun in 2002.In the Information Age, demonstration effects from NNIT-induced mobilizations are capable of bringing about dramatic changes in electoral politics. The Korean experience in 2002 suggests that, although turnout generally declined among all generational groups, NNITs can play a particularly decisive role in shaping the political cohesiveness and voting patterns of younger generational groups in electoral politics. This chapter provides data on the use of NNITs and changes in voting behavior patterns in Korea's electoral politics.

Continuing our examination of Korean cases, chapter 3, "Korea's Beef Crisis: What The Internet Portends For Democracy," illustrates how NNIT-activated younger generations in Korea changed the direction of public discourse on President Lee Myung-bak's decision to resume importing American beef to Korea. Despite the enormous popularity of President Lee, who was elected with the widest margin in the history of Korea's presidential elections, it took only 100 days for his record-high popularity to plummet to the lowest rating of all Korean presidents with so few days in office. This chapter examines how the combination of Lee's early misguided policies and staffing decisions— along with the existence of a highly "wired" young generation—quickly produced anti-Lee discourse, which, in turn, escalated into massive, ongoing street protests by a large cross-section of the population. While examining the various factors involved in such an unprecedented phenomenon, this chapter addresses two important questions regarding politics in the Information Age: (1) how do NNITs influence the political discourse and contribute to the evolution of a political crisis; and (2) who are the most critical players in NNIT-induced politics? To answer the first question, this chapter applies Situational Crisis Communication Theory, which distinguishes between four stages of crisis evolution, and the concepts underlying Heinrich's Law. To answer the second question, this chapter invokes Gidden's theory of life politics. Through all of these theoretical lenses, this chapter assesses the extent of the political impact that NNIT-mobilized young generations can have on democracy.

Chapter 4, "Obama's Presidential Campaign: How a 'Long Tail' of Young Voters Became a 'Blue Ocean' and Changed American Electoral Politics," applies the concept of the "Long Tail" to describe the Obama phenomenon and sudden influx of previously apolitical youths, mostly activated by the use of NNITs, into American electoral politics during the 2008 presidential election. In that election, young voters, motivated by a series of major national crises and events, and using NNITs (e.g., SNSs, cell phones), created a generational sense of community. This chapter traces the transformative role that technology played in the campaign and analyzes how the Obama campaign tapped the potential power of formerly apathetic young voters and created an influential Long Tail of support that redefined the political/electoral system and is now posing important questions about the future of elections and democracy in general.

Continuing our focus on the development of these issues within the United States, chapter 5, "Obama Tweeting and Tweeted," analyzes how the microblogging medium Twitter was used during President Obama's first 100 days to aid his legislation battle for healthcare reform. The HCR agenda was ostensibly divided along partisan lines, a division that is likely to be reflected among micro-content online social media users. This chapter discusses the nature and demography of this NNIT-mobilized young generation that is heavily oriented toward the Democratic Party. This chapter also measures how Obama's Long Tail reacted to these two politically important agendas as evidenced by their tweeting, replying, re-tweeting, and searching for further information. To properly identify the political reactions of the Obama Long Tail, this chapter focuses on several factors: the tweets and re-tweets sent by President Obama and the White House, as well as the replies and re-tweets sent by followers and friends of both Obama and the White House to each other.

To conclude, chapter 6, based on the case studies of both Korea and the United States, summarizes the overall impacts of NNITs upon social capital, politics and elections. Most importantly, it also evaluates how the political participation of NNIT-activated young generations is likely to evolve as more young people begin to use NNITs in the near future, and assesses the extent to which this widening of usage will affect political discourse in the politics and elections of the Information Age. Ultimately, though, this study aims to investigate one overarching, critical question: What do the Internet and other NNITs portend for democracy in the Information Age?

NOTES

1. The more generally accepted classification scheme of the evolution of human society is to start with Stone Age (with human beings' dexterity to develop stone tools), Bronze and Iron Age, Classical Period, Middle Ages, The Renaissance (15th–16th centuries), Age of Enlightenment (17th–18th centuries), Age of Industrial Revolution, and Age of Information Society. For more on this, see Saxby (1990).

2. The most important feature in the current development of information technologies is in the fact that these technologies are all "networked." Information technologies are defined as any devices involved in the process of producing, transmitting, receiving, storing, retrieving, and applying information and knowledge. When these technologies are applied in real life and politics, it facilitates the changes of the preexisting relationships among people, organizations and socioeconomic/political institutions. In this perspective, I define "information technologies" as "relationship technologies." The Internet, mobile phones, Short Message Services (SMSs), and other new networking tools, referred to collectively in this chapter as "new networked information technologies" (NNITs),are rapidly penetrating the lives of people around the globe, especially among younger generations. Because they are networked, NNITs have demonstrated the ability to spread information and mobilize large numbers of people around social or political events, speedily transforming social and political consciousness.

3. For more, see Dizard (1982), Forester (1985), Guile (1985), Fukuyama (1999), Shapiro (1999), Whitaker (1999), and Kline & Burstein (2005).

4. The 2007 Presidential election in Korea was an inverse of the 200 election in that the online campaign activities were not as active as before and the decisive shift of voters occurred from liberal to conservative candidate. The 2007 election will be briefly analyzed at the end of chapter 2.

5. There are many different translations of Zhuangzi's dream. I translated this story myself, keeping as close to the literal meanings of the original Chinese as possible.

6. [3] Plato's *Theaetetus* is presumed to have been written earlier than Zhuangzi's writing since Zhuangzi was born in 369 B.C. and Theaetetus is known to have been written in 360 B.C. when Zhuangzi was about nine years old. This excerpt is taken from Benjamin Jowett's translation of Plato's *Dialogues* and is available from http://classics.mit.edu/Plato/theatu.html.

7. This does not rule out the possibility that they can also entail a detrimental effect on existing social capital because these new mediums and spheres can accelerate the immediacy of information, which can easily lead into the viral escalation of crises or unnecessary scandals beyond reasonable control.

8. The term *long tail* was originally used in the field of statistics to indicate those portions of a particular frequency distribution that were relatively insignificant. Later, it was used to indicate an uninfluential majority of consumers within a given market. In the last ten years, however, many online businesses—including Amazon.com, Rhapsody and Netflix—have started to focus their marketing strategy on the "trivial

many" who constitute 80 percent of their total market. Due to the extensive applications of networked information technologies in these markets, products aimed at the long tail of the majority of consumers have recently gained increasing importance in these markets. Based on the analysis of such increased use of NNITs in the marketing area, Anderson (2004) observed the phenomenon of the transformation of a largely unimportant "long tail" into a newly empowered and highly influential consumers or voters—a "Long Tail." Now that the significance of the Long Tail concept has been established within economics and marketing, this article now compares the "Long Tail" of NNIT-activated, participatory young voters to the "long tail" of previously uninfluential young voters in the field of American electoral politics. For more details on the conversion of a "long tail" (lower case) to a "Long Tail" (upper case), see Han (2009).

9. See Shapiro (1999: 55)

10. Despite various interpretations of this terminology, the general consensus seems to share the idea that Information Technology enables us to move closer to the realization of "direct democracy" through plebiscitary vote on political issues.

11. Oscar Jaszi, *The Dissolution of the Habsburg Monarchy p.34* "King of Hungary, of Bohemia, of Dalmatria, Croatia, Slavonia, Galicia, Lodomeria, and Illyria; Grand Duke of Tuscany and Cracow; Duke of Loth ringia, of Salzburg, Styria, Carinthia, Carniola, and Bukovina; Grand Duke of Transylvania, Margrave of Moravia; Duke of Upper and Lower Silesia, of Modena, Parma, Piacenza, and Guastella, of Ausschwitz and Sator, of Teschen, Friaul, Ragusa, and Zara; Princely Count of Habsburg and Tyrol, of Kyburg, Gorz, and Gradiska,. . . . and so on. See Anderson (1983: 27)

12. It is classified as non-electronic information technology.

13. See Borre and Scarbrough (1995), p. 4.

14. Wharton School globalization expert Stephen J. Kobrin argues that "the more individual citizens start to feel that the locus of economic control and political decision-making on economic matters is shifting from the local level, where it can be controlled, to the global level, where no one is in charge and no one is minding the store." See Friedman (2000: 191)

15. See Sklair (1991: 6–7). "When we buy something that has been imported, when we are influenced to vote or support a cause by those whose interests are transnational, and when we are experience the need for a global product, we are engaged in a typical economic, political, and cultural-ideological transnational practices."

16. See Ong (1999: 214)

17. Ong (1999: 217) argues that "globalization has induced a situation of graduated sovereignty, whereby even as the state maintains control over its territory, it is also willing in some cases to let corporate entities set the terms for constituting and regulating some domains. . . . . What result is a system of value enjoy different kinds of rights, discipline, caring and security."

18. See Ong (1999: 221)

19. See Ong (1999: 219, 239)

20. "Populations subjected to different regimes of value enjoy different kinds of rights, discipline, caring, and security."

21. See Chosun Daily News January 26, 2001.

22. See Pierre (2000: 6)

23. Its separate and differentiated usage against that of government has recently been recognized by several literatures. See Rosenau (1992), Hirst and Thompson (1996), Alexander and Schneider (1991), and World Bank (1994). A World Bank report (1994: xvi) defines the concept of 'governance in the "manner in which power is exercised in the management of a country's economic and social resources for development." It (1994: xvi) specifies three distinct aspects of governance: "(1) the form of political regime; (2) the process by which authority is exercised in the management of a country's economic and social resources for development; and (3) the capacity of governments to design, formulate, and implement policies and discharge functions."

24. See Rosenau (1992), pp.3–4, Hirst and Thompson (1996), pp.183–184.

25. Hirst and Thompson (1996), p.184.

26. See Rosenau (1992), p.275

27. Rosenau (1992), p.291

28. By gender this committee was composed of 51 men and 49 women. By ages, 27 in age 20s, 28 in age 30s, 19 in age 40s, and 26 in age 50s. By occupation, 11 in agriculture, 12 in own business, 17in manufacturing and technicians, 14 in managerial and professionals, 5 students, 33 housewives, and 8 unemployed. By region, 25 from Seoul, 16 from Kyungnam province and Pusan, 11 from Kyungbook province and Daegu, 25 from Kyunggi province and Incheon, 11 from Cholla province, 2 from Daejeon, 2 from Choongbook province, 4 from Choongnam province, 3 from Kangwon province, and 1 from Jejoo province. Check following Web address of Joongang Daily Newspaper of Korea : http://www.joins.co.kr/news/2000/01/24/all/20000124182920102010.html.

29. Henceforth, two different terms will be used in this chapter: "long tail" (lowercase), as a general description of any ignored "trivial many" in any arena, and "Long Tail" (uppercase), to designate the formerly "trivial" but newly empowered many in those areas.

30. For more, see Dizard (1982), Forester (1985), Guile (1985), Fukuyama (1999), Shapiro (1999), Whitaker (1999), and Kline and Burstein (2005).

31. Theoretically, "N" can be replaced by 70 million, a total number of Facebook active members. As a example of (N-1)! when N equals 4, (4–1)! is 3 x 2 x 1, which is equal to 6. When "N" equals 70 million, it becomes almost impossible to calculate the total effect.

32. Regarding the tools for the young generation, Web 2.0 describes the current trend on the creative and collaborative use of the World Wide Web. This leads into Web-based online community and social networking sites such as wikis and blogs. It does not entail updates in technical specifications of web technology but, rather, changes in how this technology is used.

33. Germany except in the category of cellular subscribers per 100 inhabitants, Italy except in the category of Cellular Subscribers per 100 inhabitants, Japan except in the category of Prop. of Individuals Who Used the Internet, and United Kingdom except in the category of Cellular Subscribers per 100 Inhabitants.

34. This is the name of a Confucian university during the Yi Dynasty (1392–1910) that taught Confucian classical literature to help students pass the civil service examination and worshipped the shrines of Confucius and his students. These students were the backbone of the Confucian Yi Dynasty and Royal Court; and since they were given the role of upholding the Confucian governing ideology and institutions, they were also given the right to challenge the Royal family and governing elites whenever their governing digressed from the principal teachings of Confucius. These were the heteronomical forces (i.e., dissenting voices) built within the hegemonic forces of the Yi Dynasty.

Chapter 2

How Korea's Wired Youth Became a Political Power

NNIT-activated Experimentation and the 2002 Presidential Election in Korea[1]

The Internet, mobile phones, Short Message Services (SMSs), and other new networking tools, referred to collectively in this book as "new networked information technologies" (NNITs), are rapidly penetrating the daily lives of people around the globe, especially among the younger generations. After the terrorist attacks of September 11th, young Americans began turning to the Internet as a source of community in a way that likely "sets a pattern for the rest of their lives" (as quoted in Ludden, 2004).[2] Although it may be too soon to make these claims conclusively, NNITs seem to have demonstrated their ability to spread information and mobilize large numbers of people around social or political events, speedily transforming social and political consciousness among previously apolitical generations.

In much of the literature on youth turnout and civic engagement, the political participation of younger generations is generally analyzed in an attempt to ascertain what factors stimulate or increase their voter turnout. For this reason, it is unsurprising that political parties and political action committees co-opted NNITs during the 2004 U.S. presidential election with explicit "get out the vote" campaigns. In fact, Internet campaign activities at sites such as Meetup.com, Moveon.org, and Rockthevote.com garnered considerable media attention in their attempt to capitalize off of the younger generations' infatuation with the Internet.

Subsequently, the 2004 and 2008 U.S. presidential elections set off a flurry of academic research over certain polls that assessed young voter turnout as having increased to levels unseen since the early 1970s. According to The Center for Information and Research on Civic Learning & Engagement (2004, 1), "at least 20.9 million Americans under the age of 30 voted in 2004, an increase of 4.6 million over 2000, and the turnout rate among these voters rose from about 42.3 percent to 51.6 percent, a sharp rise of 9.3 percentage points."[3] Although it is too early to tell, it has been argued (Han 2007; Rainie 2000; Rainie, et al. 2005) that the use of the Internet and NNITs in political campaigns can increase the overall turnout among younger voters to such an extent that it may dramatically affect electoral outcomes. Although, in 2004, the use of the Internet and other NNITs did increase voter turnout among younger generations in America, the results did not match general expectations about how the participation of younger voters would affect electoral outcomes (Ludden, 2004). To claim that this new experimentation in the use of NNITs definitively increases voter turnout among younger generations, more empirical studies would be necessary, utilizing data on major elections over a more extensive period of time.

By focusing on voter turnout, though, these studies (Rainie 2000, 2005) overlook an important alternative explanation for the effect of NNITs, which was highlighted in the 2002 Korean presidential election. The data from that election suggests that NNITs can also lead to the formation of a cohesive voting bloc among otherwise indifferent younger generations, a phenomenon capable of dramatically shifting electoral outcomes.[4] In the case of Korea, what is more plausible than a causal relationship between NNITs, *increased voter turnout,* and electoral outcomes is a causal relationship between NNITs, *increased voter cohesion,* and electoral outcomes. For instance, even though the younger generations in Korea are arguably the most wired individuals on the planet, their use of NNITs alone was insufficient to reverse their declining voter turnout rate in the 2002 presidential election. Yet, despite the declining turnout and their paternalistic Confucian political culture that traditionally reserves primary political voice for respected seniors rather than inexperienced youngsters (Han and Ling 1997), the younger generations in Korea suddenly became a formidable political power. In a pattern never seen before in previous Korean elections, young voters concentrated and channeled their votes toward presidential candidate Roh. In this way, the two younger generations—the so-called "386" and the "2030" generations—ultimately cast the decisive vote in a Korean presidential election that would have otherwise been too close to call. Instead of measuring the effect of the Internet and NNITs on younger generations' political participation through overall turnout, attention should also be paid to NNITs' effects on generational voting patterns, and particularly on cohesion.

What exactly is the relationship between NNITs, generational voting patterns and electoral outcomes? In short, NNIT-induced mobilizations create the generational social capital and consciousness necessary to form a cohesive generational voting bloc with the potential to dramatically affect electoral outcomes in a tight election. Three preconditions must be met in order for NNITs to aid younger generations in making the leap from being politically indifferent and insignificant to being politically powerful and relevant:

- First, there must be rapid and broad deployment of NNITs with the highest concentration among younger generations of eligible voters;
- Second, there must be NNIT-induced, test-run mobilizations around non-political, social events salient to younger generations; and
- Third, generational consciousness and cohesion must be built up as a result of NNIT-induced mobilizations.

The political power of NNIT users in Korea could not have been realized without the deep penetration and the broad deployment of NNITs among the youth (Chang 2006; Gallup Korea 2003; Huh 2003; Kim 2003; Lee 2006; MacKinnon 2005, 331; Min 2004; Roh 2002; SICH-NMDP 2003; Song 2003, 2005; Watts 2003); however, technological infrastructure alone does not explain how previously apolitical and indifferent young generations suddenly transformed into a formidable factor in political discourse and electoral politics, which will be a key to understanding the nature of the new experimentation. Information-sharing infrastructures, public discourses and catalytic events are instrumental in the actual mobilization of social capital for specific social/political movements. Especially in electoral politics, the creation of a cohesive voting bloc by means of NNITs requires an intermediate phase where a generation mobilizes around salient events.

Successful mobilizations on political agendas lead to a series of protests, which can be conceptually understood as demonstration effects showing younger generations how to utilize NNITs as tools for political action, compelling them to form generational consciousness, and leading them to recognize their own power in the political arena. From 2000 to 2002, there was a particularly rapid and broad deployment of NNITs among younger Koreans. At the same time, members of younger generations began participating in NNIT-induced social and political movements. This phenomenon suggests that the study of NNIT usage in mobilizations is increasingly relevant. As the margin of victory over the last six presidential elections in Korea has rapidly shrunk (Gallup Korea, 2003, 269), NNIT-induced political mobilizations have created strong consciousness among younger generations and a cohesive young voting bloc that has allowed the younger generations to cast the decisive vote. Post-election analysis by Gallup Korea (2003, 271) concluded that Roh's slim victory was due not to changes in the younger generations' voter turnout but rather to changes in their overall voting patterns. In this perspective, the transformation from apolitical, disparate, and uninfluential 2030

Generation or R Generation[5] to a cohesive voting bloc can be understood as the conversion of the long tail into the Long Tail, explained in chapter 1.

To demonstrate how the increasing consolidation and cohesion of younger generations' voting patterns causally link back to the increasing prevalence of NNITs in Korea, this chapter is arranged in four sections. The first discusses theoretical arguments about social capital and its relationship to social movements and NNITs. The second outlines the characteristics of the 386 and the 2030 generations, delineates the dramatic informatization of Korea, and describes how explosive informatization has mirrored a similar explosion in civic activism. The third discusses demonstration effects as they pertain to social movements and explains how demonstration effects arising from NNIT-induced mobilizations have been relevant in Korean politics along generational lines. And the fourth section illustrates how these effects, which arose first in non-political spheres translated into political mobilization and the consolidation and cohesion of younger generations' voting patterns in the 16th Korean presidential election.

THE NEW EXPERIMENTATION AND SOCIAL CAPITAL

What will be the most important first step in understanding the nature of this new experimentation of NNIT-induced political activism? How can we assess the impact of the extensive use of NNITs upon society, politics and democracy? Furthermore, how should we measure the impacts of the new experimentation upon the existing political system, which is rooted in America's old experimentation? As pointed out during our analysis of the main features of the new experimentation in the previous chapter, the concept of social capital is a key to answering all of these questions.

First, there are several debates surrounding the relationship between social capital and NNITs as they relate to social movements. Social capital is widely regarded as one of the most important ingredients for achieving a stable democracy and successful economy (Baron, et al. 2000; Bourdieu 1986; Coleman 1988; Edwards and Foley 2001; Ehrenberg 1999; Fukuyama 1995; Putnam 1995; Wellman and Haythornthwaite 2002). While Coleman and Bourdieu emphasize the functional and instrumental aspects of social capital, Putnam discusses its impacts on collective actions, political participation and democracy. As mentioned before, for the purposes of this discussion, "social capital" will be used to mean "multiple human resources networks, either actual or potential, with certain characteristics of shared norms, values, attitudes and trust built through prior collective action that can be utilized for future social and political mobilizations" (Han 2007, 59). Social capital and social movements are closely connected (Putnam 2000, 152) and feed upon one another (Putnam 2003, 162); and Diani's (1997, 2001) argument that social capital is an outcome of a series of social movements strongly reinforces the closely interrelated nature of these two concepts.

Many other scholars, building on this theory of social capital, have also theorized about the connection between social capital and NNITs (Bimber 2000; Castells 1996; Dahlgren 2000; Delli Carpini 2000; Kraut and Kiesler 2003; Putnam 2000; Shah, et al., 2001; Wellman and Haythornthwaite, 2002). Their approaches fall into two broad schools of thought—dystopian and utopian. Dystopians claim that the new experimentation damages existing social capital by decreasing the amount of face-to-face interaction, social connectedness, and community involvement to such an extent that weakened social trust and bonds result in the waning of community and democratic fundamentals. In other words, the use of NNITs decreases the social capital, the potential for social movements, and political participation in general. In contrast, utopians hold that NNITs will enhance communication and networks so significantly that a strengthened base of shared values and trust will consolidate civic engagement, political participation and democracy in general.

Rising above the dichotomy of these two opposing views, however, Putnam asks the central question of whether "virtual social capital is itself a contradiction in terms," and he concludes that no empirical study has proven "the connection between social capital and Internet technology" (Putnam 2000, 170–1). Although Putnam acknowledges that the Internet enhances a network's capacity to activate a form of "social connectedness and civic engagement" (2000, 180), he is equivocal as to whether the effectiveness of enhanced network capacity can result in real political actions and outcomes. Along these lines of thought, he later concludes that "the Net is unlikely in itself to reverse the deterioration of our social capital" and that "the Internet and the World Wide Web . . . play a surprisingly small role" (2003, 9) in civic engagement and social capital formation. Putnam implies that social capital should be a precondition for the meaningful use of NNITs for political mobilization (2000, 177). Following Putnam's call for further empirical study on NNITs and political mobilization, attempts to address the topic have taken two main approaches—psychological and sociological. The psychological approach (Katz and Rice 2002; Kraut and Kiesler 2003; Kraut, et al. 2001), taking a dystopian stance, focuses on the deleterious impacts of the Internet and other NNITs on interpersonal relationships and social networks. Kraut and Kiesler's (2003, 9) research does not support the idea that the Internet creates more social support, nor that it creates less loneliness and stress; rather, they claim that "greater use of the Internet does not necessarily lead to larger social networks or more social support." The psychological approach goes further to argue that increased use of NNITs will endanger civic culture by consuming time that could have been spent in face-to-face community interaction. The potential for NNITs to enhance social networks and foment social movements, however, should not be ignored.

Striking a more utopian stance in their sociological approach, Wellman and Haythornthwaite (2002) find that the Internet increases social capital, civic engagement, and a sense of belonging in an online community (Kavanaugh and Patterson 2002, 329; Quan-Haase and Wellman 2002, 319). As the Internet is increasingly incorporated into individuals' daily routines, social capital is becoming further augmented and geographically dispersed. NNITs create the potential to reverse the decline in social capital by providing a medium for younger generations to cultivate social contacts, to increase their civic engagement, and to build a sense of community (Quan-Haase and Wellman 2002, 295).

This utopian perspective leaves scholars with the fundamental question: Does augmented, geographically dispersed social capital produce more political participation? In response, Quan-Haase and Wellman (2002, 312) conclude that the "Internet supplements political activities but does not change people's levels of involvement [in politics]." When it comes to the political participation of younger generations, their findings show negative, or at least neutral, outcomes. The "Internet does not appear to be impelling younger generations to be more politically involved than older generations. Although the Internet provides a viable alternative for acquiring political information and becoming politically active, the youngest and least educated remain the least active" (Quan-Hasse and Wellman 2002, 318). Overall, in the sociological approach, research findings support the claim that although Internet use can instigate social activism, increased civic activism does not seem to result in increased political participation among younger generations. While the literature implies that the Internet's impact on younger generations in politics has been inconsistent, the Korean case presents one example where NNITs have had consistent effects, both political and non-political.

YOUNG GENERATIONS, INFORMATIZATION AND SOCIAL ACTIVISM

A generation, according to Wohl (1979, 78), is defined as "an actuality [arising] only when similarly located individuals shared a common destiny and participated actively and passively in the social and intellectual movements that were shaping and transforming the historical situation." Wohl (1979, 210) attributes a generational frame of reference and identification to "great historical events like wars, revolutions, plagues, famine, and economic crisis," but can generational cohesiveness be formed in other ways? As pointed out in chapter 1, the mobilization of younger generations, especially through the use of new technologies like NNITs, requires an intermediate phase of collective action around smaller political or non-political events; and these collective actions, by demonstrating efficacy, can serve to compel young generations to recognize their potential political power as well as the rewards that their engagement and participation can bring. Often, a cycle of successful protests generates demonstration effects (Cornell and Cohn 1995; Minkoff 1997) that incite other constituencies to activism (Minkoff 1997, 779) by raising consciousness, defining occasions for action, and guiding successful tactics for protesters (Cornell and Cohn 1995, 369). In their analysis of strike imitation in France from 1890 to 1935, Cornell and Cohn (1995, 367) view the dynamic demonstration effects of protest as akin to critical information about feasibility, popular support for change and commitment to success. Nowadays, through the use of NNITs, protesters can accelerate the sharing of such critical information about feasibility, support and commitment. The next section, after briefly discussing generational characteristics of Korea's youngest voting groups and the explosion of NNITs in Korea, proceeds to tackle the broader argument about how the 386 and 2030 generations interacted to affect political outcomes.

The 386 Generation at the Core of the New Experimentation in Korea

The 386 Generation embodies many of the traits described in the definition of "social capital" above. Coined in the 1990s, the name "386 Generation" includes a "3" to represent that these individuals were primarily in their thirties at the time, an "8" to convey that they were college students in the '80s, and a "6" because they were born in the '60s. Today, the 386 Generation of activists includes college graduates in their forties and fifties; this generation played a pivotal role in a series of anti-authoritarian democratic movements that culminated in the 1987 toppling of the South Korean military regime. The events leading up to the collapse of this authoritarian regime solidified the political cohesion of the 386 Generation and caused a divergence from the Confucian state–society relations epitomized by a domineering state and a submissive civil society (Han and Ling, 1998). The 386 Generation formed networks of democratic forces that included students, labor unions and civic organizations. Their political militancy[6] emerged as a byproduct of the democratization movement and the subsequent liberalization of political culture in the 1980s (Choo and Nam 2001; Kwon and Lee 2004; Lee 2006). In other words, their generational cohesion was forged in their fight for democracy. Thus, the 386 Generation epitomizes the formation of generational political cohesion caused by major events or crises (Chang 2006; Choo and Nam 2001; Chung 2002; Huh 2003; Kelly 2004; Kwon and Lee 2004; Lee 2006; Min 2004; Nippo 2006; Roh 2002) and represents the way in which social mobilization was conventionally accomplished before the use of NNITs.

The 2030 Generation

In contrast, the "2030 Generation" refers to younger people currently in their twenties and early thirties (roughly 20 years younger than the 386 Generation), whose political memories were forged after the South Korean military dictatorship fell in the 1980s. This generation grew up with democracy and relative plenty. Before 2002, the 2030 Generation was oriented toward rampant individualism; it was technologically wired and demonstrated indifference toward politics (Kim 2002; Gallup Korea 2003; Huh 2003; Lee 2006; Roh 2002; Song 2005; Yang 2002; Yoo 2002; Watts 2003). The Hyundai Research Institute, an affiliate of Hyundai Group, named the 2030 Generation as the "R generation," borrowing from the "Red Devils," the red-clad young soccer fans who led the phenomenal stadium and street cheering for the Korean squad during the World Cup tournament in June of 2002. Red Devils is the official fan club of the national soccer team. Networking themselves through the Internet, the Red Devils club comes to represent the excitement, passion and patriotism of the Korean cheering squad. After the World Cup Games, its capacity to mobilize mass population was recognized by politicians and the Red Devils became influential in national politics.

While the 386 generation was a by-product of the 1980s' democratization process in Korean history and played a central role in the transition from military regime to civilian democratic system and has therefore exerted a great influence upon not just political but socio-economic issues in the contemporary politics in Korean society. This generation is critical of established power groups and has shown strong nationalism and group-orientation. It is often, however, also known for its excessive seriousness and formality as a result of their struggle to end the military dictatorship in the past. The N generation, which followed the 386 generation, however, is oriented toward individualism and indulges in the Internet, largely indifferent to their country and politics.

The R generation, rooted in the N generation, is a combination of the 386 and the N generations. It is group-oriented but respects individuality. This generation networked themselves through the Internet and gathered in the millions in spontaneous displays of patriotism. (Yoo, July 2, 2002). The generation has open-minded patriotism, as was clearly demonstrated in its fervent craze for Guus Hiddink, the Dutch coach of the Korean soccer team, and its support for foreign teams. A Hyundai Research Institute report points out that "this R generation helped induce harmony by attracting people from all walks of life to the streets. The new generation has given us hope that it will create harmony in Korea's future" (Kim, 2002 July 01). The generational consciousness and the political inclinations of the 2030 or R Generation dramatically shifted in the twenty-first century from being apolitical to becoming a participatory constituency, taking advantage of the explosive growth of NNITs and the demonstrated usefulness of NNITs to mobilize their peers.

Explosive Growth of NNITs and Civic Activism in Korea

Three major factors stand out as being necessary for Korea's process of informatization: (a) extensive Internet usage, (b) heavy concentration of Internet usage among the 2030 and 386 Generations, and (c) the simultaneity of the explosive growth of civic organizations and the increased penetration of the Internet among these generations. In the early 1990s, the amount of Internet users in Korean society was negligible. By 2001, however, Korea had become a full-fledged Internet society with more than half of the total population accessing and using the Internet regularly (Huh 2003; Jin 2002; Kim 2003; National Computerization Agency 2001, 2002; Roh 2002; Song 2005; Watts 2003). From 1995 to 1998, the number of Internet users doubled annually (Table 2.1) and then, in 1999, it more than tripled. In 2003, according to the Portable Internet Statistical Annex 2004, Korea was ranked number one in per capita vBNS (very high-speed Backbone Network Service) subscribers.[7] Not only the rapid pace of this expansion in Internet use, but also the generational composition and timing of this expansion, deserve attention.

Table 2.1. Number of Internet Users in Korea (in thousands)

Year	Users
1995	366
1996	731
1997	1,634
1998	3,103
1999	10,860
2000	19,040
2001	24,380
2002	26,270

Source: Korea Internet Statistics Yearbook 2004 by National Internet Development Agency of Korea (NIDA)

Table 2.2. Portion of Young Voters and Internet Penetration by Age (2002)

Age	Percentage of Total Population*	Percentage of Total Registered Voters*	Internet Penetration Rate** (Dec. 2001)
20s	16.9	23.2	84.6%
30s	18	25.1	61.6%
40s	16	22.4	35.6%
50s	9.5	12.9	8.7%
Over 60	12	16.4	N/A

Source: * The National Election Commission, Korea (www.nec.go.kr), re-quoted in Gallup Korea (2003:272), http://home.nec.go.kr:7070/ sinfo/sinfo.htm
** *National Internet White Paper* by National Computerization Agency (NCA), Seoul: NCA, 2002, p. 58

The generational composition of Internet users in Korea is remarkable. Among Korea's current population of about 47 million, those who are very active Internet users range from elementary-school-aged children to adults in their thirties; in total, they account for 48.3 percent of the total population (Table 2.2). Thus, the young generation, previously excluded from socio-political discourse, has become disproportionately poised to involve itself as a major stakeholder in the new networked public sphere.

In the late 1990s and early 2000s, there was a dramatic increase in Internet use among the young generations in Korea (Table 2.3). For students aged seven to nineteen, and also those in their twenties, Internet penetration doubled from October 1999 to June 2001. During the same time, penetration

Table 2.3. Internet Penetration Rate in Korea by Age (%)

	Age Range				
	7–19 (20%)*	20s (16.9%)*	30s (18%)*	40s (16%)*	Over 50 (9.5%)*
Oct. '99	33.6	41.9	18.5	12.8	2.9
Mar. '00	51.5	59.1	29.2	8.6	3.3
Aug. '00	65.9	65.9	35.4	18.5	4.3
Dec. '00	74.1	74.6	43.6	22.7	5.7
Mar. '01	81.6	78.4	48.4	29	6.3
Jun. '01	87.6	80.3	54.1	32.2	7.3
Sep. '01	91.1	84	61.3	36.6	8.3
Dec. '01	93.3	84.6	61.6	35.6	8.7

Source: For the data from October 1999 to December 2000, refer to *National Informatization White Paper* by National Computerization Agency (NCA), Seoul: NCA, 2001, p. 389. For the data from March 2001 to December 2001, refer to *National Internet White Paper* by National Computerization Agency (NCA), Seoul: NCA, 2002, p. 58.
* Percent of total population

for Koreans in their thirties nearly tripled. Heavy concentration of NNIT use among the young generations has a direct impact on the progress and direction of the information society in Korea.

The observation that growth in NNITs, generational trends in Internet use, and penetration levels in Korea coincide with the rapid rise in civic activism is corroborated in other scholarly work. For instance, Korean non-governmental organizations (NGOs) flourished during the late 1990s when Internet use increased explosively, as shown by Choo and Nam (2001, 25), who conducted content analysis of articles from major daily newspapers in Korea to ascertain the frequency of activities for four different groupings of civic organizations: *Shi-Min-Dan-Che* (citizen organizations), NGOs, *Min-Gan-Dan-Che* (private organizations) and *Sa-Hoi-Dan-Che* (social organizations). Until 1995, the total number of newspaper references to civic organizations remained below 500 per year (Table 2.4). Since 1996, however, the total amount of newspaper coverage almost doubled. The year 2000 marked the most rapid increase in newspaper coverage from 1,892 articles in 1999 to 3,512 articles in 2000—an increase of 85.6 percent. Rapid increases in the mobilization of civic organizations have corresponded closely to rapid informatization in Korea during the late 1990s.

Remembering Putnam's (2000) claim that social capital is a precondition for meaningful use of NNITs in social movements, it is interesting to note that the 386 Generation in Korea had already built up militant social capital and a heavily democratic consciousness as a result of democratic movements in the 1980s. Combined with the rapid growth of civic organizations, the 386 Generation provided a platform for the use of NNITs in social and political

Table 2.4.   News Coverage of Korean Civic Organizations (1991–2000)

Year	Citizen Org.	NGO	Private Org.	Social Org.	Total by Year
1991	91	0	138	189	418
1992	103	8	212	175	498
1993	102	11	151	152	416
1994	114	16	146	144	420
1995	147	63	108	138	456
1996	323	44	177	210	754
1997	510	50	234	302	1,096
1998	631	32	235	311	1,209
1999	1,183	227	204	278	1,892
2000	2,515	295	241	461	3,512

Source: Table 6-1 from *Korea NGO Report* by Choo and Nam, Seoul: Hanyang University Press, 2001, p. 25

mobilization. The following section delineates how, in the new experimentation, social capital and generational consciousness were accumulated through the mechanism of test-run mobilizations around nationalistic events that provided demonstration effects to younger generations to be utilized in future political mobilizations. Test-run mobilizations also formed, at least temporarily, a cohesiveness similar to that found in generations forged in times of crisis.

DEMONSTRATION EFFECTS AND
GENERATIONAL MOBILIZATION

Having discussed the generational factor, and having analyzed the combination of rapid informatization and explosive growth in civic activism in Korea, let us now turn toward the social movements that took place leading up to the 2002 election and examine their impact on the political indifference of the 2030 Generation, with an eye toward the influence of demonstration effects. In contrast to the arguments made by Wohl (1979) and others, I claim that a series of small, non-political mobilizations may offer a method whereby to build generational cohesion, at least in the short-term. The 386 Generation's Defeat Movement, discussed below, was the first instance of NNIT use for effective political mobilization in Korea; and smaller social and non-political movements around sporting events later served to bring the 2030 Generation more fully into the political sphere. In Korea, NNITs and the mobilizations that they helped to induce played a catalytic role in converting the 2030 Generation into a cohesive, decisive political actor in Korean politics in time for the 2002 presidential election.

THE 386 GENERATION'S DEFEAT MOVEMENT AS
AN EARLY RISER IN DEMONSTRATION *EFFECT*

Perhaps unsurprisingly, due to their strong social networks and their history of social action described above, the members of the 386 Generation played a dramatic role in the 2000 National Assembly election in Korea. On January 10, 2000, The Citizens' Council for Economic Justice (CCEJ), one of the most influential civic alliances in Korea, formed in 1989 by the 386 Generation and other activists, was joined by the Citizens' Commission for a Fair Election to issue a blacklist of unfit, corrupt National Assembly candidates (Choo and Nam 2001; Chosun.com 2000; JoongAng 2000; Korea Herald 2000). Often, in Korea, party candidates were selected based on their personal relationships to party leaders or the amount of funding they had contributed to the party. Consistent with Putnam's work on social capital, it was the 386 Generation, those with pre-existing social capital, that first used NNITs for political mobilization. The 386 Generation had learned about social capital and transferred it from their seniors, The April Nineteenth Generation, who had led a series of demonstrations against the regimes of military dictatorship starting in the early 1960s. Thereafter, the 386 Generation had accumulated social capital from their own protests leading up to their successful toppling of the military regime in 1987. The Internet, in conjunction with conventional news media, played a catalytic role in forming an alliance of over 1,104 civic organizations. Civic organizations, spearheaded by the 386 Generation, used the Internet to open a political dialogue on the reform of the nomination process and on the establishment of civil society authority over conventional political authority.[8]

The Citizens' Coalition for the 2000 General Election's homepage (www .ngokorea.org), within the first five days after it opened in January 2000, recorded approximately 50,000 hits. The site had an average of 10,569 postings per day, and a total of 856,090 as of the day before the April 13th election (JoongAng Ilbo 2000). Furthermore, 5,667 people made financial contributions on the site totaling about 350 million *won* (about US$318,000) to support civic activism, which was the first Internet fundraising in Korean electoral history (2000 General Election Citizen Alliance). *The Korea Herald* (2000), a day before the vote, claimed that the Internet had made its mark as the most influential public arena and medium for political networking. Out of a total of 299 seats, the Defeat Movement targeted 86 incumbents. Fifty-nine of these 86 lost their bids for re-election to the National Assembly, which meant that the Defeat Movement's success rate at using Internet-inspired civil disobedience was an astounding 68 percent. (http://www.redcard2004.net/).

By issuing a blacklist of unfit candidates for the April 13th, 2000 National Assembly election, civic activism fueled a heated debate in Korean politics. The Citizens' Council for Economic Justice (CCEJ), the best by-product of the 1980s democratization movement (Chosun.com, 2000; JoongAng, 2000; Korea Herald, 2000), was joined by the Citizens' Commission for a Fair Election in its efforts to encourage citizen participation. Overall, through the power of information technology, the Internet had swiftly formed an alliance of over 1104 civic organizations, enabling them to open a political dialogue on reforming the election process and on establishing the influence of civil society over conventional authority. Several web sites such as www .ngokorea.org, www.naksun.co.kr, and www.democracy.co.kr were created to list the names of those considered unfit based on evidence of crimes such as corruption or embezzlement related to past elections, political and voting records, changes in party affiliation, and personal flaws such as unethical behavior and vulgar or discriminatory statements. The old practices of selecting party candidates had been based more on personal relationships with party leaders or on the scale of funds contributed to political parties than on objective evaluations of candidates' qualifications and electability.

This unprecedented election featured changes made mostly by the Internet. First, the public policy jury system was tested for the first time in Korea, where no such system had ever been tried, even for judicial processes. The Hundred Member Jury[9] representing a diverse spectrum of total demography was set up by the Citizens' Coalition to review unfit candidates. Since then, it has become a tradition for civic alliances to establish this system when making important public decisions, which was demonstrated once again at the April 2004 National Assembly election. Of the 206 incumbants, lost their seats (63 percent) (http:// www.redcard2004.net/contents/qna-naksun.html). With the Hundred Member Jury system, the Internet has not only brought forth a new institution in Korean politics but also empowered citizens. Second, the current election law in Korea prohibits negative campaigning by any except individuals and labor unions. Reflecting the interests of incumbents, the Constitutional Court and the Central Election Management Commission upheld the current election law on the grounds that it keeps elections fair.

These unprecedented election outcomes generated through the effective use of the Internet by the 386 Generation created a learning effect for members of the younger generation who utilized the public sphere newly created by NNIs and who were later to carry out another unprecedented phenomenon in the history of Korean social capital, the Red Devils. This supports Kohut's finding that if the critical masses of early Internet adopters are more civic minded and active in communication, and they might encourage new adopters to engage in talk about community, a social capital building activity (Kavanaugh and Patterson, 2000: 329).

As Cornell and Cohn (1995, 367) argue, small groups of militants can serve as the catalyst for action by others. These groups have variously been termed *initiator movements* (Minkoff 1997) or *early risers* (Tarrow 1994). The 386 Generation's Defeat Movement served as a powerful demonstration effect for future mobilizations in Korea in its combination of off-line social capital and online networking; the movement illuminated the potential and feasibility of the Internet as a tool for political mobilization. While the formation of generations seems to require a cataclysmic event that requires long-term sacrifices or struggles, NNITs provide an effective means for expanding generational networks more quickly and deeply around salient issues within the polity. In 2002, in the wake of the successful Defeat Movement and a series of nationalistic mobilizations shaped by NNITs, the 2030 Generation was transformed from politically indifferent to politically cohesive (Kwon and Lee 2004; Min 2004; Nippo 2006; Roh 2002). While the case of Korea in 2002 may be unique in that very few countries have reached the same level of informatization, this case illustrates the impact of NNITs and the demonstration effects of mobilizations on the political cohesion of younger generations.

The First Foray: The 2030 Generation and NNIT-induced Mobilization

One of the questions this book raises is precisely how these previously apolitical but NNIT-activated young generations became involved in politics. They were not simply converted into a formidable political force overnight; there must have been some catalyst that transformed them into a focused and self-recognized generation or group. Interestingly, their recognition of themselves as a generation did not happen first in the political arena—it arose in the fields of their interests, such as sports or entertainment affairs. After acting on their own personal impulses as individuals, they later realized that they had unknowingly been part of a plenitude of likeminded individuals acting in cyberspace, and thereby came to recognize themselves as a part of a coherent group with a sense of a community.

In an effort to theorize such a conversion process, Kohut (in Kavanaugh and Patterson, 2002, 329) finds that if critical masses of early Internet users are more civic-minded and actively communicative, then they might encourage new users to engage in community-building activities and the formation of social capital. The civic-minded 386 Generation, using conventional offline mass media and the Internet effectively, spurred an unprecedented election outcome in 2000. It was this mobilization that created a model for the 2030 Generation to emulate in the next election. Unlike the 386 Generation, though, the 2030 Generation initially used the Internet primarily in the nonpolitical arena. It was two sports-related events with nationalistic undertones, occurring in 2002, that acted as catalysts for the mobilization and formation of generational consciousness among the 2030 Generation[10]—the 2002 Winter Olympic Games and the 2002 World Cup Soccer games.

During the Salt Lake City Winter Olympic Games in January 2002, a Korean speed skater named Dong-Sung Kim was disqualified in the men's 1,500-meter short track final after winning the race. Apolo Anton Ohno, a U.S. skater who had placed second behind Kim reacted negatively by throwing his hands up in disgust. Believing that Ohno's Hollywood-style histrionics had caused the disqualification of Kim for blocking Ohno's forward progress in the final turn, and presuming that Ohno had stolen Kim's gold medal, young Korean Internet users became enraged and overloaded the official website of the U.S. Olympic Committee, inadvertently causing it to shutdown through the sheer volume of their traffic (CNNSI 2002; Reuters 2006).[11] The domestic and international media attention brought on by this mobilization served to help the younger generations of Korean NNIT users realize their own potential power and the power of a cohesive cyberspace community in general.

Soon after, during the World Cup Soccer matches in May and June of 2002, a cumulative crowd of 22 million people spontaneously poured into the streets of Seoul and other major cities of Korea to support the Korean national team. This nationwide support had been mobilized by the Red Devils, an Internet-based, 120,000-member, national soccer team fan club. The Red Devils[12] were networked together through NNITs such as the Internet, instant messaging services and mobile technologies. They are also credited for having revived the national ethos of the can-do spirit that had been depressed by the Asian Financial Crisis, or IMF Crisis, of 1997 (Yoo 2002). As a result of the non-political social mobilizations emanating from these two sporting events in 2002, the 2030 Generation recognized its power to set agendas, to build consensus, to network and to organize real actions—all from the comfort of cyberspace. These events had prepared the 2030 Generation to be transformed into a cohesive political force; and that is exactly what happened when, in a shocking accident, two Korean girls died at the hands of American soldiers.[13]

From Sports to Politics—the Anti-U.S. Candlelight Protest

In June 2002, directly after the Red Devils' World Cup Soccer mobilization, a U.S. military tribunal in Korea acquitted two U.S. soldiers on charges of negligent homicide. The soldiers had been charged with killing two Korean schoolgirls while driving their armored vehicle. The acquittal, in largely ignoring Korean sentiment, spawned anti-Americanism in a mostly pro-American country. At six in the morning on November 27, a Netizen code-named *Ang-Ma*[14] appealed to the public using instant messages to "fill the *Kwanghwamoon* [the main gate of *Kyungbok* Palace, Seoul's symbolic political center] with the Korean spirit and to bring candles for the victims, *Hyosoon* and *Miseon*" (Kim 2003). Within 24 hours, 90 percent of all MSN Messenger users in Korea had posted a mourning badge on their homepages (S. K. Kim 2003) and approximately 10,000 demonstrators (Lee and Choi, 2001) gathered at the *Kwanghwamoon* on November 30 to mourn these girls' deaths.

However, what began as a gathering to mourn the two girls quickly devolved into a massive anti-U.S. demonstration. Disregarding a half-century of friendly discourse and relations between the United States and Korea, the NNIT users-turned-activists defied the pro-U.S. stance embodied by the conservative, older generations. This event forced the Korean–U.S. relationship into the political arena for the 2002 presidential election, illustrating the remarkable power of the 2030 Generation's NNIT-induced mobilizations to shift the political discourse (Lee and Choi 2001; Roh 2002; Kim 2002; S.K. Kim 2003; Watts 2003). At this point, the young generations, whose NNIT-activated and -focused approach had been initiated in the process of following athletic events, became involved in socially and politically sensitive issues — in this case, the anti-American candlelight demonstrations—and began to realize their power in major political discourse. Without cyberspace, where they had become the central players, it would have been extremely difficult for these young generations to form such a cohesive community.

Having witnessed the power of the NNITs in several movements, and having participated in non-political, social and political movements, the 2030 Generation was poised to become a major political factor in the 2002 Korean presidential election just a few short months away. These mobilizations served as the catalyst whereby veto power in domestic politics could transfer to the 386 and 2030 Generations as a result of voter cohesion. The Internet-based anti-American political movement also critically affected the presidential election set for December 19, 2002. This political movement mobilized the young generation in favor of the liberal candidate Roh. Thus, the cyber-public sphere of the 2030 Generation successfully created a cohesive counterforce to challenge entrenched, conservative politics in Korea.

Younger Generations and the 16th Presidential Election

By the end of 2002, young NNIT users had become equipped with the social capital and the generational consciousness that had emerged from mobilization for a political cause and the use of NNITs as tools for mobilization. It was a series of international athletic events that had awakened a sense of togetherness, and it was the sudden killing of two schoolgirls by an American military vehicle that transformed this sense of community into anti-American political protests. Through such mobilizations, these formerly disparate young voters came to generate social capital, sharing liberal political values, building trust to act together, and networking with each other in cyberspace. What they achieved in that presidential election was the manifestation of their newly acquired political cohesion. Simply put, without NNIT users' concerted efforts to mobilize support for Roh Moo-hyun, the election result would have been quite different (Gallup Korea 2003; H.J. Kim 2003; MacKinnon 2005; Roh 2002; Song 2005; Sutton 2006; Watts 2003). Based on survey data collected by the Korean Social Science Data Center on the day of election, H. J. Kim (2003) conducted path analysis on how three independent variables—age, Internet, and aid for North Korea—affected the outcome of the presidential election. He found that (a) the younger generation favored the Internet as a way to learn about presidential candidates, (b) the Internet influenced voters' attitudes toward the election and aid for North Korea, and (c) those voters who were greatly concerned with the election and favored aid for North Korea voted for Roh, while those who were not concerned with the election but opposed aid for North Korea voted for the conservative candidate Lee (H.J. Kim 2003, 107). Kim's analysis suggests that the Internet not only affected voter choice but also helped mobilize the 2030 Generation into a cohesive voting bloc capable of casting the deciding vote.

There have been a total of sixteen presidential elections in Korea, ten of which have been direct votes. The average voter turnout rate is 80.05 percent, with the highest (97 percent) in the fourth election of 1960 and the lowest (70.8 percent) in the most recent election of 2002 (Gallup Korea 2003, 271). The records show that, as the democratization process progressed in the late 1980s, voter turnout rates in presidential elections lowered substantially. In addition, the victory margin for presidential elections has also gradually narrowed from an average of 6.4 percent in the previous six direct elections to 2.3 percent in the latest election in 2002. Under these conditions, a well-motivated cohort of critical mass could significantly influence the outcome of an election if it coalesced around one candidate over another. The introduction of NNITs into the situation provided the tools that led to exactly this type of cohesive young voting bloc in Korea.

The 16th Korean presidential election included three major candidates: Roh Moo-hyun of the liberal New Millennium Democratic Party (NMDP), Lee Hoi-chang of the conservative Grand National Party (GNP), and independent Chung Mong-joon of the National Alliance 21 Party. As president of the Korea Football Association, Chung was boosted by his successful coordination of the 2002 World Cup and ran as an independent. Often the third wheel in the race, Chung made a deal with Roh to select a united front candidate among the two, both liberal, through a poll conducted on November 25th among their party members and the general public. Roh won the poll mainly due to support from his own Internet fan club,[15] *No-Sa-Mo*.[16] As a united front candidate, he began to take the lead over the opposition party candidate, Lee, in several pre-election polls. Despite lead fluctuations in the polls, the news media predicted Lee would win by carrying undecided voters (Gallup 2003, 311–325; SICH-NMDP 2003). Then, on the eve of Election Day, surprising everyone, Chung abruptly announced the withdrawal of his support for Roh.

Chung's last-minute withdrawal, announced just eight hours prior to the start of voting, created an urgent need for Roh's supporters to mobilize voters. This emergency situation offered two important byproducts for the study of NNITs. First, it provided an ideal opportunity to test the effectiveness of NNITs in mobilizing a large number of people in a short time. Second, it explicitly corroborates the correlation between young voters' cohesion and Roh's victory in the presidential election. In that eight-hour window, only high-speed information technology could have achieved such a result. Fearing the loss of Chung's supporters for Roh, *No-Sa-Mo* orchestrated a last-minute mobilization of young voters; and in their efforts, they maximized the use of all available NNITs, from election websites and instant messaging services to mobile phones and Web TVs.

Both direct and indirect evidence is abundant that the 2030 Generation used NNITs to build support for Roh. In the eight hours between 10 SP on December 18 and the opening of the polls in the morning, online activity broke cyberspace records (Chang 2006; Roh 2002; Song 2005; SICH-NMDP 2003; Sutton 2006, 9). Roh supporters rallied using MSN Messenger and mobile phones to encourage their peers by posting and voicing messages like "Let's pick up the phone and make a call to encourage others to vote," or "Let's make Roh president through our power" (Chang 2006; Kim 2003 a, 110; MacKinnon 2005, 331; SICH-NMDP 2003; Song 2005). OhmyNews, the first Korean website of citizen journalism, responded. Throughout the entire night, the website served as an epicenter of reform-minded citizens with 6.23 million visitors and 19.1 million page views logged during that period alone (Sutton 2006, 9).

Additionally, data from SK Telecom,[17] the largest mobile phone carrier in Korea with an average of 52.1 percent share of the total market, supports the above claim. As a result of the emergency mobilization that was prompted by Chung's unexpected withdrawal, mobile phone call volumes appear to have spiked on the day before the election and on Election Day as well. Comparing the call volumes on these two days to the normal average for December produces some stark results. Election Day, an official holiday in Korea, would normally have a call volume similar to that of other Sundays in December; however, Election Day saw the largest volume of calls with a total 16.4 percent larger (about 27.5 million calls in total) than that of an average Sunday in December.[18] Wednesday the 18th, one day before the election, and the day of Chung's withdrawal of support, exhibit a similar pattern. After controlling for the holidays of Christmas and New Year's,[19] Election Day had the highest weekday call volume for all of December.

It was predicted that lower voter turnout would benefit the opposition party conservative candidate Lee (Gallup Korea 2003, 23, 269). Indeed, with a low turnout rate of 70.8 percent on the morning of the 16th

Table 2.5. Time-stamped Exit Polls from the 16th Presidential Elections (by age)

Age	6–9 am	9–11 am	11–1 pm	1–3 pm	3–4 pm	4–5 pm	5–6 pm	Total %	N 45,477
20s	11.4	15.9	20.1	**21.6**	10.9	9.7	10.4	100	8,231
30s	11.8	16.0	**21.7**	21.1	10.7	9.6	9.1	100	12,142
40s	16.8	19.8	**20.9**	18.5	9.1	7.6	7.3	100	12,006
50s	22.4	**22.9**	21.8	16.0	6.9	5.9	4.1	100	6,595
60s	21.1	**31.5**	24.8	13.2	4.7	2.8	1.9	100	6,503

Source: Media Research
http://www.mediaresearch.co.kr/cs_center/lecture_view.asp?brd_cd=Ta_lecture&idx_bord=3;
The 16th Presidential Election Exit Poll conducted by Media Research on Election Day, December 19, 2002
(N = 45,477 from 199 voting booths).

presidential election—about 10 percent lower than the turnout of the 15th presidential election—Roh supporters had reason to worry, but they used their mobile phones and the Internet to continually galvanize support. From 11 DP to 1 SP, approximately 18 million mobile phone calls were made (Gallup Korea 2003, 13; Lee and Choi 2002; Song 2003; Song 2005). This mobilization corresponds to the increasing turnout rates throughout the day for voters in their twenties and thirties as reported by the time-stamped exit poll data (Table 2.5). Also, the ruling party website recorded 860,855 hits, which is 200,000 more than the daily average; and the number of postings to the website's bulletin board doubled on that day as well (SICH-NMDP 2003). Figure 2.1 documents the amazing increase in hits and posts to Roh's campaign website around Election Day. Specific cyber activities (e.g., official campaign website page views, postings, replies to previous posts) during the same period also correlate strongly with spikes in the overall hit data described above. For example, on November 25, as shown in Figure 2.1, Roh was selected as the united front candidate against Lee. His website subsequently received 1,254,749 hits and 6,840 postings, the highest recorded in November.

The heavy use of NNITs, especially by the 2030 Generation, however, did not result in an overall increase in voter turnout. As Table 2.6 shows, from 1992 to 2002, there was a steep drop in turnout for almost all age groups, especially in the middle and younger generational groups. In fact, the 16th presidential election marked the lowest voter turnout in Korean history. NNIT use, then, did not bring an overall increase in political participation among the younger generations. Rather, as will be shown below, it was a well-motivated, *cohesive* voting bloc that made the difference in bringing victory to Roh.

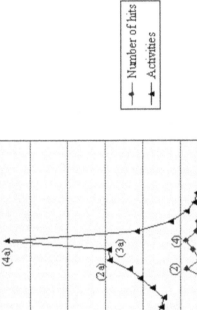

Figure 2.1 Internet Activity at the Roh Campaign Website

Table 2.6.   Voter Turnout by Age in Korean Presidential Elections (1992–2002)

Age	1992 (14th)	1997 (15th)	2002 (16th)
20–24 years old	69.8%	66.4%	57.9%
25–29 years old	73.3%	69.9%	55.2%
30–34 years old	82.1%	80.4%	64.3%
35–39 years old	85.9%	84.9%	70.8%
40–49 years old	88.8%	87.5%	76.3%
50–59 years old	89.9%	89.9%	83.7%
60 and over	83.2%	81.8%	78.7%
Total	81.9%	80.7%	70.8%

Source: National Election Commission, *An Analysis of Turnout in the 15th Presidential Election*, (Seoul: National Election Commission, 1998); National Election Commission, *An Analysis of Turnout in the 16th Presidential Election*, (Seoul: National Election Commission, 2003); found in Min (2004, 251).

According to Table 2.5, the turnout of the 2030 Generation dramatically jumped from an average of 13.78 percent (6 DP to 11 DP) to an average of 21.13 percent (11 DP to 3 SP). Table 2.7 shows that, on Election Day, the conservative opposition party candidate Lee was leading at the polls with an average of 1.6 percent until 1 SP , when the 2030 Generation's voting rate was lower than that of voters in their fifties and sixties. However, after 1 SP , as the voting rate of the 2030 Generation increased and that of older generations decreased, Rho took the lead by an average of 1.7 percent until 5 SP . While votes for Roh significantly increased from 11 DP until 5 SP , votes for the conservative party candidate, Lee, decreased from 11 DP onwards.[20]

Table 2.7 provides support for the argument that the voting patterns of the 386 and the 2030 Generations became more cohesive in their support for Roh as a result of NNIT mobilization, and suggests that the timely use of the NNITs in the wake of Chung's last-minute withdrawal dramatically affected the election outcome. The younger generations' previous collective action, use of NNITs for communication, and rapid mobilization around the presidential election in the final hours transformed them into a cohesive and decisive voting bloc for President Roh.

To illustrate the newly formed cohesiveness of the 386 and the 2030 Generations' voting bloc, Table 2.8 shows that, in the 13th and 14th presidential

Table 2.7.   Time-Stamped Exit Poll on Voting Patterns—16th Presidential Election

Candidates	6–9 am	9–11 am	11–1 pm	1–3 pm	3–4 pm	4–5 pm
Rho	47.5%	47.4%	47.7%	48.6%	48.9%	49.1%
Lee	49.3%	49.4%	48.7%	47.6%	47.1%	46.8%

Source: Media Research http://www.mediaresearch.co.kr/cs_center/lecture_view.asp?brd_cd=Ta_lecture&idx_bord=3; *The 16th Presidential Election Exit Poll* conducted by Media Research on Election Day, December 19, 2002 (N = 45,477 from 199 voting booths).

Table 2.8.   Liberal/Conservative Vote Share in Presidential Elections (1987–1997)

Presidential Election	Candidate	20s	30s	40s	Over 50
13th Election (1987)	Roh, Tae Woo (Conservative)	27.6	34.3	38.8	53.3
	Kim, Young Sam (Liberal)	28.6	26.3	23.2	18.0
	Kim, Dae Jung (Liberal)	27.6	23.9	26.3	21.0
14th Election (1992)	Kim, Young Sam (Conservative)	35.1	43.4	51.9	63.9
	Kim, Dae Jung (Liberal)	32.8	32.3	33.0	23.9
15th Election (1997)	Kim, Dae Jung (Liberal)	34.8	29.0	24.1	32.7
	Lee, Hoi Chang (Conservative)	20.0	23.4	23.6	43.7

Source: Taken from Lee & Moon (1996) on the 13th (pp. 12–13) and 14th (pp. 1617) presidential elections; also see Research and Research (December 13, 1997) on the 15th presidential election.

elections, younger generations did not display clear voting preferences for liberal or conservative candidates. In these contests, younger voters, contrary to expectations, voted evenly for the conservative Tae Woo Roh, a former military general, and the two Kims of the liberal party. However, the 15th election clearly revealed the young generations' preference for the liberal party candidate Kim over conservative party candidate Lee. This trend intensified in the 16th presidential election (Table 2.9) along with a clear distinction between the 2030 Generation and the old Korean War Generation in terms of preferences for presidential candidates. The 2030 Generation emerged as the most powerful constituent, accounting for 42.4 percent of the total votes.[21] In short, although the intensive use of NNITs cannot be said to have brought about an

Table 2.9.   Liberal/Conservative Vote Share in the 16th Presidential Election

Age Group	Rho, Moo Hyun	Lee, Hoi Chang	Totals	N (78,428)
20s	59	34.9	93.9	12,206
30s	59.3	34.2	93.5	18,396
40s	48.1	47.9	96	19,865
50s	40.1	57.9	98	13,611
60 and over	34.9	63.5	98.4	14,350

Source: Exit Poll December 19, 2002, MBC-TV and Korea Research Center (2003:12); (N=78,428 taken from a random sample of 302 voting booths).

overall increase in voter turnout in the 16th presidential election, NNITs have certainly proven how effective they can be in mobilizing a cohesive voting bloc of young supporters on the coattails of successful social and political mobilizations, as NNITs were essential to the victory of the liberal Roh.

CONCLUSION

Due to the uneven diffusion of NNITs and levels of democratization around the globe, it is too early to conclude how NNITs will affect future events in democracies; yet, younger generations' political apathy, waning civic and political participation, and low electoral turnout all seem to point in a negative direction. The literature on these issues is divided and the overall picture of cyber political discourse and its effects on political mobilization remains nebulous; however, non-political, Internet-based mobilizations of younger generations deserve scholarly attention because these mobilizations, as in Korea, may suddenly shift their focus away from social, fun-seeking activities and towards political activities. Understanding the dynamics of NNIT-induced political discourse and mobilizations will become increasingly important as new generations turn to the Internet as a source of friends, social networks and political information.

Although this chapter argues that effective use of NNITs opens the possibility of mobilizing an indifferent young constituency for collective action, the task of documenting NNIT-user mobilization activities remains difficult. One reason for this difficulty is that, since NNIT users are anonymous in ways that conventional activists never were, it is complicated to analyze whether young people are really utilizing NNITs for mobilization, especially for political purposes. However, the timing and the context of the 2002 presidential election provided an ideal opportunity for analysis because the assumption that NNIT use is deeper and broader among younger generations closely matches the reality in Korea. But as the use and deployment of NNITs continues to spread, and as populations age, this assumption may cease to hold. Therefore, data collection will become even more crucial to studying the intersection of NNIT use and politics in the future.

This analysis of the situation in Korea is only the first attempt at creating a plausible theoretical account for how NNITs affect generational civic activism and electoral outcomes in democracies. Despite differences in the level of informatization and regime type, many countries in South East Asia, such as Burma (Danitz and Strobel 1999), as well as China and Vietnam (Gan et al., 2004), are being challenged by dissenting voices equipped with NNITs (i.e., voices that would have otherwise been regarded as minor) and calling for democracy. This study focused on the demonstration effects of

NNIT-induced mobilization on the consolidation and cohesion of the young generations' consciousness and political behavior. The observations above do not corroborate claims that NNITs can increase overall voter turnout as some scholars have predicted; however, they do corroborate the claim that NNIT-induced mobilization builds generational consciousness and voting pattern cohesion, which, in a tight election, can make a difference. The specific consequences of NNIT use and mobilizations will, however, vary widely across societies and regions. Without the high level of informatization, the dense population centers, and the decreasing voter turnout that exist in Korea today, the outcome of such NNIT-induced mobilization would have likely been very different or even negligible.

The Korean case discloses three conditions that are required in order for NNITs to have a significant effect on political outcomes. First, NNITs need to penetrate deeply and be spread broadly throughout the general population, with a particularly high concentration among the young generation. Second, NNIT-induced test-run mobilizations need to occur in order to provide a series of opportunities to rally around salient, non-political social events. These events allow young generations to mobilize around issues that matter to them, to demonstrate the potential political power of the previously indifferent younger generations, and to build generational consciousness and cohesion. Third, generational consciousness and cohesion is a resource for future mobilization and can affect the voting patterns of the younger generations.

At this point, it remains unclear as to whether NNIT-induced mobilization around non-political events can create the same long-lasting social capital and voting patterns that are associated with the types of catastrophic events discussed in the literature on the creation of generations and political participation. Generations that have built up social capital and patterns of political behavior through physical interaction are very effective at using NNITs for mobilization purposes, and the 386 Generation in Korea provides a good example of this phenomenon. Despite the fact that the youngest Korean generation, the 2030 Generation, seemingly demonstrated that it possessed social capital and cohesive generational qualities, it remains unclear, due to the fragmented and volatile nature of NNIT discourse, whether their social capital and patterns of political participation are only a temporary phenomenon. Considering that the Korean mobilizations discussed above took place within about a year, can NNIT-induced mobilizations lead to the long-term build-up of social capital? Do NNIT-induced mobilizations—both those that remain electronic and those that result in physical demonstration—lead to the same type of generational cohesion that results from cataclysmic events? This book attempts to answer this question in the series of candlelight protests mobilized younger generations against Korean government decision to resume the importation of American beef in 2008.

APPENDIX A

Table 2.A1. SK Telecom Mobile Phone Call Volumes (# of Calls per Day) (Dec. 2002)

Date	Day of Week	Mobile Phone Call Volumes (# of Individual Calls)
12/1	*Sunday*	**171,138,257**
12/2	Monday	249,631,575
12/3	Tuesday	240,849,792
12/4	Wednesday	243,606,735
12/5	Thursday	244,378,163
12/6	Friday	248,857,334
12/7	Saturday	233,855,203
12/8	*Sunday*	**164,628,706**
12/9	Monday	237,780,065
12/10	Tuesday	238,629,460
12/11	Wednesday	239,930,339
12/12	Thursday	241,633,104
12/13	Friday	252,110,511
12/14	Saturday	240,050,187
12/15	*Sunday*	**169,379,759**
12/16	Monday	245,023,455
12/17	Tuesday	247,609,400
12/18	Wednesday	256,691,063
12/19	*Thursday (Election Day)*	**194,910,687**
12/20	Friday	256,582,962
12/21	Saturday	242,009,422
12/22	*Sunday*	**169,531,687**
12/23	Monday (Christmas Eve Eve)*	263,782,172
12/24	Tuesday (Christmas Eve)*	291,659,813
12/25	Wednesday (Christmas Day)*	181,937,490
12/26	Thursday	249,264,008
12/27	Friday	255,236,455
12/28	Saturday	233,712,735
12/29	*Sunday*	**162,600,802**
12/30	Monday (New Years Eve Eve)*	267,255,800
12/31	Tuesday (New Years Eve)*	298,710,782

* Not included for the purposes of statistical analysis for theoretical reasons; Christmas and the New Year's holiday are celebrated intensely by South Koreans, and spikes in cell phone volume are to be expected in the two days leading up to these two holidays.

NOTES

1. This chapter is based on my article, "From Indifference to Making the Difference: New Networked Information Technologies (NNITs) and Patterns of Political Participation Among Korea's Younger Generation," which was published in the *Journal of Information Technology & Politics*, 4(1), 2007. I want to thank the Taylor & Francis Group for their generous permission to expand this article into a chapter for this book.

2. See also Lebkowsky (2005, 35); Putnam and Feldstein (2003, 128, 285); Trippi (2004, 104, 229).

3. On the increased turnout of younger voters, also refer to The Institute of Politics, April 19, 2005, (p. 3) and The Pew Research Center, January 9, 2007 (24).

4. In the case of the United States, it has been claimed that the increased turnout among younger generations was insufficient to overcome the manufactured voter cohesion of Rovian-principled and religiously oriented "get out the base" strategies. See Altschuler and Spitzer 2006, 7; Wolfson 2006, 3); The Institute of Politics, April 19, 2005, (3, 19); The Pew Research Center, January 9, 2007, (28–30).

5. It is often used as another name of 2030 Generation. However, it is not exactly identical. Origins of this term is explained below.

6. See Kelly (2004). The influence of the 386 Generation on Korean politics, as well as the Korean–U.S. relationship, was aptly pointed out by Assistant Secretary of State, James A. Kelly: "Too young to have experienced directly the 1950–53 conflict and too often suspicious of U.S. motives, their rise to political maturity challenged us to anchor bilateral relations more deeply, and on . . . a more equal basis." The "younger generations" in Korea are loosely defined, but the term generally refers to young people in their 20s and 30s rather than those aged 18 to 29. Within South Korea, there have been two distinct "young generations" — the "2030 Generation" and the "386 Generation." The "2030 Generation" refers to people in their 20s and early 30s whose political memories were forged after the South Korean military dictatorship fell in the 1980s; the "386 Generation" was labeled as such in the 1990s because its members were primarily in the 30s ("3"), college students in the '80s ("8"), and born in the '60s ("6"), back before the Internet era (Han 2007, 61). In 2002, the term "young generations" in Korea encompassed both the 386 Generation from the 1980s and 90s and the 2030 Generation. However, in the current political crisis, teens have also begun to exert their influence, allying with the 2030 and the 386 Generations.

7. See Ministry of Information and Communications, R.O.K. (2005). Thirty-five percent of the Korean people were projected to have vBNS by 2009. Korea was ranked first in the world in 2003 with 23 vBNS subscribers out of 100. Hong Kong ranked second with 18 per 100, and Canada was third with 14.7 per 100.

8. See Rosell (1999) on new types of governance structures formed by networked civic organizations.

9. The Citizen Alliance of 412 civic organizations was established in January of 2002, published the first, the second, and the final lists of unfit candidates January 25, February 2, and April 3, respectively.

10. See Erickson and Nosanchuk (1990) on the politicization potential of apolitical association.

11. The incident, highlighted by both offline and online global news media, was still reverberating during the 2006 Torino Winter Olympics (Fleschner 2006) and the 2010 Vancouver Winter Olympics.

12. The term Red Devils dates back to 1983, the year the nation's under-20 squad advanced to the semifinals of the World Youth Championship in Mexico. Stunned by the unexpected success of the Korean side, foreign media described the players as Red Devils storming the field in reference to the color of their uniforms. It kicked off its activities in the qualifying rounds of the 1998 France World Cup. It is interesting to see that the joie de vivre of the Red Devils would not have been possible without Korea's top-notch communications infrastructure (Chung, 2002 July 1). To the amazement of soccer-crazed Europe and Latin America, a cumulative 22 million people, mostly college students, voluntarily poured onto the streets of Seoul and other major cities to root for Korea in its seven World cup matches (Yoo, July 2, 2002). In Seoul alone, about three million people flooded City Hall Plaza and Kwanghwamoon intersection in the center of the capital (Kwak, July 2, 2002). During the third-place match between Korea and Turkey, Red Devils staged its last massive flip card display in Daegu World Cup stadium showing CU@K-League, short for "See you at Korean League." It urges compatriots to redirect their enthusiastic support toward the nation's sole professional football league in somewhat cryptic Internet-style language. In fact, the K-League has long suffered from a scarcity of spectators while baseball is touted as the country's favorite pastime. It demonstrates the Internet is a thrilling channel for many soccer fans in Korea. National Police Commissioner Lee Pal-ho sent a letter to the Red Devils thanking them for their exemplary support, which contributed the hosting a "safe World Cup."

13. See Kim (2003b). Ki Bo Kim, the owner of user ID "Ang-ma," turned out to be a reporter at OhmyNews, where he had made an additional petition for demonstration under an assumed ID. This incident later became a controversy over the possibility that NNI anonymity could become a tool for scandalous, irresponsible and manipulative discourses or behaviors.

14. For images of the candlelight demonstration at Kwanghwamoon and City Hall Plaza, as well as an interview with Ang-Ma, see Ohmynews article from November 30, 2002; retrieved March 12, 2007 from http://www.ohmynews.com/articleview/

15. Roh (46.8 percent) defeated Chung (42.2 percent) with a 4.6 percent margin at the poll conducted by Research & Research on November 25, 2002. No-Sa-Mo's influence was especially highlighted in the Southeastern province of Korea, Kyungsang. See Hankook Ilbo article on February 26, 2007; retrieved March 12, 2007 from http://news.hankooki.com/lpage/society/200702/h2007022618581421950.htm

16. See Roh (2002, 13–9). No-Sa-Mo was established by Jeong-Ki Lee, user ID "Old Fox," on April 15, 2000, after the 2000 General Election. At that time, the website was named after candidate Rho, nomuhyun.org, but later changed to http://www.nosamo.org/

17. The data provided by SK Telecom is proprietary data provided only for use in this work and is presented in full in Appendix A. This limited mobile phone data for the month of December provides a partial picture of how NNITs contributed to the mobilization of young voters in the 16th Presidential Election.

18. According to Manager Yoon of SK Telecom, there is typically a big gap in the use of mobile phones between Sundays and workdays (in Korea, workdays include Saturdays). In this context, it is relevant to compare the volume of mobile phone calls on Election Day, a non-work day, to call volumes on other Sundays.

19. Korea has a Christian population of over 30 percent. Increased call volumes in the two days leading up to Christmas Day are to be expected. In addition, the New Year is celebrated quite heavily in Korea, and so the two days prior to New Year's Day are also excluded from the analysis. The mean for the sample of 20 remaining weekday workdays in December is 244,872,098. Given this sample mean, the alternative hypothesis that we would find a true mean of 256,691,063 (i.e., the Election Day total) in any given month of December can be rejected at the $p = .0005$ significance level. See Appendix A for full data set.

20. See Seong (2003) and Chang (2006) regarding the increased afternoon turnout for Roh.

21. See The National Election Commission, Korea (http://www.nec.go.kr); re-quoted in Gallup Korea (2003, 272).

Chapter 3

What the New Experimentation Portends for Democracy

Korea's Beef Crisis[1]

HONEYMOON OVER: THE NEAR COLLAPSE OF THE NEW REGIME

Lee Myung-bak was elected president by the highest margin in South Korean history on December 19, 2007. But over the next 116 days, he experienced a dramatic reversal of fortune. Lee's approval rating hit record lows as (1) calls for his impeachment, initiated by Korea's younger generations, spread throughout the country; (2) ongoing candlelight vigils of up to one million protestors drew the world's attention, objecting to Lee's new policy on the importation of American beef; (3) all of Lee's presidential secretaries resigned; and (4) presidential apologies were issued twice. These actions were the direct results of Lee's choice to re-open the Korean market to American beef—a decision satirically described as "flunkeyism" on signs held aloft by protesters at police barricades: "This is a border. From this point forward, Korea is part of the U.S.—Posted by the Governor of Korea, U.S.A., Lee Myung-bak" (Kang 2008).

In exploring the factors involved in President Lee's fall from grace, this chapter addresses three important questions regarding politics in the Information Age:

- How does experimentation with the use of NNITs influence the political discourse and contribute to the evolution of a crisis in the Information Age?
- Who are the most critical players in NNIT-induced politics?
- And did the 386 and 2030 Generations, who led the massive mobilizations in the 2002 presidential election, have any impact on the course of this beef crisis?

These three questions address the second focus of this book—namely, how the NNIT-activated but previously apolitical youth began to involve themselves in nationally important political discourse by defining occasions for action, setting the agendas, and mobilizing the masses for a series of demonstrations. So, how exactly did they bring about this transformation? And what enabled them to play such a crucial role? The previous chapter, by applying the notion of the "demonstration effect," attempted to explain the process by which such a transformation took place; the generational transfer of the militant democratic social capital from the 386 Generation to the 2030 Generation[2] in the series of test-run mobilizations that occurred between 2000 and 2002 may have served as another demonstration effect for major actors in 2008 who held a series of candlelight demonstrations against the Lee administration's decision to resume American beef imports. By applying Situational Crisis Communication Theory (SCCT) and the fundamental concepts of Heinrich's law to the first question above, and by invoking Giddens' theory of "life politics" in answering the second, this chapter explains how the newly activated young constituency during the 2002 presidential election continued to exert political influence upon the legitimately elected sitting President Lee Myung-bak and his government. In the process of addressing these questions, this chapter will also serve to illustrate the substantial political impact that NNIT-galvanized young generations can have on democracy.

Teenagers, who are the main leaders of the current candlelight demonstrations, learned how to use technology for mobilization by modeling the NNIT-equipped young generation in action during the 2002 presidential election. Use of the Internet and other NNITs accelerate the speed of information transfer, and thereby enhance the likelihood of a small accident or event developing into a political crisis or large-scale protest. As a result, such use of technology can fortify civic activities and weaken traditional political leadership, thus altering the conventional political relationship between authoritarian rule and a traditionally disempowered civil society. Such a power shift may eventually endanger the fundamentals of democratic institutions by creating, disseminating, escalating and spiraling demagogic instigations through cyberspace, which is another substantial consequence of the new experimentation.

On December, 19, 2007, when President Lee was elected the seventeenth president of the Republic of Korea (ROK) with the widest margin (5,311,326 votes) in Korea's presidential election history, it was widely regarded as a restoration of traditional ruling conservatism, which had yielded its 35-year stronghold (1963–1997) on the government to the left-leaning regimes of President Kim Dae-jung (1998–2003) and Roh Moo-hyun (2003–2007). Despite the enormity of this victory, it took little less than 200 days altogether for Lee's record-high popularity to plummet from an approval rating

80 percent in December 2007 to 17.1 percent in June 2008—the lowest rating of all Korean presidents with so few days in office, according to YTN-Hankook Research (Choe 2008; Harden 2008). In light of such a crisis for the brand new regime, experts began to worry whether the administration could continue to govern effectively for the remainder of the term.

The emerging power of the young generations, combined with their widespread, intensive use of NNITs—which clearly enhances the ability of groups to mobilize large-scale demonstrations—could well serve the political purpose of a faction or a cohesive contentious minority within the political system. For example, the conservative media within South Korea has criticized more liberal news programs for, in their view, exaggerating the threat of Mad Cow Disease and blindly linking it to the current administration's decision to resume beef imports from the United States. The possibility of such managed escalation of a political crisis feeding off of the immense power of NNITs cannot, and should not, be ruled out. Thus, future generations will have to face the grave challenge of maintaining a democratic political system within an NNIT-dominant society.

THE INTERNET, THE YOUNG GENERATION, AND NEW POLITICS IN KOREA

The critical shift from the dominance of the right-wing conservative to that of the left-wing liberal in Korean politics started with the election of the most famous opposition party leader, Kim Dai-jung, in the 1997 presidential election. The reigns of liberal Presidents Kim (1998–2003) and Roh (2003–2007), which were the byproduct of a half-century of anti-government democratic offline movements led mostly by university students, provided an unprecedented opportunity to shake the traditional conservative dominance to its very foundations. During these two administrations, left-wing-oriented political forces extended their influence and power into every realm of Korean society, while the active and wide deployment of NNITs contributed critically to the political awakening and empowerment of conventionally apolitical young generations. During the period from the early 1960s to the late 80s, these young people had either not yet been born or were too young to participate in the democratic movements, but they later grew aware of the democratic achievements that previous generations had accomplished. As mentioned in chapter 2, the groups that played a critical role in electing President Roh in 2002 (i.e., the 386 and 2030 generations) went on to become central voices in the nation's Internet-based public discourse channels. As shown in Tables 2.2 and 2.3 of that chapter, the most active Internet users in the late 1990s and early 2000s were young people ranging from elementary-school-aged children to adults in their thirties. Prior to the Internet era, these young people, who accounted for 48.3 percent of the total population, had mostly been excluded from social-political discourse, but with the rise of the new networked public sphere, they are now becoming major stakeholders. And, according to a *JoongAng Daily* poll conducted in early 2003, young generations' political identification was overwhelmingly progressive or liberal: 45.5 percent of people in their twenties considered themselves progressive, while just 21 percent characterized themselves as conservative (S. J. Lee 2006, 128). In the following section, this chapter will examine how the NNIT-induced political mobilizations of the 386 and 2030 generations contributed towards the political crisis of the candlelight demonstrations that were initiated by members of the youngest generation in their teens.

The 2002 Presidential Election and the Beef Crisis

The critical role played by young generations using NNITs in Korea's 2002 presidential election can also be said to have served as a demonstration effect for other generations in political crises elsewhere since a series of successful protests engender demonstration effects, which in turn raise cohort consciousness, define occasions for action, and provide protestors with guidance on successful tactics (Cornell and Cohn 1995; Minkoff 1997). In light of my definition of social capital "as multiple human resources networks, either actual or potential, with certain characteristics of shared norms, values, attitudes, and trust built through prior collective action that can be utilized for future social and political mobilizations" (Han 2007, 59), the role played by the 2030 Generation in the 2002 presidential election[3] serves as a demonstration effect giving teenagers confidence in their own ability to incite change through candlelight protests against President Lee. Tables 3.B1 and 3.B2 indicate that the 2002 presidential election served as a model for the current beef crisis and that protesters in the current crisis have learned from the successful mobilization of the 2002 presidential election.

By applying a perspective informed by SCCT and, to a lesser extent, Heinrich's Law, this chapter analyzes the way in which the massive use of NNITs and a series of minor but unacknowledged mistakes made by the current Lee administration have geometrically snowballed into a major crisis (Table 3.B2). Actual data on various age groups' online participation in the Daum.net online Agora, which is the second biggest Web portal and is known for online impeachment (Tables 3.3 and 3.4), is discussed below as well.

NNITs, Social/Political Mobilization and the Current Political Crisis

When analyzing the candlelight protests, which started being globally televised on May 2, 2008, the effect of Korea's informatization cannot be overstated. There are two dimensions to consider: information technology infrastructure and social capital. With regard to the first, in terms of broadband high-speed Internet usage and mobile phone subscriptions, Korea is one of the most wired and technologically savvy nations in the world; however, a true reflection of the degree to which a society is technologically oriented can be found not only in the level of its IT infrastructure but also in the actual use of NNITs in relation to social capital.

Borrowing Mario Diani's (1997; 2001) question about the causal links between social movements, political mobilization and social capital as an outcome of social movements—as well as his research on the social networks used by movement actors and the evolution of these social networks over time (Diani 2001, 208)—the arguments proposed by this book find additional support in the explosive growth of civic organizations since the June Resistance in 1987 and the world-leading index of actual Internet usage in Korea from 1999 to 2000. The Citizens' Commission for a Fair Election, through their efforts to increase citizen participation, carried out a revolutionary election campaign centering on the Citizens' Council for Economic Justice (CCEJ),[4] the nation's largest civic organization, established in 1989, and the Cyber People's Solidarity for Participatory Democracy,[5] established in 1994. This supports Diani's point that "mobilization processes rely heavily upon previous networks of exchange and solidarity" and thus, in trying to understand their operation, we need to focus on their capacity to create new forms of social capital (Diani 2001, 208).

According to the whitepaper published annually by South Korea's National Information Society Agency (NIA) and the International Telecommunication Union's annual report (2010), as described in chapter 1, Korea's NNIT indices on infrastructure and actual usage stand atop the global competition (NIA 2009; ITU 2010). As Table 3.1 displays, the growth

Table 3.1.   Internet Users in South Korea (2000–2006) (units: % and thousands)

Year	2000	2001	2002	2003	2004	2005	2006
Percent (of Total Population)	44.7	56.6	59.4	65.6	70.2	72.8	74.8
Amount of Users	19,040	24,380	26,270	29,220	31,580	33,010	34,120

Source: NIA Whitepaper (2009)

of Internet users in Korea has been continuous. Also, the total average Internet access is 13.7 hours per week with 71.9 percent of Koreans using the Internet each week for more than 7 hours, 27.9 percent for 7–14 hours, 18.9 percent for 14–21 hours, 13.9 percent for 21–35 hours, and 11.2 percent for over 35 hours. Globally, Korea ranks ninth for IPv4 (Internet Protocol version 4) addresses (5,451,000) and fifth for IPv6 (Internet Protocol version 6) addresses (4.1 × 1032). And according to this whitepaper, the household rate for Internet access climbed steadily from 68.8 percent in 2003 to 72.2 percent in 2004, 74.8 percent in 2005, and 78.4 percent in 2006 (NIA 2009). All of these data on the penetration and the diffusion of NNITs in Korea merit scholarly attention in regard to their impact upon politics and society, including their role as the foundation for a new experimentation through which a previously uninfluential constituency could exert unprecedented influence on political discourse and electoral politics.

The impact of wireless linkages between NNITs and other electronic gadgets has been enormous. High-resolution mobile camera phones, or water-cannon-resistant camcorders and laptops that have become progressively cheaper, lighter and more numerous can all be connected through wireless Internet and phone services; and this interconnectivity has resulted in the creation of the networked public sphere. Networked individuals with small NNIT gadgets have essentially become walking broadcasting companies, creating content with mobile phones and distributing it spontaneously through many layers of communication networks. At protest sites, this ability to connect empowers younger generations with the ability to monitor and instantly broadcast every action of the police. In addition, NNITs enable protesters to routinely receive constantly updated information on demonstration points, weather forecasts and riot police presence (Han and Rhee 2008). NNITs have drastically reduced the cost of broadcasting and created a mutually surveillant situation between protesting citizens and the controlling police, such that the power relationship between police and protesters is now turned upside-down as any police violence is likely to be broadcast through websites and networked information devices and thereby fall prey to national, and potentially global, criticism. According to a Reuters report on the role of electronic devices in the protests:

> The Web TV exclusively designed for this purpose, Afreeca (http://www .afreeca.com), has seen its audience almost triple since the beginning of the protests. Roughly 2 million people visited per day in April, but as of June 1, there are 5 million to 6 million people viewing Afreeca's content every day. (Benkler 2006, 219; Han and Rhee, 2008)

In this way, by organizing and sustaining the political movement, NNITs have become the linchpin for the dissenting voice (Larson 2008).

HEINRICH'S LAW AND THE EARLY SEEDS OF
CRISIS IN THE NEW REGIME

With a complex, ever-growing network of NNIT linkages, protestors' reactions to government mistakes and unanticipated incidents have been swift. On April 6, 2008, protesters of various ages, reacting to the new administration's series of small but unacknowledged policy mistakes, began to consolidate opposition forces in cyberspace and initiated the impeachment process in the Agora of Daum.net[6] (Choo 2008).

The occurrence of numerous mishaps and failed policies (Table 3.B1 and Table 3.B2) can be seen as portentous of the political resistance that would later be expressed through a series of candlelight vigil protests. From the start, though, the writing was on the wall. The first and worst disaster was in February 2008, when South Korea's most beloved national treasure, Seoul's South Gate, burned down. Soon after, a series of short-sighted policies was announced by the transition team of the newly elected and still very popular President Lee. Around the same time, severe resistance from citizens was encountered due to a series of mishaps in the implementation of reform policies: changes to English education, such as the shift from standard Korean pronunciations for popular American words such as "orange;"[7] the initiation of a series of privatizations, including the water company, public corporations, and banks; the announcement of a grand canal project to run throughout the entire Korean Peninsula; the deregulation of public schools; and an attempt to control public and private broadcasting companies (Table 3.B2).

Another failed policy had to do with Lee's appointments of cabinet members and hiring of Blue House staff members; most of his appointees were either fellow alumni of Korea University, members of his *Somang* church, or natives, like him, of *Youngnam* Province (a province in the southeast). Lee's selection of this homologous group of advisors and appointees became known as the "Disaster of *KoSoYoung*," and because most of them lived south of the *Han* River, the wealthiest district in Seoul, this group of new elites in the government was also called "*KangBooJa*" (*Kang* meaning "river" and *Boo-Ja* meaning "rich people" in Korean).

These two Korean phrases—"*KoSoYoung*" and "*KangBooJa*"—represented the early failures of the new administration. Such parochial selection of personnel with adherence to regionalism, schooling and personal relations had also been observed in the previous administrations, and has been blamed by many for the chronic failure to rectify these problems. As predicted by Heinrich's Law, which claims that a major disaster tends to occur after 300 small mistakes and 29 major incidents, this chapter considers these early missteps and misguided policies as small but sufficient signs of a major crisis approaching—signs that went unnoticed. This period during which signs of a major crisis go unnoticed also exemplifies the prodromal stage in Fink's (1986) four stages of crisis evolution, which will be discussed in greater detail below.

A very bad situation was made worse when, during a trip to the United States in April, Lee reversed the government's position and agreed to resume importing American beef of cattle older than 30 months. This decision unleashed a firestorm of protest as teens, with the support of the 2030 and 386 Generations (Song 2008), initiated massive candlelight demonstrations against the government. The effect of such widespread and successful opposition from regular citizens was clearly reflected in the by-elections for local government heads and council members on June 4th. The ruling party—the Grand National Party—won only nine of the 52 local positions and suffered significant losses even in its traditional stronghold, Gyungsang Province in the southeast of the country, where it only won five of the 15 seats available (Lim 2008). Also, the turnout had been 21.4 percent—lower than the 22.5 percent of the previous local elections (Lee 2008)—reflecting general disappointment, even in the region that had strongly supported the Lee regime. Although Lee's decision on American beef clearly met with vociferous, widespread opposition, it was not the only reason for this overwhelming loss of popularity; the loss was the predictable result of the aforementioned poor decisions in the regime's first days, an outcome very much in keeping with the Heinrich's Law ratio of 1:29:300, as will be discussed below.

The combination of Lee's misguided early policies and staffing decisions, along with the highly wired nature of the young generations, quickly produced anti-Lee discourse, which in turn escalated into massive, continuing street protests by a large cross-section of the population.

Applying Heinrich's Law to the Beef Crisis

In 1931, an expert in industrial safety with a keen interest in putting a stop to the mounting number of accidents published a seminal work, *Industrial Accident Prevention: A Scientific Approach* (Heinrich 1931), which became a classic in the field. Based on his seventeen years of experience as an engineer in the Inspection Division of the Travelers Insurance Company, Herbert Heinrich argued that the application of scientific knowledge and preventive measures could help society to greatly lower the rates of accidents in the workplace. Though commonsensical in nature, his research offered a more detailed illustration of the theory that most major accidents are preceded by a great number of warning signs and small-scale accidents, which, if unheeded, are likely to lead to serious consequences.

To simplify the results of his research, Heinrich formulated a fundamental law of accidents—1:29:300. According to Heinrich, "The person who suffers a disabling injury caused by an unsafe act, in the average case, has had over 300 narrow escapes from serious injury as a result of committing the very same unsafe act . . . 29 minor injuries . . . [and] 1 in a major or lost-time injury," (Heinrich 1950, 10, 24). In other words, Heinrich's research suggested that, based on 75,000 cases, 88 percent of "unsafe acts of [individual] persons" and 10 percent of "unsafe mechanical or physical conditions" from the total of 75,000 cases were preventable (1950, 17–8).

Although Heinrich's Law has been somewhat discredited in recent years (e.g., E. Scott Geller, in his 2001 work *The Psychology of Safety*, calls the figure 300 a "mythical value," and other industrial safety experts, such as Frank Bird, have shown the number of narrow escapes to be generally much higher than 300), Heinrich's main point remains true that a series of small errors enable an eventual major accident, whether in a factory or an administration. Like the situations Heinrich studied in which people failed to recognize dangerous situations and preclude serious problems, so too the South Korean regime and its political institutions failed to recognize opportunities to change course and prevent further erosion of support for the president. More specifically, the Lee administration faced a political impasse marked by a near complete loss of trust from citizens, a series of massive protests, and an online impeachment process. If we apply Heinrich's Law to this political crisis, the major crisis that the regime must overcome is the massive resistance that was initiated by the beef decision.

Were there, in fact, 29 small incidents and 300 warnings prior to this major political catastrophe? Possibly not, but what matters most is to recognize that there were enough small mistakes and warnings to indicate an impending crisis. Heinrich's Law was formulated to reduce the number of industrial accidents and protect insurance companies from litigation; thus, the application of this law to social movements and political upheavals requires adjustments in variables. Heinrich's Law is used here to conceptualize the causes of the current crisis in government and to analyze how small, cumulative incidents and warnings can produce a major political crisis.

Among the differences between the origin of Heinrich's Law and its application to the political situation in the twenty-first century is that NNITs massively redefine the warnings–accidents–crisis sequence. Unlike the top-down, one-way communication of a factory setting, the interactive nature of the relationship between the political regime and its citizens is critically mediated by the Internet, mobile phones and other NNITs such as online social media, which allows—or even encourages—bottom-up, exuberant and, at times, chaotic dissemination of information.

TECHNOLOGICAL TRANSFORMATION OF
KOREAN POLITICS

In the twenty-five years between President Park Chung-hee's seizure of power in the 1961 military coup and the 1987 election of civilian Kim Young-sam, Korean citizens lived under a military dictatorship. Korea's first civilian president, Kim Young-sam, was elected by an alliance between conservative military interests who wanted to maintain their power base and traditional opposition forces who wanted to seize power. Eleven years later, a more puissant power shift from a conservative to a liberal constituency occurred when Kim Dae-jung was inaugurated in 1998 and then succeeded by President Roh in 2002. Contrary to the general expectation that Lee's wide margin of victory in the 2007 presidential election would reverse the newly emerging liberal, left-wing political forces and restore a conservative government that placed a premium on stability, what emerged instead was a new political dynamic galvanized by NNITs. The conservative ruling party and the administration were at a loss, suddenly subject to the ever-increasing demands of a high-tech citizenry. The combination of NNITs and a previously apolitical younger generation has cultivated a new political dynamic in which the traditional power structure and system often yields to, or at least shares power with, this new political force.

In this new political experimentation, a concept of "life politics" has arisen as an especially significant variable. The main reason that Korean teens have been on the frontlines of these candlelight vigils is because the imported American beef that could, purportedly, transmit Mad Cow Disease would be served in their school lunches (Song, 2008). Although teens have never before played a significant role in political discourse, they have now become the eye of a political hurricane because they are aware of the issue and are capable of rapidly mobilizing for a cause and connecting with offline protests through websites and text messaging. Their awareness and widespread use of NNITs have together made them the central players in this new NPS and political dynamic.

Seemingly consistent with the general perspective of adolescents, their primary concern is how politics affect their daily lives. Referring to this concern as "life politics," Giddens (1994, 90–91) states that "[l]ife politics are about how we should live in a world where everything that used to be natural (or traditional) now has in some sense to be chosen, or decided about." Giddens sees life politics as focusing on issues less related to equality or emancipation and more about how one should construct one's life in a context of rapid detraditionalization (Mouzelis 2001, 439). The emerging global agenda of life politics entails "unintended consequences of escaping rational control by state agencies" (Flitner and Heins 2002, 321) and creates a situation in which "state and societies cannot any longer be walled off from other spatially discrete bodies and polities" (Flitner and Heins 2002, 334). A phenomenon arises where "individuals can resort to neither traditional truths nor collective ideologies when making decisions in their everyday lives" (Mouzelis 2001, 438). Giddens' notion of life politics is being realized in current Korean politics by otherwise indifferent teens entering cyberspace; and cyberspace is liberating and empowering those who have never perceived themselves as capable of influencing political issues. The following section analyzes the volatility of life politics and discusses how the current situation in South Korea can be put into a theoretical perspective. Coombs' Situational Crisis Communication Theory and Fink's stages of crisis evolution will be applied to help explain the current political free-for-all in Korea, which is taking the form of a new political experimentation in the networked public sphere.

SCCT AND THE REVOLUTION OF THE CURRENT CRISIS

Situational Crisis Communication Theory (SCCT) was originally intended "to articulate a theory-based system for *matching crisis response strategies* to the crisis situation to best preserve the organizational reputation" (Coombs 2004, 266; emphasis mine); however, this theory can serve as a useful tool to conceptualize the current crisis of the Lee administration. An important presumption underlying this theory is that "information about a past crisis can shape perceptions of the current crisis" (Coombs 2004, 266). Furthermore, SCCT suggests that a "manager should use response strategies that demonstrate acceptance of responsibility for the crisis and that address victim's concerns" (Coombs 2004, 265). Working from this tenet of SCCT, and with input from Heinrich's Law, this book argues that South Korean protesters, well aware of the prior accidents and mistakes made by the Lee regime, have attributed the current beef crisis to prior mishaps and misguided reform policy options suggested by the Presidential Transition Committee, pointing to the origin of the current crisis in the administration's earlier accidents and missteps. These two theories—Heinrich's Law and SCCT—were developed in the context of private industry and, due to their focus on small accidents or crises, provide a relevant frame of reference for the crisis now occurring in South Korea due to the NNIT-induced politics of the new experimentation.

Coombs (1999, 2004) presents ten types of crises, one of which is the category of "challenge." In his view, this type of crisis arises when an "organization is confronted by discontented stakeholders who challenge the organization because they believe it is operating in an inappropriate manner"

(1999, 61). The candlelight demonstrations against the importation of U.S. beef fall into this category. What has exacerbated this challenge is the existence of NNITs and a new political constituency—an NNIT-equipped young generation operating in a new cyber version of the agora, which was the ancient symbol of democratic governance through public deliberation. The central feature of this NNIT-induced new experimentation is that previously apolitical youths are now taking a central position in cyberspace by initiating an impeachment process against the most popularly elected president in Korean history; angered that their interests did not factor into their president's decision to import American beef, they suddenly became involved in a form of "life politics." Interestingly, the initiation of this impeachment process would have been impossible had they not already centered themselves in the new networked public sphere.

In SCCT, the "perceptions of the causality or the perceived reasons for a particular event's occurrence" are termed "attributions" and are seen as having three dimensions—stability, external control and personal control (Coombs 2004, 267). An attribution is seen as stable only if the cause of the event occurs regularly—e.g., if the same mistakes are made repeatedly by a person, organization or regime. An attribution marked by external control is one in which others cause the event, while one attributed to personal control is one in which the main actor controls the event. Based on these criteria, the current challenge in South Korea appears to have been seeded by an external accident (i.e., the burning of the South Gate) during the administration's transition period, but was primarily caused by internal and personal mistakes in the form of faulty policy decision making and mismanagement of the crisis at each stage; thus, the locus of control was not external but personal. The current crisis is rare in that it started within the very early days of the new regime, as summarized in Table 3.2.

Table 3.2.   Dimensions of the Current Crisis in the Lee Administration

	Random ←			→	*Predictable*	
	South Gate Accident	Transition Team's Mistakes & Canal Project	High-level Appointments (Cabinet and Blue House)	General Election Politics	Beef FTA	Impeachment
Stability	Low	Low	Medium	Low	Low	
External Control	High	Low	Low	High	High	
Personal Control	High	High	High	High	High	

Fink (1986) describes crisis evolution as having four stages: prodromal (hints of future crisis appear), breakout (triggering events appear), chronic (crisis develops and continues), and then resolution. To this classical stage-approach, Mitroff (1994) adds a fifth category in between the breakout and chronic stages—namely, "actions" by the main participants in the crisis. As explained in the previous chapter, the 2030 Generation, which made such a difference in the 2002 presidential election, was comprised of formerly disparate young "Netizens" who gradually realized their collective power in cyberspace through several intermediate stages of learning. Between 2000 and 2002, the 2030 Generation learned from the demonstration effects of the 386 Generation's attempts to combine offline social capital with online power in their efforts to defeat those politicians whom they considered unfit for National Assembly seats in the 2000 general election. Following their success, members of the 2030 generation soon realized their own potential power in cyberspace—during the 2002 Utah Winter Olympics in January 2002, the Soccer World Cup in May, the candlelight anti-American demonstration in November, and, finally, the presidential election in December (Table 3.B1 and Table 3.B2).

In 2000, a negative campaign was initiated to defeat corrupt politicians, and within four months, it had accomplished its objective. A series of sports-oriented events that fortuitously led to massive mobilizations for the liberal candidate Roh occurred throughout the year of 2002. In comparison, the time between President Lee's inauguration on February 25, 2008 and the impeachment process in the Daum.net Agora in April 2008 was much shorter—110 days. In terms of Fink's four stages of crisis evolution, the current crisis can be seen as having a prodromal stage that occurred during the new administration's transition period from December 2007 to February 2008; a breakout stage that began with the beef import decision in April; and a stage of chronic confrontations between the government and protesters, which began in May (Appendix B).

The amount and speed of information exchange among dissenting stakeholders exceeded the ability of the current government to control. With two-thirds of Koreans equipped with mobile phones and near-complete Internet penetration, the government lost control of all three dimensions of the current crisis: "perceived importance, immediacy, and uncertainty" (Coombs 1999, 92). With this type of NNIT-induced challenge, it took merely 57 days from the South Gate disaster on February 10th for the impeachment Agora Web-based petition against President Lee to be created, and only 15 days after his beef import decision for angry citizens to initiate a series of candlelight vigils. Furthermore, it took only 69 days from the first prodromal accident to the breakout of a challenge, and only 20 days from the first candlelight vigil until Lee's first apology, as illustrated in Appendix B. This case provides a glimpse into how NNIT-induced mobilizations can shorten the entire crisis–evolution cycle and precipitate the rise and demise of a political regime or leadership.

The major difference between the crisis and the well-known theories of Heinrich's Law and SCCT is that the evolutionary cycle of the current political crisis is much shorter; also, a major catastrophe can be created because NNITs attract more attention from the parties involved and are capable of escalating instigations virally. In this way, such NNIT-induced new political experimentation can endanger the fundamentals of political stability in democratic institutions. Additionally, the use of NNITs shortens the intervals between major crises and demonstration effects. For example, the cycle of candlelight demonstrations was expected to intensify in 2008 with a number of important events: the twenty-first anniversary of the June 10th Resistance of 1987, which had deposed the military dictatorship and established a substantive democracy in South Korea; the sixth anniversary of the deaths of *Hyo-sun* and *Mi-son*, whose killing by an American military vehicle on June 13, 2002 ignited anti-American candlelight vigils that led to a small victory in 2002 for liberal presidential candidate Roh; the scheduled strike of the Democratic Labor Union (*Minjoo nochong*) on June 16, 2008; and a visit to South Korea by U.S. President Bush in early August 2008. A rapid succession of major political events, any of which could provide an opportunity to escalate the current crisis, now carries increased political weight because of NNITs. The following section concentrates on the outbreak of the political crisis that arose from the decision to resume beef imports and the reaction from citizens utilizing NNITs.

AGORA IN DAUM.NET AND PRODROME
FOR DISASTER (300:29:1)

In contrast to the old experimentation of American face-to-face, volunteer associational activities in local communities, the new experimentation of "online impeachment" is being led in cyberspace by the youth who had formerly been apolitical and uninterested. Originally, in ancient Greece, the agora was both the location and the mechanism for democratic decision-making processes. Its high-tech namesake, a petition webpage on Daum.net (<www.daum.net>, the second largest Web portal in Korea), was established in December 2004 to encourage citizens' participation in national political discourse in the networked public sphere. Since 2004, a total of about 1,400 topics have been petitioned; among them, the one that attracted the most supporters was the Petition against the Negotiations between South Korea and the United States on the Free Trade Agreement, which, on June 2, 2006, had 192,075 signatures (Choo 2008). Almost two years later, the Petition for the Impeachment of President Lee was

Table 3.3.   Daum.net Traffic Total on Impeachment against President Lee

Activity on Daum.net	12/12/07	05/14/08	06/04/08	06/10/08	06/11/08
Major events	Before Presidential Election	Period of Candlelight Vigils	Defeated in the By-election	Reaction to Lee's 5/22 Apology	Immediately before 2nd Apology
Pageviews	7,705,387	15,895,789	41,670,437	37,267,856	32,779,655
Adjusted Pageviews	6,959,693	14,643,863	39,026,737	34,942,935	30,740,159
Unique Visitors	436,452	631,807	953,091	830,216	847,659
Visits	618,313	978,304	1,615,191	1,429,495	1,442,734
PVs per UV	17.65	25.16	43.72	44.89	38.67
Login #	154,678	158,296	346,078	284,735	285,507

Source: www.daum.net

established on April 6, 2008 by a Netizen with the ID 40221 (Andante). Since then, an average of 27,000 citizens signed the petition each day, producing a total of 1,334,711 signatures by May 27, 2008. Such extraordinary online civic disobedience was ignited by President Lee's swift agreement with President Bush on April 18, 2008 to reopen the Korean market to American beef—beef that had earlier been banned because of the 2003 outbreak of Mad Cow Disease in America.

Table 3.3 provides a dynamic depiction of online, non-face-to-face, interactions among mostly young generations with an exponential jump in traffic from December 2007 to May and June of 2008 in terms of page views and adjusted page views; and it shows the highest amount of traffic in early June, around the time when the new administration had been in office for 100 days and the U.S. Ambassador to South Korea, Alexander Vershbow, commented (on June 4th) that Koreans needed to learn more science about mad cow disease, which incited an escalation of protests from Koreans. Compared to the old experimentation of America's face-to-face civic participation in the late nineteenth century, this new experimentation is indeed quite different.

Another interesting finding is that, as Table 3.4 shows, teenage involvement in the early stage of the Agora petition in cyberspace and the candlelight vigils soon began to inspire the involvement of other age groups, especially the 2030 Generation, after the initial candlelight demonstrations peaked in early June. There is still a remarkably high percentage of online

Table 3.4. Impeachment Webpage Agora: User Analysis by Age Group

Date	Total	0–9	10–19	20s	30s	40s	50s	60+
June 4	174,913	160	8,378	57,273	69,098	29,821	10,183	0
June 5	172,767	146	7,713	56,234	68,432	29,789	10,453	0
June 6	139,739	133	12,171	46,670	48,671	23,588	8,506	0
June 7	135,163	124	8,843	41,955	49,022	25,699	9,520	0
June 8	123,245	108	10,096	39,535	43,778	21,704	8,024	0
June 9	144,769	113	5,221	41,807	58,995	28,272	10,361	0
June 10	144,058	133	6,153	43,708	57,681	26,816	9,567	0

Source: www.daum.net

Agora petitioners in their teens or even younger—a fact that deserves additional scholarly attention in terms of both the positive and negative effects of NNITs upon the political process. Also, participants in their fifties show relatively strong participation in the petition process, implying that the resistance against the new administration is gaining legitimacy throughout all age groups of the population.

Bilateral negotiations between the two countries on beef imports had been deadlocked until, during President Lee's April 2008 visit to the United States, a hurried decision was made to resume the import. Since then, Korean citizens have been demonstrating against the government's decision, which was widely considered a betrayal that endangered the nation's health. According to Harden (2008):

> [President Lee] moved to lift the beef ban, without consulting many of his own advisors, his party or the public. He did so shortly before a meeting on trade with President Bush in Washington. New public discontent quickly surfaced. Nearly two weeks ago, Lee apologized for failing to consider South Koreans' fears about Mad Cow Disease. But until this week, his government had insisted it would stick with completely removing the ban on U.S. beef . . . As the public anger grew, Lee was unmoved. "You don't have to eat American beef if you don't like it," he said. He has since paid a high political price. His party is now warning him to shake up his cabinet and jettison ministers associated in the public mind with U.S. beef. Changes are expected later this week.

On May 22nd, President Lee issued a formal apology to the nation, and then on June 19th, he issued a second apology and announced that he would replace the entire Blue House staff. However, to date, the issue of importing American beef remains unresolved, and the candlelight vigils have continued on a weekly basis since May 2nd, when approximately 400,000 angry citizens launched the first vigil. Although Lee's decision to import American beef has certainly been the flashpoint for much of the current discontent with his administration, it appears that the his administration's failure is actually rooted in its transitional and inaugural stages, during which, as Heinrich's Law suggests, many early warning signs occurred but were disregarded. Clearly, the mobilization of such powerful opposition would never have been possible, especially by young generations in so short a time, if they had not been conscious of their power in cyberspace, which demonstrates the effectiveness of this new experimentation in NNIT-induced political dynamics in the Information Age.

PRODROME (300:29:1) FOR THE CURRENT CRISIS

The prodromal accident that preceded the regime's current crisis happened to be an external disaster: it was on February 10, 2008, about two weeks before President-elect Lee was to be inaugurated, when the nation's most prized treasure, the *Sungnyemun* (also known as *Namdaemoon* or South Gate), burned down. By many, the fire has been considered a precursor of later problems: "It happened right after New Year's Day and right before the inauguration day of new Korean President, Myung-bak Lee. So such coincidence is being regarded as a sign of calamity" (Chung 2008).

For decades, the South Gate, the oldest wooden structure in Seoul, had been off-limits to the public, as it was situated in the center of a traffic rotary; but in 2004, then-Seoul Mayor Lee Myung-bak restored pedestrians' walk-up access to the gate, which to many seemed like a fine improvement. However, after it suddenly caught fire, popular opinion shifted sharply (Carr 2008). At that time, the fire's cause was still up for debate—some believed it had been started by a homeless person seeking shelter inside the structure, while others viewed it as an act of vandalism, possibly by Japan. An American lawyer named Brendon Carr, who happened to be working in Seoul at the time, visited the site and was impressed by the goodwill of then-President elect Lee's leadership to restore the burned-down national treasure by starting a fundraising campaign to collect the 20 billion *won* ($21.1 million) needed. In response, though, hundreds of critics in cyberspace immediately asked why they should open their pockets and pay for the government's failure to protect the national treasure. Backtracking, the transition team promptly scrapped their plans for a national fundraising campaign (Carr 2008b); Chairwoman Lee of the transition team retracted the team's initial announcement, explaining that the cost of the "restoration plan will be dealt with by the government's budget" (Carr 2008b). Carr wondered what the difference was between the government budget and money from the people's pockets; however, the citizens' main point was that President Lee seemed to be shirking the government's responsibility by creating a national fundraising effort to restore the damage. This totally unexpected and clearly external disaster served as a prodrome of the government's subsequent failure to address the nation's needs in other areas and correct the misguided policy recommendations from his transition team and, in particular, subsequent political moves related to South Korea's relationship with the United States. This relationship can be viewed with great clarity due to the way in which widespread use of NNITs accelerated the evolution of the current crisis.

CONCLUSION

This chapter aimed to describe the nature of the new political experimentation that is now manifesting as the NNIT-induced young generations' participation in politics. Korea's history of democracy is short—the first democratic civilian government was established only recently in 1993—however, a series of militant, democratic, anti-dictatorship movements resulted in the accumulation of social capital represented by the 386 Generation, which was transferred first to the 2030 Generation through a series of test-run mobilizations between 2000 and 2002 and then finally to Korea's teenagers in 2008. Although the 2030 and younger generations were initially apolitical, disparate and indifferent toward politics, after recognizing their power in the networked public sphere, they began reacting to decisions being made on issues related to their health and, through their organization and mobilization of candlelight demonstrations, ultimately drove national politics into a crisis. It comes as no surprise, however, that the impeachment process was conducted in cyberspace, as this is the main space of the young generations' activities; this is the Korean version of the new experimentation that is being induced by the youth's use of NNITs.

Since 2000, Korea has undergone dramatic and unprecedented changes in its political environment. The two most important elements underlying these changes are a) the ubiquitous and transformative use of NNITs in the political process and b) the young generations' explosive reactions as a decisive power bloc and leader of opinion groups in social and political movements. Lessons about the 386 Generation's leadership in their democratic opposition to the authoritarian regime during the late twentieth century were transferred through a series of demonstration effects, first to the younger 2030 Generation during the 2002 presidential election, and then to teens through candlelight vigils and the online impeachment movement. The transmission of demonstration effects through intermediate events to otherwise apolitical younger generations in the new political environment of NNIT-induced participation is central to this transformation of political discourse and participation. The dramatic effect of this technology cannot be overstated.

In an attempt to understand how the Internet and other NNITs have affected the dynamics of social and political movements in South Korea today, this chapter finds that NNIT-induced mobilizations can accelerate a political crisis or challenge political leadership under the following two conditions: (a) the widespread and rapid deployment of NNITs in society and (b) the strong presence of generations who use NNITs for political discourse and participation. The application of Heinrich's Law and Situational Crisis Communication Theory to this political crisis that originated in cyberspace and was accelerated by NNITs reveals two contradictory points: on the one hand, a panoramic view of the escalation cycle illustrates how a small accident can mushroom into a major crisis; on the other hand, the application of Heinrich's Law points to the seeds of the political crisis early in its development. In regard to Situational Crisis Communication Theory, this case also contributes new insight into how new actors equipped with NNITs can dramatically shorten the cycle of crisis evolution and cause a chain reaction of crises. Another important point that became apparent through this research was that an NNIT-induced mobilization can precipitate a crisis in the Information Era by ensuring that citizens remember other mistakes previously made by the same persons; in the current technological environment, past mistakes are never truly in the past.

Heinrich's Law suggests that a major crisis can be predicted after a sufficient numbers of mistakes, events and warnings. The ubiquitousness of the Internet and other NNIT-based environments has intensified the overall cycle of escalation from small accidents to a major crisis; and by so doing, has increased the predictability of such escalation in political and social movements. This point carries particular import for democracy in the twenty-first century. Will NNIT-induced social or political movements imperil the stability of democracies by instigating pointless protests and mobilizing people in support of demagogic agendas? Or will they advance the democratic process by challenging authoritarian regimes, primarily in under-democratized countries? This question calls to mind Nobel Prize winner for Economics Amartya Sen's razor-sharp point on democracy: "Democracy is a demanding system, and not just a mechanical condition [like majority rule] taken in isolation" (Sen 1999, 10). With respect to these questions, this chapter has discussed the likelihood of a series of negative impacts on the core principles of modern democratic institutions.

First, the hyperactivity of the NNIT-fueled reactive political action may shake the republican principle of constitutionalism because the escalated NNIT-induced protests of the type seen in Korea seem to undermine the constitutional legitimacy of the presidency by almost effortlessly initiating an impeachment process in cyberspace. Second, a constituency of NNIT-created "chiefs" can significantly hamper the executive power needed to implement national policy agendas, regardless of the advisability or inadvisability of individual policies. As a case in point, the initiatives described during Lee's campaign—i.e., the canal, privatization and deregulation—seem now to be deadlocked for the foreseeable future. Third, the heightened civic engagement of a high-tech civil society empowered with NNITs and led by younger generations now suggests the emergence of a fifth estate, superimposed above the fourth estate of mass media. The influence of this emerging power may eventually grow to such an extent that no other institution can counterbalance it. Indeed, with few procedural guarantees of representative political dialog, the whole democratic political system may become vulnerable to demagogic behind-the-scenes manipulation.

Finally, this chapter finds that, simultaneous with the emergence of newly powerful young generations, older generations have also begun to play more significant roles in NNIT-spawned social and political experimentation. It was younger generations who played a pivotal role in electing progressive and liberal candidate Roh in the 2002 presidential election; however, the constituency over the age of 50 showed strong and increasing participation in the political mobilizations in cyberspace. It is my belief that, as informatization increases in the coming years, a political equilibrium will be established between young and old generations in terms of their influence in cyber politics. With so many eyes watching, and the ever-increasing availability of information in an endless "now," it will be hard for this dynamic to be otherwise.

APPENDIX B

Table 3.B1   Demonstration Effect: What Happened in Korean Presidential Election (NNITs and Young Generations)

Table 3.B2   Panoramic View of the Current Political Crisis.

Table 3.B1. Demonstration Effect: What Happened in 2002 Korean Presidential Election (NNITs and Young Generations)

	2000	2002			
Events	Defeat Movement in General Election	Utah Winter Olympics	World Cup Games	Hyosun and Misun	Presidential Election
When	April 19	January	May–June	June 13 and November 27	December 19
Who	386 Generation and Civic Alliance	2030 Generation	2030 and 386 Generations	2030 and 386 Generations	2030 and 386 Generations
What	First negative election campaign through Internet to defeat unfit politicians in the National Assembly	Individuals attack the official Olympic website complaining about the incorrect decision by umpire in short track speed skating competition	Led by The Red Devils (Internet soccer fan club), 22 million fill the streets to cheer for the national team	Two schoolgirls killed by American military vehicle in June, Anti-American candlelight vigil in city center in November	Young generations experienced with NNITs cast decisive votes as a voting bloc in the presidential election for the first time
Stages & Impact	The first Demonstration Effect (386 Generation and Internet)	• Consolidation of 2030 Generation • NNIT-induced consolidation and mobilizations experimentation period	Breakout (triggering event) for political participation in presidential election		Byproduct of a year-long mobilization
Outcomes	68% defeated	Official website collapsed, globally recognized	Globally highlighted role of Red Devils	Candlelight protest culture established	• President Roh elected • 2030 Generation with NNITs emerge as a new political force

Agora (Internet Petition Page on December 17, 2004)

Table 3.B2. Panoramic View of the Current Political Crisis

	December 19, 2007–July 2008		
Stages	**Prodrome:** Events during Transition and Inauguration	**Breakout:** Summit in the U.S. and Beef Import (Breakout)	**Chronic:** Candlelight Protests
Time Period	December 2007–April 2008	April 2008	May 2, 2008–Present
Major Players	Netizens	Teens	Teens $\longrightarrow$ 386 $\longrightarrow$ all generations
Failed Policies, External Disasters, Mistakes	• South Gate burned (2/10) • Education policy on English • Blue House & Cabinet appointment mishap • Failed policies of privatization, canal construction • School deregulation (4/15) • Control of public broadcasting companies	• Beef negotiations in Seoul underway (4/1) • Agora Impeachment initiated (4/6) • Lee visits U.S. (4/15-19) • Lee's decision to resume importing of beef at Camp David (4/18)	• 1,368,311 signed the petition for impeachment by early July on Internet Agora (Daum.net) • 100 leaders' declaration against regime on 100th day of regime (6/2) • Defeated in by-election (6/4) • Two apologies by president (5/22, 6/19) • Reshuffle Blue House staff (6/20) • Canal & privatization projects abandoned • President Bush's visit cancelled due to continuous protests but occurred on August 5
Applications	Prodromal (Heinrich's 300: 29: 1)	Breakout (Triggering Events)	Chronic Resolution?

NOTES

1. This chapter is based on my article, "Korea's Beef Crisis: The Internet and Democracy," which was published in the *Australian Journal of International Affairs,* 63(4), 2009. I want to thank the Taylor & Francis group for their generous permission to expand this article into a chapter for this book.

2. The 386 Generation is about 20 years older than the 2030 Generation. For more detailed explanations of these two generations, refer to chapter 2 (p. 2).

3. On how young generations in 2002 found themselves connected to each other and recognized their power as a voting bloc in the presidential election, see Kwon and Lee (2004), Watts (2003), and Yoon (2007), in addition to chapter 2 (p. 8).

4. *Kyung-shil-lyun* in Korean. It is the most powerful and largest civic organization on socio-economic justice in Korea. See the URL www.ccej.or.kr/main.htm.

5. *Cham-yeo-yeon-dae* in Korean. It is the most powerful civic organization on political issues in Korea. See the URL www.peoplepower21.org.

6. See http://agora.media.daum.net/petition/view?id=40221.

7. Chairperson Lee, Kyungsook of the Presidential Transition Committee for the current President Lee pronounced the word "orange" as "arinji" as an example of its new education reform policy for Koreans to learn real pronunciations in English. Her pronunciation and approach caught national attention and became a laughingstock. Later, this education reform idea was completely dropped, and this incident was referred to as an unrealistic policy vision of the new government.

Chapter 4

NNITs and the Obama Phenomenon

Transforming Electoral Politics of the Youth

Having successfully used new networked information technologies, such as the Internet and mobile phones, as well as new online social networks, such as Facebook, MySpace, YouTube and Twitter, the Obama campaign consolidated these various avenues of support into the website WhiteHouse.gov on January 20, 2009 through the intermediate entity of Change.gov, which was established by president-elect Barack Obama's transition team on November 5, 2008 and maintained until his inauguration. Under the header of "Open Government," Change.gov stated that "[t]he story of the campaign and this historic moment has been your story," and asked readers to "Share Your Vision" via email and become a "part of bringing positive lasting change to this country." Serving as a consolidated Web portal, Change.gov was designed to maintain unprecedented levels of support from users of NNITs during the campaign and prompt their continued involvement in the Obama White House agendas.

This chapter explains the Obama phenomenon by attempting to link young generations' increased participation in electoral politics and voting turnout with their dominance in the use of NNITs and their strong gravitation toward Democratic candidate Senator Obama. The main focus of this chapter will be Generation Y, ages 18 to 32, who have been allegedly apolitical but have arguably transformed themselves into active political constituency. By examining the main features of NNIT-activated Generation Y in the 2008 Presidential campaign, this chapter presents empirical evidence regarding whether NNIT-activated increased participation of young generations produced a decisive contribution to the victory of candidate Barack Obama in the 2008 Presidential election. even though it may require an extensive survey data to corroborate a causal link between the use of NNITs and increased voter turnout.

Compared to the main features of major generations in American politics such as the Greatest Generation, active in the 1940s and 1950s, the Baby Boom Generation, active in the 1960s and 1970s, and Generation X, active in the late 1980s and 1990s (Keller 1978; Strauss and Howe, 1991; Jennings 2004; Strauss and Howe, 2006), members of Generation Y:

1. Are the most high-tech savvy and interconnected national constituency in history;
2. Are interacting both face-to-face offline and online cyberspace;
3. Are members of ethnically diverse groups that are socially engaged through individual profiles via online social media;
4. Have become involved in politics following the 9/11 terrorist attack in 2001, having developed a "politics-matter-to-me" attitude and demon-strating clear signs of an increasing voting rate;
5. Are in direct contacts with candidates by bypassing the conventional media gate-keepers;
6. Are actively participating in Internet fundraising and electoral politics with peer production and distribution of campaign materials they gener-ated using online social media;
7. Have increased their electoral turnout during the last two presidential elections from 1996 to 2008.

The most significant aspect of the changes occurring among Generation Y is the way in which their unprecedented use of NNITs has facilitated their increased participation in the highly contested presidential elections of 2004 and 2008. There are two conflicting studies on the relationship between social capital and voter turnout by generation. Putnam (2000, 2003, and 2008) attributes the decline in the young generations' voting turnout to the overall demise of civic culture since the late 1960s. However, in his seminal study on the voter turnout and the dynamics of electoral competition in established democracies since 1945, Franklin (2004: 171) contends that "commentators who see in the falling turnout a reflection on the civic-mindedness of citizens, or on their commitment to democracy, appear to be mistaken." Among many variables that have affected voter turnout in the Western democracies since 1945, the nature of a specific election matters most. (Franklin, 2004: 251). On the other hand, in their analysis of British general elections, O'Toole et al (2003: 58) argue that most of the existing literature on low participation of young generations in electoral politics is flawed due to its narrow defini-tion of politics and conventional research design that does not reflect young people's distinctive views on politics. Though these debates require further empirical research on the controversy, it is clear that in recent presidential election outcomes Generation Y (born in the mid-1980 and became a new cohort in the 2004 Presidential Election) has actively engaged in electoral campaigns and has voted more than the same age cohorts in previous elections as demonstrated in both Table 4.3 and Table 4.4.

The 2008 U.S. presidential election resulted in the great transformation and redefinition of U.S. electoral politics and overall political landscape. President Barack Obama's accomplishments in this election include: (1) transforming certain red states into the blue states; (2) cultivating a Blue Ocean of previously untapped young voters; (3) demonstrating the critical power of new networked information technologies (NNITs) in election campaigns; (4) winning previously anti-democrat demographics including frequent churchgoers, military, independents, white men, Hispanics, and even gun owners. Overall, this election observed a turnout rate of 62.5 percent, the highest in 44 years (a total of 133 million votes which means about 11 million more than voted in 2004). For example, The Exit Poll by CNN and CBS News (*et al*, 2008) poll noticeably shows that the 2008 U.S. presidential election demonstrated far more increased turnout among both general youth voters from ages 18 to 29 and specifically college students, as well as their stalwart leaning toward liberal Democratic candidate Barack Obama. The CNN Exit Polls confirm:

- 66 percent of voters from ages 18 to 29 voted for Obama while 32 percent voted for McCain [which is not much different in the House election with 63 percent for Democrats and 34 percent for Republicans, (Ruffini, 2008)];
- Obama's support from young voters cut across the racial divisions (by 54 percent against McCain's 44 percent from the same White age group, 95 percent vs 4 percent from African Americans, and 76 percent vs. 19 percent from Latino voters);
- Obama outperformed McCain in terms of support from first-time voters 68 percent to 31 percent.

The CBS News, UNWIRE, and Chronicle of Higher Education Student Voter Poll, sampled from college voters in 30 counties released three days after the election, indicates that:

- 44 percent identified as Democrats, 28 percent as Independent, 28 percent as Republican;
- Higher voter totals in 24 of the 30 counties sampled;
- Obama's increased his share of youth votes by 10 percent or compared to Kerry in states like Indiana;

- Obama won constituencies that went for Bush in 2004, including 13 of 18 Bush counties in college town counties in swing states like Indiana (Ball State, Purdue), North Carolina (WCU, ECU, Appalachian State), Ohio (Bowling Green State), Pennsylvania (Penn State), and Virginia (JMU, Virginia Tech).

Overall, this election produced both increases of total voter turnouts in general and among the young constituency aged 18–29 in particular, including a "gargantuan 25 percent swing among existing young voters" (Ruffini, 2008). Ruffini's argument is that Obama's landslide winning margin of 25 percent for the youth vote equals "73 electoral votes from Florida, Ohio, North Carolina, or Indiana" (Ruffini, 2008). His calculation is "18 percent times a 25 percent increase in the Democratic margin equals 4.5 points, or a majority of Obama's popular vote margin. Had the Democratic 18–29 vote stayed the same as 2004's already impressive percentage, Obama would have won by about 2 points" (Ruffini, 2008).

Despite such a sweeping victory, the country remains ideologically remained divided along the political spectrum. According to Rove's (2008) interpretation of the exit polls: "America remains ideologically stable, with 34 percent of voters saying they are conservative—unchanged from 2004. Moderates went to 44 percent from 45 percent of the electorate, while liberals went to 22 percent from 21 percent." Two factors can explain this seemingly ironic phenomenon of a candidate like Obama winning voters across the political spectrum and while the country remains ideologically divided. First, the sudden collapse of the Wall Street financial institutions redirected the flow of votes. Second, Obama campaign outperformed McCain despite the latter's strategy of juxtaposing arguments about experience and character with Obama's emphasis on change.

Obama's victory in the historic election of 2008, which can be attributed to a panoply of factors, including race, the Wall Street collapse, the Iraq War, and eight years of Bush fatigue, was also aided greatly by the participation of an unprecedentedly high number of young voters and their use of NNITs. Writing in March 2008 about the heated primary contest between Obama and Clinton, Putnam (2008, (1) observed the increased participation of young voters, noting that "Primaries and caucuses [from] coast to coast in the last two months have evinced the sharpest increase in civic engagement among American youth in at least a half-century, portending a remarkable revitalization of American democracy." Confirming Putnam's observation, Williams and Gulati (2008, 5) found that young voters in Iowa had turned out "at three times their level in 2004, representing 22 percent of the total caucus turnout; in New Hampshire, the youth turnout doubled over 2004 levels and represented 18 percent of the total primary vote." Similarly, Kirby et al. (2008) found that the national youth turnout rate practically doubled from 9 percent in the 2000 primaries and caucuses to 17 percent in those of 2008 with more than 6.5 million voters under the age of 30 participating. Evidence abounds for the increased turnout of younger voters (18–29 years old): a 3 percent jump in the congressional elections from 2002 to 2006; a 9 percent increase in the presidential election from 2000 to 2004; and an average increase of 8.8 percent in the primaries and caucuses of 16 states from 2000 to 2008 (Kirby, et al. 2008).

An overall increase in civic engagement as well as a strong gravitation toward a particular candidate was observed as these NNIT-activated young voters evinced a noticeable inclination toward Senator Obama among other democratic candidates in the primary elections and over Republican McCain in the general election. Since 1980, a trend of strong gravitation toward the Democratic Party can be identified in voters aged 18 to 29 as compared to voters of all other age groups. In fact, according to the exit polls from CBS/ NYT (1980–1988), Voter News Service (1992–2000), and National Election Pool (2004–2008), young voters (ages 18 to 29) have consistently gravitated more toward the Democratic party than towards the Republican party, especially since 2000. Despite the fact that the Democratic share of the votes alternated erratically since 1960s among voters ages 18 to 29, there has been an overall increase from 44 percent in 1980 to 53 percent in 1996.

As mentioned above, one of the factors responsible for Obama's astounding success was his campaign's skillful use of NNITs. For example, the video titled "Dear Mr. Obama" (www.youtube.com/watch?v=TG4fe9GlWS8) recorded the most popular election film in YouTube, attracting 13 million hits by November 11 (Vaidyanathan, 2008). NNITs are transforming the relationship between candidates and constituency. Citizens using YouTube can distribute their own messages "faster in a 15 minute news cycle than traditional media can in a 24-hour news cycle" (Vaidyanathan, 2008). In fact, these digital social networking technologies do not decrease but rather increase subsequent face-to-face interactions among users and make these interactions more meaningful by relating and matching the temporal and spatial contexts of agents.

In fact, one of the biggest differences between Obama's campaign and those of his opponents was their overall strategy in regard to the role of NNITs, including new online social media. Among these media, social network sites (SNSs) are Web-based services that enable users to "construct a public or semi-public profile . . . articulate a list of other users . . . [and/or] view and traverse their list of connections and those made by others within the system" (Boyd and Ellison 2007, 2). Through social network sites, members can interact with peers in cyberspace, maintain friendships, and build relationships with the friends of their friends. The most important contribution of these SNSs, in terms of their impact upon users, is that they equip users with a convenient means of producing and broadcasting content. By making use of numerous mega-membership networks that cross cultural, national, political, religious and ethnic backgrounds, the young generations have established a cyber, or networked, public sphere. The success of Obama's presidential campaign is purported to have arisen, in part, from the strategic use of mobile phones and online social media as a way to reach the youth. Whereas Obama's campaign derived much of its support from state-of-the-art *digital network power*, the campaigns of Clinton and McCain were both based on more traditional *analog power*. In other words, Obama's campaign strategy was designed to excel in the new environments of the Information Age experimentation, while the campaigns of Clinton and McCain were both focused on the political capital of the old American experimentation. This chapter focuses on Obama's success in tapping into the potential power of the youth in this new digital era.

Obama's high-tech approach led to his enormous popularity among young generations on an ever-widening array of new social media sites, including Facebook, MySpace, YouTube and Twitter. By contrast, both McCain's and Clinton's "top-down, command-and-control" approach involved locking down the support of "party stalwarts" and assembling an "all-star team of consultants" (Green 2008, 7; Abroms and Lefebvre 2009, 415). Cohen (2008) attributes Obama's victory in the Democratic primary to his campaign's "grasp of the central place of Internet-driven social networking," and Clinton's loss, in part, to her campaign's "most crippling blindness to [the power of digital] networks." For example, Obama's campaign produced 1,982 campaign online videos that received 900 million hits, whereas McCain's team used 376 videos that received only 500 million hits. So it should come as no surprise that in the eighteen months leading up to the election, the total video watch time[1] for Obama (14,548,810 hours) completely outstripped that of McCain (488,093 hours) (Owen 2009, 24).

According to Figure 4.1 above, Compete.com recorded almost 5 million visitors to Senator Obama's website near election day and only about 1.5 million visitors to McCain's at its highest point in early November. Overall, throughout the entire election campaign period in 2008, neither McCain nor Clinton could match Senator Obama in the competition to attract the attention of the American youth in cyberspace. Figure 4.1 indicates how, by tapping into the enormous power of NNITs, a first-term Senator was able to outflank vested interests and glittering political stars, creating what later came to be known as the "Obama Phenomenon" (Han 2007, 2009, 2010).

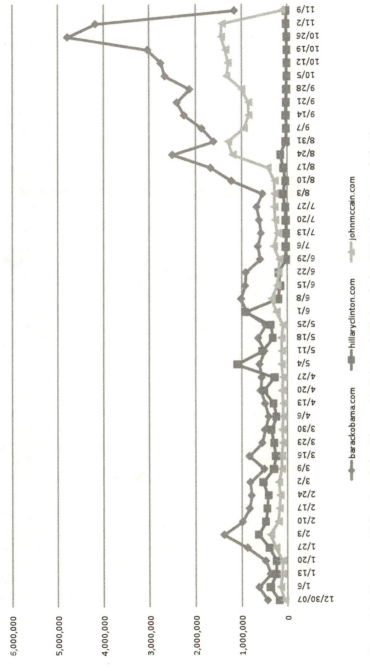

Figure 4.1 Homepage Visitor Trends for Obama, McCain, and Clinton during 2008 Primaries and Election

This success can also be attributed in part to several additional factors not mentioned above: a significant overall increase in participation and voter turnout in the primaries, mostly by young generations; their rapidly growing use of digital social network sites; and the resulting explosive growth of small-scale donations on the Internet. Since this chapter serves as a case study examining the essence of the new experimentation that is occurring in the United States, what matters most is how we conceptualize the changes currently occurring in electoral politics as a result of the young generations' use of NNITs.

CONCEPTUALIZING THE OBAMA PHENOMENON

This chapter applies two concepts—that of the "Blue Ocean" and the "Long Tail"—as metaphors as detailed in the Chapter 1 to help us understand this unprecedented success utilizing NNITs in a presidential election campaign. The first concept comes from the field of marketing, and the latter from statistics. The juxtaposition of these two terms may initially seem like a mixed metaphor, but they represent distinct perspectives that can be coupled to perceive the inner workings of the Obama phenomenon in greater depth.

As explained in the section "Conceptualizing the Obama Phenomenon: Blue Ocean of Long Tail of NNIT-Activated Young Constituency" in chapter 1, the concept of the Long Tail originated in the use of database technology in the sales and marketing of books in Amazon.com. *Wired*'s editor in chief Chris Anderson formulated this concept of "Long Tail" from his observation of how an almost forgotten book later became a bestseller in Amazon. com. *Touching the Void*, a book written by Joe Simpson in 1998 about a harrowing account of a mountain-climbing tragedy, was only a modest success but soon forgotten. However, a decade later, it became a *New York Times* bestseller because of the popularity of a similar book, *Into Thin Air* written by Jon Krakauer. How did this happen? Anderson (2004) points to the power of Amazon.com's software, which tracked the buying patterns of consumers and suggested a recommendation list, suggesting that readers who liked Krakauer's book would also like Simpson's *Touching the Void*. Online consumers took that suggestion and even wrote rhapsodic reviews, which generated huge sales. It was highly unlikely that readers of Krakauer would know about Simpson's book a only few years ago. Anderson describes how Amazon.com "created the *Touching the Void* phenomenon by combining infinite shelf space with real-time information about buying trends and public opinion. The result: rising demand for an obscure book." In other words, NNITs have converted a forgotten book to a bestseller overnight by intermediating booksellers and readers, and, more importantly, by matching readers with similar interests. This phenomenon creates a new market, or Blue Ocean with new rules of the game, that is not restricted to online book-selling but can apply to other industries such as media and entertainment as explained in chapter 1.

Here, this notion of increased book sales online marketing capabilities seems to provide a relevant analogy into electoral politics where members of the lowest voting age group begins to convert themselves into a more formi-dable constituency. This formerly disparate and apolitical young generation, previously an ignored element of the electorate, now appear to attract more attentions from politicians because they engage in online discourse on issues on the national agenda and electoral topics, produce/share/distribute cam-paign materials, and increasingly participate in voting. Anderson explains the increased power of Long Tail that:

> What's really amazing about the Long Tail is the sheer size of it. Combine enough nonhits on the Long Tail and you've got a market bigger than the hits. Take books: The average Barnes & Noble carries 130,000 titles. Yet more than half of Amazon's book sales come from outside its top 130,000 titles. Consider the implication: If the Amazon statistics are any guide, the market for books that are not even sold in the average bookstore is larger than the market for those that are (see "Anatomy of the Long Tail"). In other words, the potential book market may be twice as big as it appears to be, if only we can get over the economics of scarcity.

Two points are noteworthy. Those non-hits in the book industry and other entertainment industries become the newest factor in the increased sales of this industry and their potential size is bigger than that of the hits. According to venture capitalist and former music industry consultant Kevin Laws, the biggest money is in these kinds of smallest sales items. This observation is applicable to electoral politics and campaigns that formerly disinterested and non-voting young generations are now reached by candidates and campaigns through online media and they begin to pay attention to campaign agendas and national politics. The young age group from 18 to 39 contains the largest reserve army of potential voters. How do we explain such a transformation of an apolitical generation to one that participates in electoral politics and influences voter groups, and why is this shift occurring now? This group of citizens was largely excluded in the public sphere dominated by the Industrial Age media that has been so dominant for so long. But now they are active in the newly rising cyberspace regarding their own interests of activities, mostly non-political areas such as sports, entertainment, and personal information exchanges, all of which can be converted to political and campaign issues through test-run mobilizations with demonstration effects when such issues affect their lives. They also form a sense of online- or cyber-community separated from older generations so that they can talk about political issues within themselves. Thus, it is not that this generation was necessarily apolitical but rather that they felt excluded from the conventional public discourse which is mostly tailored by and for older generations. The chances for their voices to be reflected in the traditional public sphere and medium such as the *New York Times*, network television, and major magazines are slim. They don't feel that they belong to these pre-existing media outlets. However, they are central players in the NNIT-activated public spheres and their potential to become political activists in that space can be realized at any time as long as political issues appear relevant to them. They do talk about politics, not in the conventional medium but in their own spheres. Nothing is free from politics. Thus, when a new online music site, such as Napster for example, became a public issue due to a conflict of intellectual property rights, young cyber-community members voices and deliberated their opinions on the issue and began to convince others through what they are good at cyberspace: investigating the issues online, writing their opinions, making videos to promote their opinions, spreading their opinions using their networks of friends, and building a network of supporters. These activities are what they were accustomed to engaging in everyday. It is just a matter of changing the topics: from daily routines to political and campaign issues.

In addition to the concept of demonstration effect in studying the transformation process, Giddens' theory of 'life politics' appears to be a good theoretical tool to explain why these young generations with NNITs become involved in politics and how different their motivation in participating in politics is from that of their seniors. Giddens starts his theory by explaining the nature of the modern set of relationships between human and institutions, especially between citizens (agent) and the state (structure), approximately from the 1920s through to the 1970s were "treated as 'fate' and fixed rather than as something based on negotiation and choices that had to be worked at" (Ferguson, 2001: 42). Emancipated from conventional or "pure relationship" in the relationship with the state called by Giddens (1994), 'reflexive modernity' resulted in the structural transformation in the meaning of life: acquiring "sense of having choices as to how to live, who to be, and how to plan one's life were not on lay or professional agendas" (Ferguson, 2001: 43). Relying on the concepts like "transnationalism" (Itzigsohn, 2000; Waters, 2003) or "distributed public governance" (Flinders, 2004), Giddens argues that the process of "reflexive modernity" "separates" and "divorces" each individual from fixed identities and hierarchical political authority. Itzigsohn (2000: 1128) argument that "the rise of networks and institutions that create new forms of social relations and action across national borders" can certainly be applied to the domestic political context and this new experimentation of networks provides an optimal environment for the youth to engage in politics on their own terms.

To young generations, politics and elections have to be matters specifically affecting their lives rather than big political causes such as emancipatory movements or nationalism. Giddens' notion of life politics seems relevant in explaining young generations' sudden interests in political participation. According to Giddens (1994b, pp.90–1), life politics are "about how we should live in a world where everything that used to be natural (or traditional) now has in some sense to be chosen, or decided about" (Giddens, 1994b, pp.90–1) as explained in chapter 3 on Korea's beef crisis. It is about life choices and involves viewing power as generative rather than hierarchical. It is a politics of self-actualization in a reflexively ordered environment where reflexivity links self and body to systems of global scope" (Giddens, 1991, p. 214; re-quoted in Ferguson, 2001: 47). The new life political agenda involves the notions of governmentality and citizenships among many other areas such as "ethnic groups, abilities, sexualities and genders (Ferguson, 2001: 49). Giddens sees life politics as focusing on issues that are less related to equality or emancipation, and more to how one should construct one's life in a context of rapid detraditionalization. It has to do, in other words, with identity construction, with competing life styles, with whether or not work should continue to be the basic organizing principle of our lives, with contested practices like abortion, in-vitro fertilization, genetic engineering, and so on (Mouzelis, 2001: 439).

As was the case in the emerging global agenda of life politics, NNIT-activated young generations and their participation in politics entails unintended consequences of escaping rational control of conventional politics and preexisting major stakeholders such as senior citizens, gate-keeping forces of industrial news and media and other state agencies. Interests in life politics create a situation where individuals can resort to neither traditional truths nor collective ideologies when taking decisions in their everyday lives" (Mouzelis, 2001: 438).

Such a transformation of disinterested youth voters requires NNIT-infrastructure and test-run mobilizations through series of demonstration effects. Thus, previously uninfluential youth voters (long tail) become more influential in the campaign process (Long Tail). The birth of the Long Tail catalyzed through the use of NNITs becomes a new market for candidates while older age groups with higher voting rates and less use of NNITs become a kind of Red Ocean in the sense that rules of games in mobilizing these groups of voters are fairly fixed within the Industrial Age medium.

The term "Blue Ocean" (Kim and Mauborgne 2005) is used to describe an emerging market of great importance that is ripe for exploration and cultivation. In this case, the Blue Ocean of digital technology-oriented electoral campaign strategy is wide-open for competition, and Senator Obama was the first candidate to enter this new arena. The new experimentation with using NNITs in electoral politics and campaigning is a Blue Ocean both for candidates who understand the power of NNITs among the constituency, especially the apolitical youth, and voters who previously lacked an effective means to voice their opinion.

The statistical concept of a "long tail" was originally used in reference to uninfluential majority in a particular frequency distribution; however, within the context of this discussion, as discussed in the Introduction (chapter 1). This chapter explores how NNITs have transformed the younger generations from a conventionally uninfluential "long tail" into an increasingly participatory and influential group in electoral politics of the 2008 presidential election.

Base on the conceptual framework of the Blue Ocean of NNIT-activated young generations of Long Tail, this chapter begins by referring an analysis of the new players in this rising Blue Ocean, and explains how the Obama campaign cultivated this market that had previously been untapped. I then proceed to analyze how, as a result of their support and widespread use of NNITs, Obama generated a "Blue Ocean" in the form of a newly empowered young voting bloc. Next, the section entitled "Obama"s Gold Mine: Unprecedented Fundraising Records," analyzes how Obama's NNIT-based campaign produced such an unprecedented amount of contributions. After that, "Generational Activism Increases Voter Turnout" explains how digital social networking and the mobilization of young voters resulted in a more cohesive voting bloc that gravitated toward Obama and served as a factor contributing to his decisive win. Finally, "Continuing Relevance of the Long Tail in the Years Ahead?" suggests that the use of NNITs by Generation Y has not only remained strong but will continue to play an increasingly critical role in the possible creation of an enormous, cohesive voting bloc.

NNITs, YOUNG VOTERS, AND POLITICAL PARTICIPATION

Has the voter turnout of young generations really decreased? If so, what are the reasons for such decline? Overall, turnout in established democracies had declined by just 4 percent on average between the decades of the 1970s and the 1990s, according to the Institute for Democracy and Electoral Assistance (Franklin, 2004: 10–11). However, Franklin (2004) argues that such decline over a twenty-year period is not significant; rather, turnout has been remarkably "stable." Many scholars (Strauss and Howe, 1991; Franklin, et al., 2004; Jennings and Stoker, 2004; Hooghe 2004; Blais, 2006; Rubenson, et al., 2004; Blais et al., 2004) as well as Putnam (2000, 2003) confirm a general trend of declining social capital among young generations in the established Western democracies. However, the findings by the former group of scholars are not the same as that of Putnam's regarding the causal linkage between age, social capital, and voting turnout. Analyzing the longitudinal surveys of three generations on their level of social capital (social trust and civic engagement), Jennings and Stoker (2004: 353–355) present an interesting finding that the Baby Boomer Generation outranks the Greatest Generation in the categories of social trust and stronger associations with civic, neighborhood, and sports organizations while Generation X trails far behind these two predecessors in these categories. Their three-generation, longitudinal study from a 1965 national sample of high school seniors who were subsequently resurveyed in 1973, 1982, and finally in 1997 reveals that the conventional belief of consistent decline of social capital from Greatest Generation to Baby Boomer Generation to finally X Generation is mistaken. Their research finds that "any analysis of the changing trust levels of Americans must take both life-cycle and generational differences into account" (Jennings and Stoker, 2004: 352). Thus, Jennings and Stoker confirm that: (1) X Generation clearly lags behind its predecessors in every aspect of social capital, (2) the Baby Boomers are not always trailing behind the Greatest Generation, (3) trust levels first falls with the transitional period from adolescence to adulthood, then climbing again in the late 20s and subsequently (Jennings and Stoker, 2004: 371–375). They conclude that social trust is a disposition that is quite malleable among young adults and quite unstable across the early years of adulthood (2004: 374). Accordingly, the youth's image as "passive citizenry" with low voting turnout is mostly derived from Generation X (Strauss and Howe, 1991; Jennings and Stoke, 2004; Hooghe, 2004) and misrepresents reality of the current young generation.

In this context, it is important to explain the sizeable increases in both voter registration and actual votes among voters from 18 to 34, the official age group bracket of young voters in the Bureau of Census statistics closely matching with the age span of Generation Y, for both 2004 and 2008 Presidential elections (Table 4.3 and Table 4.4). Franklin's research finding seems to provide a significant insight on this issue that voting turnout is mostly decided by "not something about the way people approach elections but something about how elections appear to people" (Franklin, 2004: 215). This chapter argues that it was the characters of these two latest contested elections that attracted young generations (Blais, 2006; Blais, et al., 2004; Franklin 2004, Hooghe, 2004), mostly by the awakening effect of 9/11 terrorist attack, two wars with Islamic countries and economic fallout that engendered a politics-matter-to-me attitude among the young genertion (Han, 2007).

In general, lower voting rates among young generations are explained by three effects: a period effect (something particular about an election); a life-cycle effect (voting rate shifts as young voters grow older); and a generational effect (cohorts differ even when compared at the same time in their life cycle) (Rubenson, et al., 2004; Blais, et al., 2004, Hooghe, 2004). While most of these scholars agree that political cynicism, lack of political interests, and a less engaged citizenry are the main features of Generation X, no definitive empirical study is available on the latest young cohort, Generation Y. However, Generation Y has been described as more democratic, tolerant, and both critical of and skeptical toward established power than Generation X (Inglehart 2003; Norris 1999). Through 2008 Presidential Election, Generation Y has demonstrated a sense of civic obligation, heated political interests and trust on the power of votes.

How did this previously indifferent young long tail transform into empowered Long Tail? What has made the young generations more involved in the political discourse and how do we explain such transformation? To grasp the importance of the Long Tail's role in the recent presidential election, it is important first to understand how uninvolved the young voters had actually been in politics and how NNITs have helped cause this dramatic transformation. As has been noted by many authors (Putnam 2008, 37; Han 2007, 58; Dutta-Bergman 2006; Lebkowsky 2005, 35; Trippi 2004, 104; Putnam, et al. 2003, 128, 285), the new attitude that "politics-matter-to-me," which has become more common since 9/11, has altered the traditional indifference of Generation Y (18–32 year olds) (Jones and Fox 2009, 1) toward politics and public issues. In chapter 2, I argued that a transformation of this magnitude is generally preceded by an intermediate phase of successive, collective actions that serve as test-run mobilizations through which participants come to recognize their potential power and the rewards that their participation can bring. To demonstrate this point, I cited the case of the 2000 South Korean General Assembly election, during which young Koreans in their twenties and thirties (the 2030 Generation), having learned the rewards of political activism from their immediate elders (i.e., the 386 Generation),[2] used Web technology to help defeat corrupt members of the General Assembly. Having demonstrated their expertise in online games, this generation turned their attention to political issues, such as the important anti-American candlelight demonstrations in November 2002 and the presidential election in December 2002. Based on these cases, I (Han 2007, 61) support Cornell and Cohn's view (1995) that "a cycle of successful protest generates a demonstration effect by raising consciousness, defining occasions for action, and successful tactics for protesters." To this, I would like to add that one byproduct of a cycle of successful protests is the creation of a politically-active generation.

Wohl (1979, 78), in his book *The Generation of 1914*, defines a "generation" as "a sense of common destiny shared by similarly located individuals who share the same values and [participate] actively and passively in the social and intellectual movements that [are] shaping and transforming their historical situation." Examples of dramatic historical events that awaken the generational sense of community and identity are "great historical events like wars, revolutions, plagues, famine, and economic crisis" (Wohl 1979, 210). In twenty-first century America, a series of major political events in the early 2000s—the 9/11 terrorist attacks, the Iraq War, the meteoric rise and fall of candidate Howard Dean in the 2004 Democratic presidential primaries (Williams and Gulati 2008; Abroms and Lefebvre 2008, 415), the 2006 mid-term elections, and primaries and caucuses in the 2008 presidential election—collectively contributed to the formation of a new post-9/11 generational consciousness. A series of test-run mobilizations—such as the 2004 presidential campaign and the 2006 mid-term election—may have increased young people's propensity to vote in subsequent elections (youngvoterstrategies.org 2006, 7). Now that they are digitally connected and becoming increasingly aware of their political power in an expanded networked public sphere, young constituents in the United States are beginning to recognize their ability to make a difference and are taking this role more seriously, as evidenced by their consistent activities on social network sites such as Twitter (Han and Kim 2009). They were "at the forefront of these innovations, which contributed to their increased engagement in the election" (Owen 2009, 19).

Even after the 2008 Presidential election, the number of Obama Twitter followers grew explosively between December 2007 and December 2009, as illustrated in Figure 4.2 (Han and Kim 2009). Compared to the average number of Obama tweet followers during the 2008 Presidential election (i.e., 59,000), the average number of followers of President Obama's Twitter account by the end of August 2009—over 1.5 million—clearly shows a growing engagement in the Twitter network. Han and Kim (2009) also found that, between April and September of 2009, Twitter users were reacting increasingly to one major aspect of the Obama Administration's political agenda in particular—health care reform—as I will examine in greater detail in the next chapter.

Prior to the 2004 presidential election, scholars' opinions were divided about the impact of NNITs upon social capital (Han 2007, 60). Since, according to the psychological perspective, the notion of social capital is based on face-to-face interaction, psychologists generally considered NNITs detrimental to

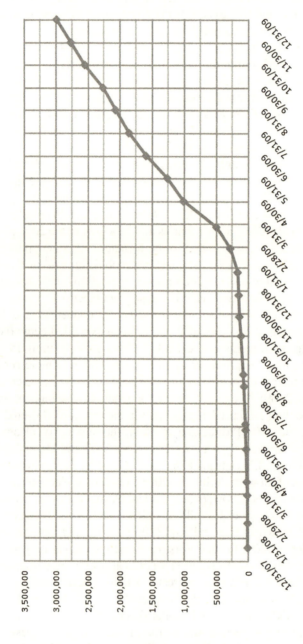

Figure 4.2 Obama Twitter Follower Trend (2008–2009)

social capital as NNITs involve none of the face-to-face physical interaction presumed necessary for bonding and bridging social capital; however, the increasing extent to which NNITs are penetrating daily life is now beginning to convince another group of scholars, comprised mostly of sociologists and political scientists, that social capital is, in fact, being augmented and geographically broadened through the use of NNITs (Benkler 2006; Boyd and Ellison 2007; Dutta-Bergman 2006; Ellison and Steinfield 2007; Han 2007; Huysman and Wulf 2004; Williams 2006). This is how a new experimentation is occurring. Dutta-Bergman (2006), in particular, found a strong correlation between the amount of activity in online communities (e.g., posting information, participating in discussions) after the 9/11 attack and the amount of offline community participation (e.g., attending meetings, volunteering for political causes, writing letters to the editor, signing petitions). In his view, there is a general complementarity between the use of NNITs and the increase in offline community involvement around the national crisis caused by the 9/11 terrorist attacks. Meetup.com, for example, a website that enables users to meet with other likeminded individuals and groups in their local area, clearly illustrates this ability to transform online contacts into offline interaction.

It has been noted that the transformation of the youth from an indifferent generation into a more focused bloc correlates with their explosive use of new social media, as evidenced by the high membership numbers of SixDegrees. com, Cyworld, Friendster (90 million),[3] LinkedIn (35 million), MySpace (253 million), Flickr, Facebook (175 million) and Twitter (2.2 million) (Boyd and Ellison 2007; Benkler 2006). The Rapleaf report (2008) reveals that the primary age group using these new social media is between the ages of 18 and 34 (which is very close to the current ages of Generation Y) and accounts for 70.45 percent of Facebook, 65.27 percent of Flickr, 75.62 percent of Friendster, 61.7 percent of LinkedIn and 60.8 percent of MySpace. And considering that the age group from 14 to 17 in 2008 accounted for about 16 percent of the total users on Facebook, MySpace, Friendster and Flickr, the dominance of the youth in these new social network sites is getting stronger. Even though the link between cyberactivism and the proportionate increase in the number of votes still requires more thorough investigation, a quick comparison of traffic trends between the websites of Obama and McCain in the closing weeks of the race shows a surge of support for Obama in the last week versus only a modest gain by McCain, according to the Candidate Sites Traffic Comparison website Compete.com (Pace 2008). Based on the Compete.com comparison of weekly unique visitors to BarackObama. com and JohnMcCain.com during the weeks from May 31 to November 1, 2008 (Fig. 4.1), Pace observed that, for the week ending on November 1, "nearly 4.9 million people visited Obama's website, a 60 percent rise over the previous week, and twice the level Obama reached on the heels of his August convention speech," while "McCain saw just a 9 percent increase in his site traffic last week to 1.4 million, meaning that in the final week of the race, McCain finally reached the level of traffic he enjoyed after announcing Sarah Palin as his running mate."

Benkler (2006) argues that this expanded and networked public sphere creates a unique space for discourse among peers, enabling them to bypass the gate-keeping forces of established mass media, build consensus for a national agenda, and mobilize forces to support it. As civic and political engagement among younger generations was awakened by a series of milestone events with demonstration effects, and as these youths became increasingly aware of their influence within the expanded public sphere (e.g., as in the 2008 Democratic primaries and election), skepticism regarding the positive impact of NNITs upon social capital seems to have dwindled.

So, how exactly did NNITs transform the pre-Obama long tail of indifferent young voters into the politically significant Long Tail that played such an important role in the outcome of the 2008 election? Dale and Strauss (2007) found that new technology bridges the historical gap between young people and the voting booth, thereby directly affecting campaign mobilization. Using field experiments and a mobile phone survey conducted during the 2006 election, Dale and Strauss divided over 12,000 newly registered young voters into two equal groups: a treatment group, whose members received a text message reminding them to vote; and a control group, whose members did not. More specifically, on the day before the November 2006 mid-term election:

> . . . researchers sent text message voting reminders to over 4,000 mobile phone numbers chosen at random from a pool of over 8,000 mostly young people who had completed voter registration applications. Afterwards, participants were matched to voter records to determine if they had voted in the election, and a sample was surveyed to gauge their reaction to the messages. (Dale and Strauss 2007)

The researchers found that the treatment group voted 3.1 percent more than the control group (56.3 percent vs. 53.2 percent), and they concluded that "text messaging is an effective tool for driving young voters to the ballot box" when used with more passive messages, such as "Polling place info@866–687–8683," but relatively ineffective when used with interactive or soliciting campaign messages, which seems to be a strong sign of young generations' self-motivated political behavior patterns and reliance on the knowledge and political orientation that they had developed through cyber interactions. The Public Interest Research Group (PIRG) survey of the 2006 election similarly

Table 4.1. Comparison of Mobilization Effects and Costs/Votes Generated

Tactics	Mobilization Effect	Costs/Votes Generated
Text/SMS Messages	4–5%	$1.56
Quality Phone Calls	4–5%	$ 20
Door-to-Door Canvassing	7–9%	~ $ 30
Leafleting	1.2%	$ 32
Direct Mail	~ 0.6%	$ 67

Source: PIRG "Fact Sheet on Youth Vote and Text Messaging" http://www.newvotersproject.org/text-messaging (accessed on March 12, 2009)

revealed that simple text message reminders increased the likelihood of voting by 4.2 percent. This study also found, as indicated in Table 4.1 below, that text/SMS messages are the most effective technique in terms of cost and second most effective in terms of mobilization, second only to door-to-door canvassing.

One of the major factors, and possibly the most important, of Obama's success was his early understanding of how new social media and other NNITs were changing the rules of the game in electoral politics. Whereas McCain's and Clinton's campaign databases were strictly proprietary, Obama's was open source and thereby capitalized on the viral proliferation of young users of new social media. Obama's campaign database[4] included over 175 million registered users of Facebook, most of them under the age of thirty. Thus, once Obama's message went out, it was immediately sent to as many as 70 million (in 2008) active users of Facebook, who then disseminated it further at no cost to the campaign. These and other generally young technophiles comprised the a networked army that served as the foot soldiers of the Obama campaign. Obama's Blue Ocean of computer- and network-savvy young volunteers maximized software power when organizing campaign operations in the fields and gained increasing amounts of supporters as a result. For example, according to Isaac Garcia, CEO of Central Desktop, the precinct captains in Obama's campaign volunteered to use Central Desktop's social software, a wiki- or Web-based collaboration platform, for the Texas primary and caucus, which included "254 counties, over 8,000 voting precincts, and a population of all different ethnic, economic and age demographics" (Catone 2008, March 4). Taking advantage of digital open source technology in this way, the Obama campaign gained a distinct advantage over the campaigns of his opponents who continued to use analog tools. President Obama's campaign capitalized on this Blue Ocean—this sudden influx of massive numbers of new, young, electronically linked voters—by tapping into it. The

next section examines the characteristics of the individuals comprising the
Long Tail, which created a network effect and conducted fundraising over
the Internet.

THE IMMEDIACY OF THE NETWORK

The closely interwoven social networking web now penetrates every realm
of our social life and, thus, mediates the relationship between the campaign
supporters of the Long Tail and the candidates. Specifically, this web empowers the constituency by allowing its members to monitor the candidates'
every move. It also dramatically shortens the cycle of campaign stories being
developed, disseminated, and even occasionally contested. Examples from
the recent 2008 presidential election are abundant. Obama's comment to an
audience at a private fundraising event in San Fanscisco in April 2008 that
"bitter" people "cling to guns, or religion, or antipathy" was first recorded as
an MP3 and published by a blogger the same day. Similarly, Obama's Pastor
Jeremiah Wright's "God damn America" sermon was posted by ABC News on
March 13, 2008, and was soon viewed millions of times on YouTube.
Likewise, the anti-Semitic audio-taped comment by McCain supporter, Pastor
John Hagee, was posted on the Internet by liberal blogger Bruce Wilson the
same day and was viewed and commented on by millions.

Perhaps the most sensational example of the immediacy of the network
was how quickly and devastatingly Senator Clinton's remark on Robert
Kennedy's assassination was transmitted over the networks. In an interview
with the editorial board members of the Sioux Falls, S.D. newspaper *Argus
Leader* on May 23, Clinton, said "[m]y husband did not wrap up the nomination in 1992 until he won the California primary somewhere in the middle
of June, right? We all remember Bobby Kennedy was assassinated in June
in California. I don't understand it." This interview was conducted via live
video-streaming. While the reporters who were with Senator Clinton had only
a poor Internet connection, other outlets such as the *New York Post* immediately began to spread its own interpretation of Clinton's remarks, stating that
"[s]he is still in the Presidential race, she said today, because historically, it
makes no sense to quit, and added that, 'Bobby Kennedy was assassinated
in June,' making an odd comparison between the dead candidate and Barack
Obama."[5] The *Post* item was linked to on the Drudge Report within several
hours, and the Obama campaign responded that her comment was "unfortu-
nate and has no place in this campaign." The video clip of Clinton's interview
was available by 4 s p , and Clinton issued a public apology for her perceived
mistake by 5 s p the same day. These examples show how the unprecedented

immediacy of network power has put candidates in a roller-coaster in the primaries and caucuses.

A general network theory in economics describes the number of network links as (N-1) factorial (!). For example, if we had 6 people in a network, the number of network links would be $(6–1)*(4)*(3)*(2)*(1)$, or 120 links. In January 2008 alone, according to CNNMoney.com, "nearly 79 million viewers, or a third of all online viewers in the U.S., watched more than three billion user-posted videos on YouTube, according to comScore's latest report."[6] Also, Facebook's statistics indicate more than 70 million active users as of May of 2008 (www.facebook.com/press/info.php?statistics). A quick Google search for "Clinton's comment on Kennedy assassination," done on May 27, five days after Clinton's remark indicated that 1,970,000 individuals had viewed the comment. This example indicates how dramatically activity on this network can influence the course of a campaign.

PROFILE OF THE LONG TAIL

This new electoral market, formed by the sudden introduction of a massive, electronically connected, young constituency, is the central force in this new experimentation. Thus, in order to understand the impacts of this new American experimentation, it is critical to examine the characteristics of these young voters. A closer look at the individuals that comprise Obama's Long Tail reveals that they, for the most part,

- belong to ethnically diverse groups, with 31 percent non-White or Latino membership (Dale and Strauss 2007, 20);
- have a highly mobile lifestyle, relying almost exclusively on mobile phones (Smith and Rainie 2008);
- had experienced a series of test-run mobilizations following 9/11 and had changed from being politically indifferent to highly invested in politics, exemplifying a "politics-matter-to-me attitude" (Han 2007, 58; Putnam 2008, 37; Dutta-Bergman 2006; Lebkowsky 2005, 35; Trippi 2004, 104; Putnam, et al. 2003, 128, 285);
- are the most high-tech and interconnected national constituency in American history, and have begun to use networks for various aspects of political participation—sharing profiles via online social media (including micro-content online social networking tools, such as Twitter and SNSs), engaging in entertainment activities via SNSs, using cyberspace to network socially, and organizing with others for political events, issues or causes (Jones and Fox 2009, 3, 5; Lenhart 2009, 4, 6; Melber 2009);

- are creating new modes of campaign engagement by making their own blogs, videos, text messages and emails (Abroms and Lefebvre 2009, 419) unlike the modes of older generations that utilized conventional campaign tools;
- are learning campaign-related information from people whom they know and trust, which is more influential in shaping beliefs, attitudes and behavior (Abroms and Lefebvre 2009, 419) than the way in which older generations obtain their information from official political institutions and industrial news and media;
- prefer simple, passive and short political messages sent through more personally trusted peer-to-peer communications (e.g., e-mails and text-messages) to more interactive and traditional avenues (e.g., landline phone calls or door-to-door canvassing) (Youngvoterstrategies.org, 5; Dale and Strauss 2007, 4); and
- voted in greater numbers in the 2008 election than in the 2000 and 2004 elections, but still recorded a lower voter turnout than any other age group, and thus still possess potential to be cultivated for more votes in the future, compared to older voters, who have much less room for improved voting participation.

Regarding the generational change of using of new online social media for political purposes, Abroms and Lefebvre (2009, 419) claim that young generations' direct involvement in making election campaign materials through the use of NNITs, such as YouTube videos, represents "an important increase in the power of self-expression by the public, a power that had been noted to be on the decline with the rise of mass communications." They conclude that "[w]ith these new tools of engagement, a much wider range of supporters than in previous campaigns could now publicly demonstrate support for a candidate and be called upon for additional support in the future" (2009, 420).

Next, it is important to substantiate the presence and influence of the sudden influx of massive numbers of new, young, electronically linked voters by examining changes in the youth's voter turnout record over the decades. If the newly created NNIT environment can boost the youth's interest in politics and transform them into a focused and consistent voting group, then NNIT-activated young generations and their participation in electoral politics can restore the crumbling foundations of politics and democracy that were built on the old American experimentation, before young generations were a major factor in electoral politics. Putnam (2008) cited a UCLA poll of college freshmen nationwide to point out that young voters' interest in politics actually plummeted from 1966, when 60 percent reported a high degree of concern and saw politics as very important, to 2000, when only 28 percent made such a claim. The voting rate for this age group, which in 1972 had been 52 percent, dropped dramatically to just 36 percent by 2000. According to Han (2007) and Andrew et al. (2008), in the 2004 Presidential election, the voter turnout visibly increased: "In 2004, we saw an increase, a 9 percentage point increase—larger than that of any other age group. We saw another increase in 2006 from the midterm in 2002 of 3 percentage points" (Andrew, et al. 2008). Among these newly increased young voters, Steinhaur (2008) finds that "[i]n many states, Democrats have benefited from a rise in younger potential voters, after declines or small increases in the number of those voters in the 1980s and '90s. The population of 18- to 24-year-olds rose from about 27 million in 2000 to nearly 30 million in 2006, according to Census figures."

Similarly, Lopez et al. (2005, 2) found that in 2004, voter turnout among young people had surged to its highest level in a decade. An overview of the voter turnout rates for various age groups in 2000 and 2004 (Table 4.2 and Table 4.3) shows that the greatest increases in both the number of registered voters (6.9 percent) and the number of registered voters who voted (10.6 percent) occurred among voters aged 18–24, with the next greatest increases (2.7 percent and 5 percent, respectively) occurring among voters aged 25–34, and the smallest increases (0.7 percent and 1.1 percent, respectively) occurring among adults aged 65–74. One variable that explains such explosive increases in voter turnout among young constituency is education. A CIRCLE report (2008, December 19) reveals some of the factors that contributed to such increased voter turnout among young voters (18–29), which offer insight in the analysis of the main features of the emerging cohesive voting bloc. This report concludes that education seems to have been the far most important variable in the creation of such a bloc. For example, Table 4.2 below, indicates a sharp contrast between young voters having less than a high school education and those who have a high school education or higher.

Still, despite these increases in both voter registration and voter turnout for all ages, from 18 to 75 and older, the youngest is the lowest among all voting groups, reaffirming this chapter's major claim that younger voters have the greatest potential to be transformed from an apathetic long tail into an active and formidable Long Tail capable of bringing about change through active involvement in election campaigns and increased voting turnout. In fact, many young voters were first-time voters: 64 percent of 18- to 24-year-olds and 43 percent of 18- to 29-year-olds were first-time voters as compared to just 11 percent of voters from all other age groups (CIRCLE, 2008, 6). From this perspective, the 2004 Presidential election exhibited the highest increase in voting—not just an overall increase of 4 percent for all ages but, more importantly, an impressive proportional increase for young voters overall. Marcelo

Table 4.2.   Voting Rates & Educational Levels among Young Adults Age 18–29

	Less than High School	High School Diploma	Some College	College Degree	Post Graduate
% of Population	14%	29%	38%	16%	3%
% of Voters	6%	24%	38%	24%	8%

Source: CIRCLE (2008, December 19)

and Kirby (2008) also point out that, in the 2004 election, the share of actual voters aged 18–29 actually increased from 14 percent in 2000 to 16 percent, while the percentage of voters aged 30 and older actually decreased over the same period, from 86 percent to 84 percent.

Table 4.3 clearly illustrates that increases in voter registration and actual vote among young generations are becoming a trend since 2000 presidential election. Table 4.4 evidently illustrates that the trends of considerable fluctuations in voter registration and actual votes in the presidential elections since 1972 among young voters from 18 to 24 have considerably fluctuated since 1976 have been changed to a steady increase since 1996.

Focusing on the age group from 18 to 29 enables us to appreciate how quickly voting turnout rates have increased for this group. According to Tufts University's Center for Information and Research on Civic Learning and Engagement, an estimated 23 million young Americans aged 18 to 29 voted in the 2008 election—an increase of 3.4 million over the amount in 2004. Perhaps more notably, over each of the four presidential elections from 1996 to 2008, there has been an average 5 percent increase in voter turnout for young voters (CIRCLE, December 19, 2008).

In the 2000 election, only 32.3 percent of 18- to 24-year-olds voted, a number far below the national figure of 51.3 percent for the entire voting age population (VAP). Voters under the age of 30 cast 48 percent of their votes for Gore and 46 percent for Bush. However, in the 2004 election, with the increased turnout of 56.7 percent, the percent of voters under the age of 30 increased to approximately 42 percent. The democratic candidate's margin grew as well in 2004 with Kerry winning 54 percent and Bush 45 percent. Bush beat Kerry with a little more than 3 million votes (3 percent). The 2008 presidential election had a higher turnout overall, recently-activated young voters could well cast very decisive votes in an election with a small, but very significant, margin of victory. Table 4.5, below, reveals the consolidated voting behavior among members of the young generations. Between 2000 and 2004, the Youth Share of Votes Cast increased somewhat while the Youth Share of Citizens among the 18–29 groups decreased, indicating that

Table 4.3. Reported Rates of Voting Registration and Votes Cast in 2000, 2004, and 2008 Presidential Elections (noted in thousands and in percent of total)

Ages	2000			2004			2008		
	Total # Citizen	Total # Regist.	Total # Voted	Total # Citizen	Total # Regist.	Total # Voted	Total # Citizen	Total # Regist.	Total # Voted
18–24	23,915	12,122 (50.7%)	8,635 (36.1%)	24,898	14,334 (57.6%)	11,639 (46.7%)	25,791	15,082 (58.5)	12,515 (48.5)
25–34	32,233	20,403 (63.3%)	16,286 (50.5%)	32,842	21,690 (66.0%)	18,285 (55.7%)	34,218	22,736 (66.4)	19,501 (57.0)
35–44	40,434	28,366 (70.2%)	24,452 (60.5%)	38,389	27,681 (72.1%)	24,560 (64.0%)	36,397	25,449 (69.9)	22,865 (62.8)
45–54	35,230	26,158 (74.2%)	23,362 (66.3%)	39,011	29,448 (75.5%)	26,813 (68.7%)	41,085	30,210 (73.5)	27,673 (67.4)
55–64	22,737	17,551 (77.2%)	15,939 (70.1%)	61,865	48,918 (79.1%)	44,438 (71.8%)	32,228	24,734 (76.6)	23,071 (71.5)
65–74	17,233	13,573 (78.8%)	12,450 (72.2%)	17,759	14,125 (79.5%)	13,010 (73.3%)	19,571	15,290 (78.1)	14,176 (72.4)
≥75	14,582	11,375 (78.0%)	9,702 (66.5%)	15,933	12,581 (79.0%)	10,915 (68.5%)	16,724	12,810 (76.6)	11,344 (67.8)

Source: Voting and Registration in the Election of November 2000, 2004, 2008 (published 2002, 2006, 2010 respectively by U.S. Census Bureau)

Table 4.4.   Changes in Reported Registration and Voting (Voters from 18 to 24 from 1972 to 2008 Presidential Elections) in Percentage

	'72	'76	'80	'84	'88	'92	'96	'00	'04	'08
Registration	58.9	51.3	49.2	51.3	48.2	52.5	48.8	50.7	57.6	58.5
Vote	49.6	42.2	39.9	40.8	36.2	42.8	32.4	36.1	46.7	48.5

Sources: (1) "Voting and Registration in the Election of November 1996," which covers the Reported Registration and Voting from 1972 to 1996 Presidential elections, by Lynne M. Casper and Loretta E. Bass, U.S. Census Bureau, Economics and Statistics Administration, U.S. Department of Commerce. (2) "Voting and Registration in the Election of November 2000, 2004, 2008" (published 2002, 2006, 2010 respectively by U.S. census Bureau.

participation continues to grow among this group. It remains unclear whether such an increase will become a trend.

What really has made this phenomenon unique is how young generations' usage of NNITs in their daily lives has affected the process of campaigning. One particularly important finding is that members of Generation Y or "Millennials"—born between 1977 and 1990 and currently aged 18 to 32—tend to dominate the Internet, using it not just for individual purposes but also for social and political networking, acquiring information and communicating about elections (Jones and Fox 2009). The success of this new experimentation, which will become the linchpin of the future of American democracy, will mostly depend upon Generation Y when they become the

Table 4.5.   Youth Share of the Electorate and Citizen Populations, for Presidential Election Years 1972–2004

	Youth Share of Citizens		Youth Share of Votes Cast		Difference Between Share of Cit. Pop. And Share of Votes Cast	
Age	*18–24*	*18–29*	*18–24*	*18–29*	*18–24*	*18–29*
1972	17.9%	28.6%	14.2%	24.2%	3.7%	4.4%
1976	18.2%	29.8%	13.1%	23.6%	5.1%	6.2%
1980	17.8%	29.5%	12.1%	22.3%	5.7%	7.3%
1984	16.4%	28.7%	11.2%	21.7%	5.2%	7.0%
1988	14.1%	25.7%	9.1%	18.1%	5.1%	7.6%
1992	12.8%	23.0%	9.2%	17.7%	3.6%	5.3%
1996	12.5%	22.0%	7.6%	14.9%	4.9%	7.1%
2000	12.8%	21.1%	7.8%	14.3%	5.0%	6.8%
2004	12.6%	20.9%	9.3%	16.0%	3.4%	4.8%

Source: Lopez (*et al*) The Youth Vote 2004: With a Historical Look at Youth Voting Patterns, 1972–2004, The Center for Information & Research on Civic Learning & Engagement (CIRCLE), Working Paper 35, July 2005, p. 4.

major socio-economic force in America—that is, what they do on the Internet and how they use it to involve their political voice in national discourse, electoral politics and civic organizations. As the most active Internet users in the United States, they account for 26 percent of the total adult population but only 30 percent of Internet users. The next most active group, members of Generation X—born between 1965 and 1976 and currently aged 33 to 44—account for 20 percent of the total adult population but comprise only 23 percent of Internet users (Jones and Fox 2009).

For Millennials, SNSs function as a networked public sphere, which will serve as the nervous system of the new experimentation, comprised not "of tools, but of the social production practices that these tools enable" (Benkler 2006, 219). During the 2008 election, through the use of online social media such as SNSs, "this basic model of peer production of investigation, reportage, analysis and communication indeed worked" (Benkler 2006, 228) and became a part of their daily Internet activities described above. In contrast to the Millennials, members of older generations, such as Generation X, mostly use the Internet for individual activities, such as researching health issues or doing online shopping or banking. The differences in Internet use between Generation Y and other generations are summarized in Table 4.6 below.

Generation Y can truly claim cyberspace as their living space as they use it for such a wide range of activities—not just for their individual chores but also to create a social and political community as they establish their own rules for cyberactivism (Abroms and Lefebvre 2009; Jones and Fox 2008; Benkler 2006). This phenomenon differs greatly from the ways of nineteenth-century

Table 4.6. Percent of Each Generation That Uses the Internet for Various Online Activities

Online Activity	Generation Y (18–32)	Generation X (33–44)	Young Boomers (45–54)	Old Boomers (55–63)
Play games	50%	38%	26%	28%
Watch videos	72%	57%	49%	30%
Use SNSs	67%	36%	20%	9%
Download music	58%	46%	22%	21%
Create SNS profiles	60%	29%	16%	9%
Read blogs	43%	34%	27%	25%
Create blogs	20%	10%	6%	7%

Source: excerpted from Jones and Fox (2009: 5)

Americans whose major interactions were conducted in brick-and-mortar locations such as bars, restaurants, town halls, and churches—all within the boundaries of the local community. In the new experimentation, it is variables such as digital connectedness and education that matter most. In Generation Y, the social network users are primarily students; 68 percent of full-time students and 71 percent of part-time students have a social network profile, while just 28 percent of older Internet users who are not students use social networks (Lenhart 2009, 4), confirming the claim made by the CIRCLE report (2008, December 19) that education is the most important factor in the activation of young voters with intensive use of NNITs. As older adult Internet users have become more involved in SNSs—from just 8 percent in 2005 to 6 percent in 2006, and then 35 percent in 2008—their use of online social media for political purposes has also expanded to include activities such as discovering friends' political interests or affiliations (29 percent), obtaining campaign or candidate information (22 percent), signing up as a friend of a candidate (10 percent), and joining a political group (9 percent) (Lenhart 2009, 11).

In August 2007, Obama outstripped Clinton in terms of both MySpace friends (169,397 vs. 133,684) and YouTube channel views (11,098,217 vs. 849,842). Similarly, Obama's March 18th speech on race was viewed over 5.3 million times,[7] surpassing the viewership for all of the cable channels for that week combined (Melber 2008). By the summer of 2008, Obama could claim an astounding 750,000 active volunteers, 8,000 affinity groups, and 30,000 fundraising events (Green 2008). Obama's unquestionable dominance in securing a Blue Ocean or sudden influx of massive numbers of new, young, electronically linked voters, as compared to McCain and Clinton, was evident in the number of unique visitors to the candidate's website during the 2008 presidential campaign and election (Fig. 4.1). Although impressive, these numbers represent just a portion of the long list of campaign tools used by the Obama campaign's Long Tail, comprised of those who, not long before, had been the trivial many. The following excerpt represents how this Blue Ocean of Obama's Long Tail engaged in the 2008 presidential election campaign via cyberactivism of the type described below:

> More than a million young voters asked for campaign text messages on their cellphones. Two million joined MyBO [the online community My BarackObama], a website fusing social networking with volunteer work, while more than 5 million supported Obama's profile on social sites like Facebook. Most famously, 13 million voters signed up for regular e-mails, fundraising pitches and other communications. On election day, a staggering 25 percent of Obama voters were already directly linked to him—and one another—through these networks . . . During the campaign, [the student network] held 19,633 grassroots

events, raised more than $1.7 million and hosted a constant stream of many-to-many communication through more than 170,000 blog entries. (Melber 2009, 6, 8)

The relationship between the Long Tail and digital technology is especially evident in one Pew Internet poll (Smith and Rainie 2008, 4, 5, 10) which summarizes how young voters' use of NNITs is creating a new genre of political activism, as noted by Anderson (2004), Lopez and Kirby (2005), Brynjolfsson et al. (2006), Catone (2007 2008) and Abroms and Lefebvre (2009).

Most importantly, the Pew Internet survey (Smith and Rainie 2008) and other reliable exit polls show that the Long Tail of young voters tended to gravitate toward the Democratic Party. For example, more Democrats than Republicans viewed online videos (51 percent vs. 42 percent), and more Democrats than Republicans posted social networking profiles (93.6 percent vs. 21 percent) (Smith and Rainie 2008, iii, 15). Furthermore, among Democrats Obama's supporters were found to be much more Internet-oriented than Clinton's: 74 percent of wired Obama supporters reported that they had received political news and information online, as compared to just 57 percent of online Clinton supporters (Smith and Rainie 2008, iii, 13). In the future, however, the tendency of the youth to gravitate toward the Democratic Party may shift toward the Republican Party or any political party for that matter, depending upon the political situations of the time and the relative appeal of political leaders from different segments of the political spectrum.

This analysis of Obama supporters during the 2008 presidential campaign shows the dramatic role played by voters aged 18 to 29, whose dramatic transition from being apathetic and uninfluential to strongly committed and very influential created a new kind of high-tech, socially oriented politics due, in large part, to these voters' social networking capacity, both on- and offline.

OBAMA'S GOLDMINE: UNPRECEDENTED FUNDRAISING RECORDS

Another impact of this new experimentation stems from its method of campaign fundraising as well as its scale and speed. During the Industrial Age, campaign fundraising was conducted through the political party and other political institutions, and relied primarily on paper and the postal system; donations were mostly made by mailing in checks. In the Information Age, election campaign methods have changed somewhat, but regulations on the contribution limits and individual qualifications have remained the same. In the 2008 presidential election, however, the Internet transformed the scale and speed of the fundraising campaign and created a phenomenal, massive influx of young small donors, breaking fundraising records in scale and speed. In this way, Obama succeeded in tapping into this Blue Ocean of the NNIT-activated Long Tail of young small donors. Joshua Green, in his 2008 discussion of the dramatic changes that electoral politics had undergone in the preceding eight years as a result of increased participation by previously apathetic young voters and the pervasive use of NNITs, compares Obama's Long Tail with the young armies of supporters that formed during the 2000 Gore and 2004 Kerry presidential campaigns stating:

> If the typical Gore event was 20 people in a living room writing six-figure checks and the Kerry event was 2,000 people in a hotel ballroom writing four-figure checks, this year for Obama we have stadium rallies of 20,000 people who pay absolutely nothing, and then go home and contribute a few dollars online. Obama himself skillfully capitalizes on both the turnout and the connectivity of his stadium crowds by routinely asking them to hold up their cell phones and punch in a five-digit number to text their contact information to the campaign—to win their commitment right there on the spot. (Green 2008, 7)

By tapping into the support of NNIT-activated young voters who share a common social network, Obama appears to have unleashed a political juggernaut.

During the 2008 presidential election, the widespread use of NNITs not only intensified political participation but also boosted campaign contributions by making Internet fundraising easier and co-opting more donors, more quickly, and in a more cost-effective way than in the past. In the 1992 presidential election, before the Internet era, the total contribution to presidential candidates was $331.1 million. In the four elections preceding that, it had been $324.4 million in 1988, $202 million in 1984, $161.9 million in 1980, and $171 million in 1976. This compares with post-Internet figures of $425.7 million in 1996, $528.9 in 2000, $880.5 million in 2004, and $1.8129 billion in 2008 (OpenSecret.org 2009). The combined total of $192.2 million spent by all the presidential candidates in 1992 is a mere fraction of the $833.8 million spent in just the first 6 months of the 2008 primaries and caucuses.

Although more empirical studies are needed to confirm the causal link between the use of NNITs and the phenomenal increase in campaign funding, the use of NNITs clearly impacted campaign fundraising in the 2008 presidential election as evidenced by the speed of the fundraising and the unprecedented increase in small-scale donations, both of which, this study argues, are clearly linked to the Blue Ocean of Obama's Long Tail. For example, Representative Ron Paul, who was regarded as the most active on

Table 4.7. Monthly Fundraising Totals of Obama and Clinton Campaigns from January 2007 to April 2008 (in millions)

	1/07	2	3	4	5	6	7	8	9	10	11	12	1/08	2/08	3/08	4/08
Obama	1.2	3.2	15.6	4.7	7.6	12.2	1.6	3.8	8.5	2.1	4.3	6.5	20.3	25.4	17.7	11.6
Clinton	2.3	3.8	17.6	1.9	5.0	17.0	1.7	5.3	14.1	5.5	6.0	9.9	9.3	17.7	9.2	9.8

Source: Center for Responsive Politics, OpenSecret.org (Totals include only itemized contributions, which typically exceed $200, available at http://www.opensecrets.org/pres08/weekly.php?type=M&cand1=N00009638&cand2=N00000019&cycle = 2008 (accessed on May 31, 2008).

the Internet among the Republican presidential candidates, broke a record for the maximum amount any candidate had raised in a day, securing $6 million over a 24-hour period online in December 2007. Overall, Senator Obama had over one million campaign donors at the end of the campaign period, 26 percent of whom had contributed amounts of $200 or less.[8] In February of 2008, he raised $45 million of his $55 million total for the month online (William and Gulati 2008, 6). As of June 2008, nearly 1.5 million people had donated to Obama. By contrast, and as reflected in Table 4.7, from the start, Clinton's formidable fund-raising machine relied almost exclusively on wealthy donors, who generally gave donations of $2,300 or more.

A glance at the type of contributions that Obama received indicates how the Internet enabled him to cultivate a Blue Ocean of NNIT-galvanized young supporters who filled his campaign's war chest through many small contributions. As shown in Table 4.8 below, which contains data from the Center for Responsive Politics (OpenSecret.org 2009), Obama received

Table 4.8. Itemized Categories of Contributions by Individuals in 2008 U.S. Presidential Primaries (top) and General Election (bottom)

Candidate	No. of $200+ Contributors	% from Donors of $200 or less	No. of $2,300+ Contributors	% from Donors of $2,300+	No. of $4,600 Contributors	% from Donors of $4,600
Obama	141,658	45%	28,215	28%	2,652	5%
Clinton	102,381	30%	26,634	44%	8,230	20%
McCain	52,564	24%	15,953	46%	1,386	8%
Obama	362,952	54%	66,034	32%	13,120	9%
McCain	145,299	34%	34,461	49%	6,654	16%

Source: The Center for Responsive Politics (OpenSecret.org) 2009: http://www.opensecrets.org/pres08/donordems.php?cycle=2008
NB: All the data on this page are for the 2008 election cycle and based on Federal Election Commission data released electronically on Monday, July 13, 2009.

more contributions in the category of "$2,300 or less" than both Clinton and McCain but received the lowest portion in the category of "$4,600 or more." In April of 2008, Obama surpassed both Clinton and McCain in contributions, receiving $31.3 million to Clinton's $22 million and McCain's $18.5 million.

The Obama campaign attracted small donors who donated $91 on average. Of the 200,000 new donors to the Obama campaign, the vast majority (i.e., 94 percent) gave less than $200. In fact, out of the total $32 million that was raised for Obama in January 2008, $28 million was raised through the Internet, 90 percent of which came from donations of $100 or less (Catone 2007). Upon examining patterns of fundraising during the campaign, it becomes apparent that Obama successfully tapped into a new culture of social networking that resulted in the young generation's involvement in the primaries and caucuses. Obama's campaign slogan of "change politics," combined with intensive and widespread use of online media, outpaced McCain's efforts to appeal to the young voters. It is quite noticeable that the difference of 20 percent in the category of "Donors of $200 or less" between Obama and McCain was far more than that of 5 percent between Bush and Kerry in the same category in the 2004 presidential election, according to the Campaign Finance Institute.

So, other than the obvious advantage of raising funds, what is the benefit of securing many new donors of less than $200? The Obama campaign did not have to report to the Federal Election Committee the names of those tens of thousands of small donors that they had newly retained, nor the amounts of their donations. This undisclosed donor information gave a huge advantage to the Obama campaign over Clinton's since other politicians, mostly Democratic Party superdelegates in a primary season, would have been given access to that donor list for their own campaign purposes if superdelegates supported Obama over Clinton (Lasky 2008; Gerstein 2008). It is notable that during the period from 2005 to 2008, Obama donated three times as much as Clinton to superdelegates (Faughnan 2008). In this way, Obama's influence over superdelegates in the 2008 primaries and caucuses was dramatically augmented, as was that of his donors. Despite the fact that large-scale donors also played a significant role in Obama's fundraising, Boatright (2009, 146, 158) argues that "the narrative accepted by the media was that Obama's campaign was driven by small donors," and "For the moment, the Democratic Party, and Democratic candidates, are the clear beneficiaries of the maturation of the Internet as a fund-raising medium." Over time, and in small increments, Obama's Long Tail seems have been the most significant contributor to the unprecedented success of his campaign fundraising.

INFLUENCE OF OBAMA'S LONG TAIL

The ultimate question of this chapter is whether the Obama Long Tail of generational activism among NNIT-galvanized young voters produced any visible influence in the outcome of the 2008 presidential election. Many indicators suggest that it did. For example, in 2004, Democrats registered more voters than Republicans in four of seven states, often by a small margin (Table 4.9). By contrast, in 2008, Democrats registered more voters in five of the seven states, and generally by large numbers, whereas the Republican Party suffered losses in all but New Jersey. In the two states where Bush had won over Kerry in 2004 (Iowa and Nevada), Obama won by a 10.5 percent margin on average. Overall, Obama secured all of these swing states with an average margin of 13.57 percent. The jumps in voter registration prior to the 2008 election eventually led to a decisive Democratic victory in the swing states.

The same question of the potential impact of the NNIT-activated Obama Long Tail of generational activism and its visible influence in the outcome of the 2008 presidential election might be much more convincing if the margins of victory were smaller in the contests between Obama and McCain in the following five battleground states as in Table 4.10

Another significant difference between the '04 and '08 elections that contributed toward the election of Obama can be seen in the number of voters reporting a strong preference for the candidate. As Table 4.11 shows, in the 2008 election, about 3.6 million more voters from the 18–29 age group reported an inclination to vote for Obama (68 percent) than for McCain (32 percent), a difference of 36 percent—far more than the 2 percent and 9 percent reported for the 2000 and 2004 elections, respectively. Forty-five percent of those young voters identified themselves as Democrats. Among voters aged 30 to 44, 38 percent of whom identified themselves as Democrats, Obama beat McCain by 6 percent (52 percent vs. 46 percent); and among voters aged 45 to 59, 37 percent of whom identified themselves as Democrats, he tied (49 percent vs. 49 percent) (CIRCLE, 2008: 3).

Such strong gravitation toward Obama is also clearly reflected in the combined indicators of race and age, especially among voters aged 18 to 29. The CIRCLE Report (2008, 4) found that an average of 92.25 percent of all African American voters voted for Obama, and 66.25 percent of all Latinos, with the highest rate of 76 percent among Latino voters aged 18–29. Obama won 54 percent of whites aged 18–29 with an average of 41 percent from whites of all other age groups.

Since the early 1960s, young American voters have rarely been active enough to be recognized as a critical factor in a national election. With the

Table 4.9. Increase in Percent of Registered Voters for Each Party and 2004 Presidential Results

Registered Voters	New Jersey		Oregon		Iowa		New Hampshire		Connecticut		Pennsylvania		Nevada	
	D	R	D	R	D	R	D	R	D	R	D	R	D	R
2004	23.2	17.7	38.7	35.6	30.8	31.0	26.7	31.2	33.7	22.0	47.6	40.7	40.1	40.5
2008	34.0	20.8	43.2	33.0	34.9	30.2	30.5	31.1	36.8	21.1	50.7	38.0	43.2	37.8
Changes	10.7	3.1	4.5	-2.5	4.1	-0.8	3.9	-0.1	3.1	-0.8	3.1	-2.7	3.1	-2.7
'04 Presidential Results	K	B	K	B	K	B	K	B	K	B	K	B	K	B
	52.9	46.2	51.4	47.2	49.2	50.0	50.2	48.9	54.3	44.0	50.9	48.4	47.9	50.5
'08 Presidential Results	O	M	O	M	O	M	O	M	O	M	O	M	O	M
	57	42	57	41	54	45	54	45	61	38	55	44	55	43

Source: Dave Leip's 'Atlas of U.S. Presidential Election', aggregated from Secretary of State's Offices in 50 states. K: John Kerry, B: George W. Bush 2008 Presidential election result from http://www.cnn.com/ELECTION/2008/results/president/

Table 4.10. Smallest Margins of Victory in Swing States

State	Obama	McCain	Margin (%)	Total	Others
MO	1,441,911	1,445,814	–0.13%	2,925,205	37,480
MT	231,667	242,763	–2.26%	490,302	15,872
NC	2,142,651	2,128,474	0.33%	4,310,789	39,664
IN	1,374,039	1,345,648	1.03%	2,751,054	31,367
FL	4,282,074	4,045,624	2.82%	8,390,744	63,046
OH	2,933,388	2,674,491	4.54%	5,698,260	90,381

Source: Calculated from official numbers of Federal Election Commission

Table 4.11. 2008 Presidential Election Voter Inclination as Reported in Exit Poll

	2000		2004		2008	
Age	Bush	Gore	Bush	Kerry	Obama ( )*	McCain
18–29	46%	48%	45%	54%	68% (45%)	32%
30–44	49%	48%	53%	46%	52% (38%)	46%
45–59	49%	48%	51%	48%	49% (37%)	49%
≥ 60	47%	51%	54%	46%	47% (39%)	51%

Source: CNN Exit Polls, 2000, 2004 and November 4, 2008.
* Numbers in parentheses represent the percentage identified as Democrats in each age group.

exception of Bill Clinton's first run for president in 1992, the political power of the younger generations had, until recently, remained largely untapped. In the 2008 presidential election, this Long Tail of supporters, formerly the trivial many, became a new campaign market for Obama, became activated, and played a significant role in determining the election outcome. This analysis of the means by which Obama's Long Tail was activated, and the important role that it served in the election, has shown that, by increasing the participation of younger voters in swing states through the use of NNITs, the Obama campaign has seemed to take advantage of the Long Tail as an influential voting group. Especially in light of the constraints that are imposed by the Electoral College system, the strong leaning of youths toward candidate Obama appears to have been a critical factor in his victory in previous battleground swing states, such as New Mexico, Nevada, and Colorado—all of which Bush had won in 2004, by 1 percent, 3 percent and 5 percent, respectively.

Additional studies will be required to assess whether current Blue Oceans, created by Long Tails of young voters, will prove to be important determinants in future elections. According to the U.S. Census Bureau's population projection from 2000 to 2050, members of Generation Y currently number about 50 million people. Over the next several years, young voters belonging to the Millennial Generation (currently ages 9–17) will gain influence as they join with members of Generation Y, numbering approximately 82 million citizens out of an adult citizen population of just over 225 million, representing over 36 percent of the entire voting population. By 2015, when this entire Millennial cohort reaches voting age, it will comprise approximately one-third of the electorate. And though it remains uncertain whether Generation Y will join the political Long Tail, it is quite clear that the recent increase in the political participation of young constituents equipped with NNITs will factor importantly in national politics and elections of years to come, for the 2008 presidential election demonstrated the power of the new experimentation in the electoral politics of America.

NOTES

1. This is equivalent to the number of video views multiplied by the length of each spot posted by a campaign.

2. As mentioned in chapter 2, it is named "386" because they were in their 30s at the time, were undergrads in the '80s, and were born in the '60s.

3. Numbers in parentheses are the numbers of registered users in 2009. These sites are listed in the order in which they were established, and the statistical information is from www.alexa.com, a website-ranking service. To give a sense of their growth rate, Friendster began in mid-2002 and grew to 300,000 users by May 2003; LinkedIn began at the end of 2002; Facebook demonstrated explosive growth from 69.3 million in August 2008 to more than 120 million by October (Owen 2009, 24).

4. It was constructed by Chris Hughes, the then-24-year-old co-founder of Facebook.

5. Seelye, Katharine. (2008, May 24, 9:40 SP). On the Road: Clinton's Very Bad Day, New York Times, (accessed on May 26, 2008), thecaucus.blogs.nytimes.com/2008/05/24/on-the-road-clintons-very-bad-day/.

6. Yen, Yi-Wyn. (2008, May 25) YouTube looks for the money clip. techland.blogs.fortune.cnn.com/2008/03/25/youtube-looks-for-the-money-clip/.

7. "Obama Girl" got more than 11 million views on YouTube; "Yes, We Can" got over 16 million views on YouTube and other sites; and "Dear Mr. Obama" got over 13 million views on YouTube. See Owen (2009, 23).

8. Obama's fundraising in the beginning of his campaign in January 2008 had already begun to cultivate a new source of campaign funds for the presidential race. For example, in that month, Obama raised $28 million online with 90 percent of those transactions coming from donors of $100 or less. See Luo (2008).

Chapter 5

Obama Tweeting and Tweeted

The Sotomayor Nomination and Health Care Reform

Having established the significance of the role played by young voters in the election of President Obama—as a new electoral market (i.e., Blue Ocean) comprised of the formerly trivial many (i.e., Long Tail)[1]—this chapter now shifts focus toward the issue of how, by using the micro-blogging social network site Twitter, these young voters have maintained their involvement in the political discourse of the Obama administration. This chapter examines the way in which the Obama administration successfully mobilized this Long Tail to influence the political discourse to successfully pursue two of the most controversial items on his agenda: the passage of his health care reform (HCR) bill and his appointment and approval of the first Hispanic female Supreme Court Justice Sonya Sotomayor. By showing that NNIT users have continued to work as a focused constituency, this chapter will also show that this new experimentation with NNITs by the young generation has continued. One way to demonstrate this continuation is to measure how Obama supporters have reacted to these two politically important agendas as evidenced by their tweeting, replying, re-tweeting and searching for further information.

Micro-content online social networks (MC-OSNs) are short message services with a limit of 140 characters that use multiple delivery channels (e.g., instant messaging, cell phones, email, Web) for informal, real-time communication and broadcasting among friends and strangers who voluntarily subscribe for any of several reasons: in order to maintain acquaintances, to receive and distribute valuable information, to promote certain agendas that are of particular interest to subscribing groups, to sustain a sense of connectedness, and to release emotional stress (Zhao and Rosson 2009, 245). Twitter.com is one such real-time short messaging service (SMS), a kind of "what-are-you-doing-now" site that allows users to send out text-based instant messages of 140 characters or less to update followers on agendas of interest.

Despite a big difference between the total number of tweets sent by President Obama and the amount of followers on the issues of health care reform and the Sotomayor nomination, as of early 2010, the fact that there were more than 1.5 million followers of President Obama's account and 450,000 followers of the White House account clearly shows continued and growing engagement in the Twitter network as compared to the average number of Obama tweet followers during the 2008 presidential election—59,000.

Due to the recent rapid development of seamlessly interconnected matrices of digital technologies, online social networking (OSN) services are currently converging into the highly integrated central communication platforms upon which the new experimentation has been based. Considering that communication channels outside the centralized system of the conventional news media are likely to be replaced over time, and that attention is focusing increasingly on networks as opposed to single entities, this book argues that this new experimentation is contributing to the establishment of expanded social capital and a new networked public sphere (NPS). The NPS carries with it expectations of centering around younger generations, and of playing a crucial role in future electoral politics, campaigns and the democratization of the Information Age (Benkler 2006; Han 2007). The importance of NNITs in electoral politics was exemplified by Democratic Party candidate Barack Obama's digital campaign strategy, which outflanked vested interests and glittering political stars such as Hilary Clinton and John McCain in the 2008 presidential election (Han 2011).

Since his election, President Obama has dominated the NPS as a public figure and has effectively used Twitter and other online social media for a diversity of purposes: to share information, to announce campaign schedules, to convince supporters and stakeholders, to encourage dissemination of information, to apply political pressure on Congressmen and to solicit feedback from Twitter members on his reform agendas. On September 13, 2009, for example, President Obama began mobilizing support for the passage of the HCR bill by sending out the following tweet: "Please watch this special message, and if you haven't already, tell your members of Congress you support reform: http://bit.ly/9RHAe." Another tweet was issued on September 15, 2009: "Your voice on Twitter can help pass health reform—tweet your reps today: http://bit.ly/LA253 #hc09." This is how the Blue Ocean that Senator Obama cultivated during his Presidential campaign has continued to participate in major aspects of the political agenda.

It is crucial to understand the nature of microblogged information (Java and Song 2007; Zhao and Rosson 2009) and the impact of the recent dramatic increases in NNIT use on political discourse and electoral campaigns in the United States (Han 2007, 2009; Lenhart and Fox 2009; Lusoli 2005; Kluver, 2007). Though the growth and impact of NNIT-based political communication has been discussed recently (Han 2009; Abroms and Lefebvre 2009; Catone 2007, 2008; Dale and Strauss 2007; Melber 2009; Owen 2009; Pace 2008; Smith and Rainie 2008), the scarcity of major research on this topic has left many questions on the use of NNITs in political contexts unanswered. More specifically, questions remain as to whether the new experimentation activates political participation in general and that of the young generations in particular, increases voting turnouts, affects Congressional behavior, and ultimately transforms electoral politics. Or, in contrast, does it only create a temporary hype around the political issue, leaving room for demagogues to maneuver according to their own agendas? Since the history of NNIT use is still short, no clear knowledge has been established on the following issues:

- Whether NNITs were used effectively for Obama's HCR legislation efforts; and
- Whether the use of NNITs contributed to the passage of HCR legislation.

BACKGROUND: HEALTH CARE REFORM AND TWITTER

During the 2008 presidential election campaign, the successful use of NNITs proved nothing less than transformative. On November 5, 2008, Change.gov was established by President-elect Barack Obama's transition team to continue social media interaction, and on January 20, 2009, all such efforts were integrated into WhiteHouse.gov. Both Change.gov and WhiteHouse.gov served as consolidated Web portals, designed to maintain support from the users of NNITs and online social media during the campaign and to maintain their involvement in the major political and reform agendas of the Obama White House and Administration.

One current indicator of public support for political usage of NNITs is the growing number of Twitter users who "follow" political leaders and famous public figures. Based on a limited collection of tweet data, it has been observed (Han and Kim 2009) that the number of Obama Twitter followers skyrocketed from less than 10,000 in December 2007 to almost 3 million in December 2009. More specifically, the fact that, by August 2009, there were more than 1.5 million followers of the President's Twitter account and around 450,000 followers of the White House account clearly demonstrates people's growing engagement in the social networking tool of the Twitter network (especially in comparison to the 59,000 tweet followers that Obama had during the 2008 presidential election). Among Twitter users, there have also been increasing reactions to the major political and reform agendas of the Obama Administration (Han and Kim 2009), and specifically to HCR tweets (e.g., from April to September 2009, as shown in Fig. 5.1) with hashtags, such as #obamahealth care and #healthcare, which function as short address tags for specific messages.

Figure 5.2 specifically illustrates how Twitter users responded to political events during the recent legislative battle, summarized in Diagram 5.1, *Chronology of Major Political Events*. The correlations seem clear between the highlighted spikes in the use of Twitter (Fig. 5.2) and major political milestones in the process of passing HCR legislation. For example, Figure 5.2 clearly shows that the use of Twitter spiked on December 21, 2009 before the Senate approved the bill, with explosive growth in Twitter user activity during March 2010 when the House of Representatives passed the bill (March 22) and it was signed by President Obama (March 23).

Here, it is worth recalling that the intrinsic nature of political community is theoretically *virtual* in the sense that no political community is based 100 percent on face-to-face interactions but rather is imagined through the virtual projection of loyalty and the political consciousness of being together in a community, which corresponds with Anderson's (1983) "imagined communities," Minkoff's (2001) "mediated collective identity" and Smith's (2001) "symbolic affiliation." The virtual nature of the actual relationships among the members of a political community can effectively be activated by the use of NNITs, including OSNs, especially by younger generations; and this is precisely what constitutes the new experimentation of using NNITs for social and political participation, as discussed in chapter 1. When young users of NNITs demonstrate their power to mobilize peers through test-run mobilizations, as in the cases of the 2004 Democratic primaries and the Howard Dean phenomenon, such NNIT-galvanized mobilizations are expected to result in the bonding and bridging of the social capital, as an outcome of a "demonstration effect" in the cases of both the United States and South Korea.

An important theoretical issue in American politics in the Information Age, and an example of the impact of this new experimentation, relates to the linkage between constituent opinion and congressional behavior, and especially the potential influence of NNIT-based constituency pressure on the passage of HCR legislation. Miller and Stoke's classic study (1958) revealed that members of the House do vote according to both their own policy views and their perception of their constituents' views, but did not explain the means by which constituents and representatives share their views with each other nor what main tool the two groups use to communicate. Kuklinski's 1978 study, as well as Cover and Brumberg's (1982) study on the impact of congressional

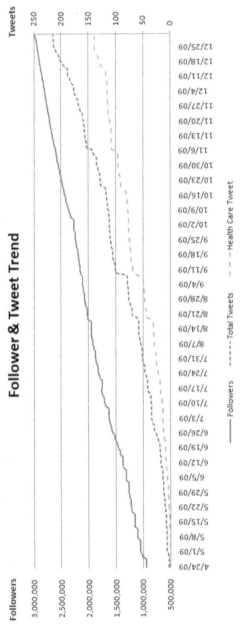

Figure 5.1 Amount of Obama Followers and Total Tweets on Obama and Health Care

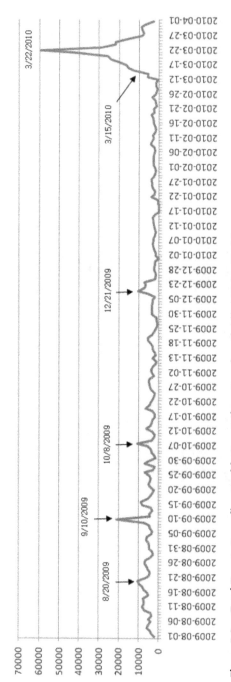

Figure 5.2 Total Tweets Regarding Health Care Reform Based on the Five Major Hashtags

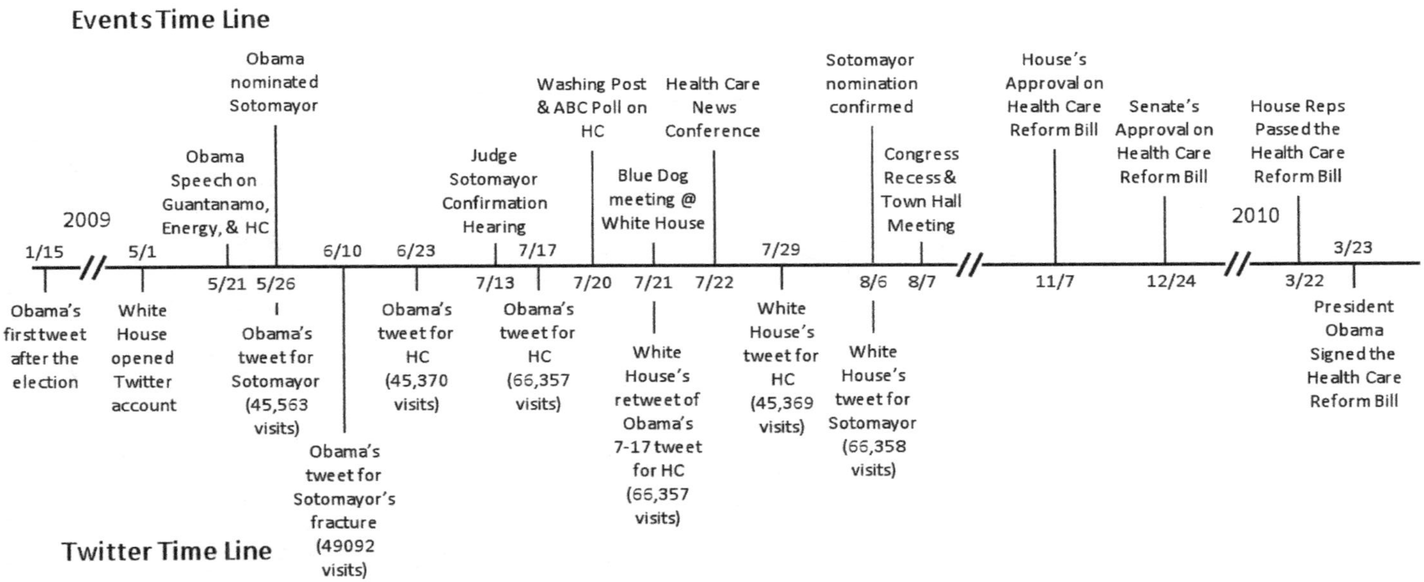

Diagram 5.1 Chronology of Major Political Events

mail, disclosed that representatives influence the policy preferences of their constituencies by controlling communicative channels of the mass public, opinion leaders and mass media; however, no empirical study has been conducted on the impact of constituents' use of NNITs upon the legislation process. Thus, an analysis of the tweets exchanged during the HCR legislation battle, and a series of interviews with key representatives and their staff, will contribute towards a deeper understanding of this issue.

In our investigation of the linkage between Congressional behavior and Twitter users' involvement in the national discourse on the passage of HCR legislation, the question naturally arises as to how we can determine whether Twitter messages on health care reform (e.g., the new experimentation) have affected the national discourse on this agenda and the passage of the legislation in the Congress. One of the answers can be found by tracing the distribution of tweets between President Obama, his followers, his followers' followers, and Congressmen. Social Network Analysis (SNA) has been widely used to study the patterns of people's connections and their interactions within social groups, and it is well-known for its use as a key research technique in fields such as sociology, organizational studies, medicine, information science and political science. SNA views the social relations that exist among a set of actors as a network in which the nodes are the individual actors and ties are the relationships between the actors (Scott 1988). With the advent of the Web, the study of OSNs has interacted with information networks embodied in the Web, and models of this interaction have been proposed (Romero and Kleinberg 2010).

Of particular interest, in the case of President Obama's HCR process and the use of Twitter, is the dissemination of information through OSNs, including the idea of the cascading of information (Leskovec, et al. 2007). These ideas have been motivated by applications such as viral marketing (Leskovec, et al. 2007), the spread of online news (Leskovec, et al. 2007; Lerman and Ghosh 2010), and the growth of online communities (Backstrom, et al. 2006). From the perspective of political science, scholars view massive OSNs as representations of social interactions that can be used to study the propagation of ideas (Huberman, et al. 2009). Social network analysis of Twitter will identify the routes by which information flows from one node to many others, and by which people communicate about the HCR issue.

Tweet data can be used to show patterns of social networks and information distribution, (see, e.g., Java, et al. 2007). The social network of Twitter fundamentally differs from that of other major OSNs such as MySpace and Facebook because Twitter does not require mutual authentication in order to set up a connection between tweet originators and followers, whereas the others do. Such Twitter connections function as one-way networks unless the sender follows the recipient as well. Thus, the information distribution pattern is most often one-way, which enables us to keep track of information distribution, that is, from President Obama to his immediate and subsequent followers, and ultimately to representatives and vice versa.

A colleague and I (Han and Kim 2009) developed a tweet-retrieving crawler (an automated application that retrieves all data specified) on the Linux server by using the Twitter API (Application Programming Interface), on which Twitter exposes its data for 8 to 10 days. Using the API, we downloaded all HCR-related tweets that included President Obama's original 6 hashtags specified below. Obama followers on health care have used these hashtags as well. The tweet data was downloaded and stored in the Linux server database and then converted into Excel format for further analysis, which includes the unique tweet ID, the date on which each tweet was sent, the content, and the Twitter ID of the user who sent the tweet. Sometimes, these tweets included the recipients' user IDs (if the sender specified it), which enabled us to identify Twitter users for a survey.

The current tweet dataset that was collected with regard to the Obama administration's HCR agenda contains a total of 1,062,082 tweets sent between August 1, 2009 and April 1, 2010. This data was secured by using six hashtags: #obamahealthcare, #healthcare, #healthcare09, #healthreform, #hicp and #hcr.

OSN, SOCIAL CAPITAL AND POLITICAL PARTICIPATION

As discussed in chapter 1, Putnam (2000, 25–6) characterizes the collapse of social capital and the waning of civic-mindedness as a "generational" or "intercohort" phenomenon. He also mentions that the infusion of new technology, such as phones and the Internet, is typically slowed by the generational gap since older generations tend to be more reluctant to adopt new technologies. As discussed earlier, the main user of these NNITs is the youth, who had previously been blamed for lower voting turnout rates and the overall decline of social capital. The new experimentation on which this study focuses begins with the youth's recent engagement in political discourse and the great potential for their political participation to be cultivated.

As to the impact of the Internet in general, and OSNs such as Facebook and MySpace in particular, many scholars have found ample evidence that greater use of OSNs would result in the formation of social capital. First of all, Zhao (2006, 846) claims that "there are no single Internet effects," meaning that the impact of the Internet on social capital will depend on the specific contexts of existing social ties. Based on the assumption that "the online world is a site for social activity, both original and extended from offline life," Williams (2006, 596) argues that the use of online sites can affect the process of bonding and bridging social capital. Further, to measure the positive impact of OSNs upon social capital, Williams (2006) develops a subscale of both bonding and bridging processes. Based on their empirical research on college students' use of Facebook and social capital, Ellison, Steinfield and Lampe (2007, 1164) conclude that there is "a robust connection between Facebook usage and indicators of social capital, especially of the bridging type. Internet use alone did not predict social capital accumulation, but intensive use of Facebook did." Such positively associated findings on the relationship between OSN use social capital, and electoral politics, will be reinforced by the fundamental changes that have come from the predominance of wireless and mobile communication technology over wired communication systems.

Online social network users have begun to form a seamless matrix of social and political connections linking individuals to each other on personal and public issues, especially through MC-OSNs such as Twitter. NNIT-mobilized social capital affects electoral politics too. As Anderson (2004), Lopez et al. (2005), and Brynjolfsson et al. (2006) have concurred, "[p]olitical activism isn't just about going door-to-door anymore. It's also about making the videos, posting on blogs, tying everything together, commenting, and sending text messages. All of these are new waves of political activism" (PBS 2008, 3). More than older voters, Generation Y voters (ages 18–32) were found to dominate in political and electoral activities carried out via social networking sites. These activities fall into the following categories: posting their own political commentary, signing up as a friend of a candidate, or starting/joining a political group (Smith and Rainie 2008, 10–1).

Even after Obama's inauguration on January 25, 2009, this Long Tail of Obama supporters seems to have maintained their support and interest in the political discourse, continuing to utilize OSNs (e.g., Facebook, MySpace, YouTube), as well as SMSs, micro-blogs and MC-OSNs, (e.g., Twitter, Qik, Jaiku, dodgeball). The next section analyzes demographic information on the Long Tail of NNIT-galvanized young voters who were active participants in post-election politics.

DOMINANT PLAYERS IN MC-OSNv AND TWITTER

In 2008, the use of MC-OSNs like Twitter steadily increased among adult American Internet users, from 6 percent in May to 9 percent in November and then 11 percent in December, according to Pew Internet Research (Lenhart and Fox 2009, 3). Surprisingly, Twitter users have a median age of 31, which

Table 5.1. Percentage of MC-OSN Users among American Internet Users

Age	Percentage
18–24	19%
25–34	20%
35–44	10%
45–54	5%
55–64	4%
65+	2%

* *Source:* Pew Internet (Lenhart and Fox 2009: 4)

is a bit higher than the age range chosen by the U.S. Census and other studies to represent young voters (i.e., 18–29); the median ages for MySpace and Facebook, however, fall within this age range (27 and 26, respectively). Voters ages 25 to 34 account for 20 percent of all MC-OSN users, which is the biggest percentage; the next largest age bracket is the youngest (i.e., 18–24). Overall, MC-OSNs like Twitter make up the dominant form of real-time communication for the young generations. Most MC-OSNs users typically use SNSs such as Facebook, MySpace, YouTube and LinkedIn. SNSs users dominate this new communication channel (23 percent of SNSs users are actively involved in MC-OSNs as opposed to just 4 percent of non-SNS users), which implies that their interests and important agendas in politics would also carry through into MC-OSNs. So, who exactly are the dominant players in these social network sites, and what is their political orientation?

Who were these numerous young voters who had gravitated toward Obama so strongly when he was the Democratic candidate and whose overwhelming participation in the 2008 presidential campaign proved so significant? As discussed in the previous chapter, a closer look at the people who constituted Obama's Long Tail reveals the following general trends:

- Through a series of test-run mobilizations, they changed from being politically indifferent to highly invested in politics and began to demonstrate a "politics-matter-to-me" attitude;
- Their voter turnout was dramatically higher in the 2008 presidential election than in 2000 and 2004 with much more potential to be cultivated for higher voter registration and turnout in upcoming major elections;
- They had a highly mobile lifestyle, relying almost exclusively on mobile phones;
- They were the most high-tech and connected national constituency in history, sharing profiles and engaging in entertainment activities via SNSs,

using cyberspace to network socially, and organizing with others for political events, issues, and causes (Jones and Fox 2009, 3–5; Lenhart 2009, 4, 6; Melber 2009);

- They preferred short, simple political messages that were communicated through personally trusted peer-to-peer communications and required no response (e.g., e-mails, text messages) (Youngvoterstrategies.org, 5; Dale and Strauss 2007, 4).

The fact that, out of all age groups, the youngest shows the lowest increase in both voter registration and turnout supports the major argument of this book—namely, that it is these voters who have the greatest potential to transform, or be transformed, from an apathetic "long tail" into a vibrantly active "Long Tail."

The profiles of these young generations, with their specific styles of NNIT use, including OSNs, clearly indicate that this new phenomenon will likely make a tremendous impact on the campaign process and political discourse once they take interest. As discussed in chapter 4, Millennials (ages 18–32) may play a central role in future electoral politics and politics in general since this new experimentation has successfully turned them on to public affairs and they use these networks to acquire information and communicate about elections. However, Generation X (born between 1965 and 1976 and currently ages 33–44) mostly uses NNITs to engage in online shopping or information retrieval on personal issues, as discussed in chapter 4.

In addition to using the Internet for activities directly related to elections, members of Generation Y, more than other generations, also use the Internet for entertainment—viewing videos, playing games, blogging, downloading music and participating in SNSs such as Facebook, MySpace, YouTube and Twitter (Table 4.6 in chapter 4). For Generation Y, SNSs together function as a networked public sphere made up not "of tools, but of social production practices that these tools enable" (Benkler 2006, 219). Through the use of SNSs, the NNIT-activated youth's cyber peer production of socio-politically sensitive materials had a significant impact on the 2008 presidential election. This new experimentation has placed Generation Y at the center of cyberspace, with the potential to impact the course of major elections in the future.

FEATURES OF MC-OSNv: TWITTER

Micro-content online social network sites are unique in that their instantaneity and convenience are unparalleled by other existing channels, mainly due to the brevity of their messages and the technical compatibility of existing digital media in securing multiple delivery channels. In addition, the flow and influence of information in MC-OSNs is largely determined by the subscribers.

MC-OSNs create a cybercommunity mainly comprised of two groups of people—those who want to maintain pre-existing relationships and those who want to share topics of interest and valuable information. In this space of tweeting, two types of actors exist—tweet senders and tweet receivers. Because both types can follow tweets and have followers of their own, Twitter creates a matrix of spiral information-sharing patterns; furthermore, a third party can monitor, by downloading the whole record of tweets on a given topic, the dynamics and patterns of this information flow and thereby measure the popularity and influence of certain tweets.

Users participate in this community to "achieve a level of cyber presence, being 'out there' and to feel another layer of connection with friends and world" (Zhao and Rosson 2009, 243). Technically speaking, MC-OSNs fundamentally depend upon the pervasiveness and mobility of *networked* wireless information technology. Due to the seamless nature of this matrix of multiple delivery channels, as well as their open architecture, Twitter and other MC-OSNs are able to overcome the exclusiveness of conventional Web-based blogging and thereby empower tweet followers. Because of these technical and architectural features, Twitter theoretically generates an opportunity for indiscriminate tweets to be available to indiscriminate tweet followers. This may result in the creation of untrustworthy information; however, followers filter information by subscribing and unsubscribing to certain tweets along the lines of their interests. This filtering process significantly enhances the level of trust and relevancy in the spiral of information exchanged through MC-OSNs. Accordingly, the process of filtering information through each user's choice of sources provides multiple contexts by which to measure the value of each tweet and the reliability of tweet providers.

When Zhao and Rosson (2009, 248) conducted phone interviews on trust with 11 Twitter users between September and December 2008, one interviewee commented that information from Twitter was valuable and credible because "it provides me a filter for the best types of information in the topics that I am most interested in. Because, more often, the people I monitor in Twitter are people who have similar interests with me, so I find them very valuable."

The Twitter Directory in 2008, and Twitterholic.com in 2009, serve as repositories of statistical information on how many users follow each member's messages. For example, a search on November 11, 2008 of the Twitter Directory revealed that Barack Obama's updates were the most followed, with 131,233 recorded as "following" and 127,294 as "followers," while 99 other identities fall far below Obama's level of popularity, reaching a maximum of only five figures in most cases. In fact, the second most followed is Kevin Rose with 107 "following" and 72,539 "followers" as of that day.[2] As of August 8, 2009, the same Obama site ranked 7th with 1,900,945 followers, the most friends (765,546) out of the top 100 twitterholics listed, and 314 updates. As of August 12, 2009, the former Vice President Al Gore ranked 21st with 1,398,190 followers and 8 friends; and Senator John McCain ranked 43rd with 1,145,694 followers and 63 friends. Although these numbers are impressive, they represent just one item on the long list of campaign tools used by the Obama campaign's Long Tail. This illustrates how the widespread use of the most up-to-date digital technology can contribute to social and political networking.

Due to certain features of the rules of the information-sharing pattern, data from Twitter is much more accessible and analyzable than data from mobile phones or SNSs, such as Facebook or MySpace. This study finds that there are three different tracks in the life cycle of a tweet. As illustrated in Diagram 5.2, Obama's tweet on health care reform was delivered to Obama's followers, who could either reply to him or re-tweet the message onward to their own followers. At this point, various things can happen—President Obama can re-tweet the replies from his followers, or the second loop of Obama followers ("OFF" in the Diagram) and their followers can re-tweet or reply to each other to discuss the issue amongst themselves. In the life cycle of a tweet, the first track is used to simply receive and check certain tweets. The commitment of those followers is limited to that stage of checking the tweets they receive. This first track reveals the total volume of followers; however, the total volume of the first track does not provide information on how many followers actually read the tweet or how that tweet impacted each follower.

Track 2 is the process of re-tweeting (RT), where the impact of a tweet can be measured in terms of the following categories: (1) frequency, (2) tweet flow and transfer, and (3) the size of the RT nodes. In the re-tweet process, followers of certain topics are filtered and the popularity of the topic becomes visible to general users. At this stage, tweeters deepen their commitment by not only checking the tweets but also distributing the information of the original tweet sender to their followers. In this stage, tweet distribution multiplies exponentially. This study finds that the initial stage of re-tweeting has the most impact because the total volume of re-tweets slows down with time.

Track 3 includes more detailed information on topics of interest for further reference, mostly in the form of shortened URLs, due to the limitation of each tweet to 140 characters. Bit.ly is a Web service that enables MC-OSNs users to shorten, share and track links to webpages where more substantial amounts of information are available. Thus, the third track presents researchers with

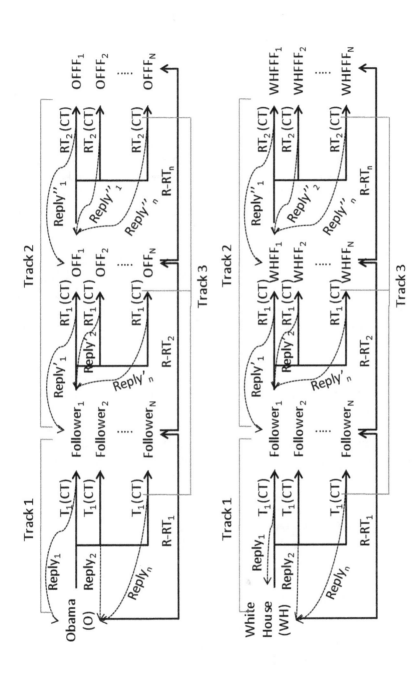

Diagram 5.2   The Life Cycle of a Tweet

valuable data about each tweet, such as how many followers checked for the second loop of substantial information over time, what kind of follow-up conversations occurred at this final destination, and who the visitors were. To give an example, a re-tweet (May 1, 2009) of an original White House tweet on swine flu "smgFi" contained the URL http://bit.ly/smgFi, which linked to a webpage providing detailed information on swine flu. The "bit.ly" offers profiles on that specific site through http://bit.ly/info/smgFi with information on how many visits were made over time, the visitors' locations, the content of conversations on this topic within this website, and other metadata.

This back-trafficking is made possible by the rules of tweeting; the @ sign is always followed by a username, which allows users to send messages directly to each other if they desire. For example, a message with @example would be directed at the user named "example" although the message could still be read by anyone. Therefore, even without specifying the return address, an author can receive replies without the need of identifying demographic information on recipients. In the process of exchanging tweets, third parties can also easily identify who the original and following users are, which may also increase the amount of follow-up offline face-to-face meetings and consequently contribute to the building of trust among Twitter users.

Twitter also has a search function that uses hashtags, which are words or phrases prefixed with a number sign (#). For example, a search for "Obama" would bring up all of the messages that included "#Obama." And a re-tweeting of Obama's original tweet can be executed by using the return address "RT@Obama." Currently, the White House and President Obama both use the following hashtags with regards to healthcare reform: #obama-healthcare, #healthcare, #healthcare09, #healthreform, #hicp, and #hcr. In summary, due to the nature of how Twitter facilitates an enormous amount of information exchanges (e.g., using different types of tweet transmissions, a shortened URL link using bit.ly, and back-trafficking using @ signs or hashtags), Twitter data provides better opportunities than other NNITs, such as SNSs or mobile phones, for discerning the way in which Twitter was used by the Obama Long Tail of supporters on two major post-election issues—Sotomayor's nomination and the HCR battle.

OBAMA TWEETING AND TWEETED

On "Organizing for America," the official website for Obama's main reform agendas, an "Obama Everywhere" section offers 16 channels, all of which are either OSNs or MC-OSNs. This section examines Obama's usage of Twitter in his effort to share information, convince supporters and stakeholders, announce campaign schedules, encourage dissemination of information, apply political pressure on Congressmen in each district, and solicit feedback from Twitter members on these two political agendas. Important milestones in the evolution of Obama's HCR policy and nomination of Judge Sonia Sotomayor are illustrated in Diagram 5.1, along with critical moments that boosted tweet activity, including click-throughs to additional information on these two issues.

Both issues are ostensibly divided along partisan lines, which is likely to be reflected among MC-OSNs users. In order to properly identify the political reactions of the Obama Long Tail, this chapter focused on the tweets and re-tweets sent by President Obama and the White House as well as the replies and re-tweets sent by followers and friends of both Obama and the White House to each other and back to both President Obama and the White House (Diagram 2).

As displayed in Table 5.2, this study tracked the total number of followers who had clicked-through the shortened URL using "bit.ly" (http://bit.ly) in search of further references on HCR issues. From January 15 to August 7, 2009, a total of 54 tweets originated from Obama's personal Twitter account. Out of these, 29 dealt with health care reform, and all but one contained URLs as shortened bit.ly-forms. Each of these 28 URLs is unique and features distinctive information. On the topic of Supreme Court Justice nominee Sonia Sotomayor, Obama sent out four tweets. The remaining 21 tweets sent by Obama were on diverse topics.

Figure 5.3 shows trends in the amount of "click-throughs" received by URLs that Obama included in his personal tweets on health care reform; these URLs redirected his followers to further references for supplementary information on this issue. Displaying the intensity of the reaction of Obama's Long Tail, the figure represents not only how many people use Twitter but

Table 5.2.   Tweets under Investigation

	Obama	*The White House*
Periods	Jan. 15–Aug. 7	May 1–Aug. 7
Total Number of Tweets	54	384
Health Care Reform	29	82
Shortened URL attached	28	26
Sotomayor	4	15
Shortened URL attached	4	5
Other tweets	21	287

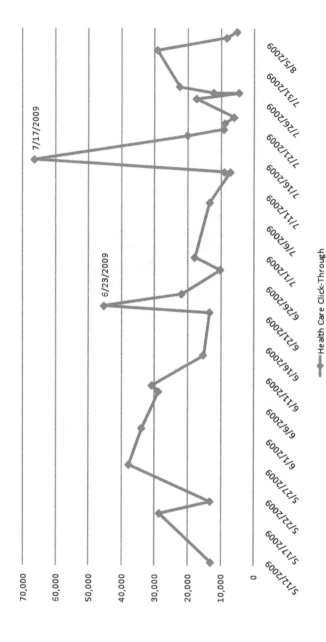

Figure 5.3 Number of Click-throughs on URLs in Obama's Tweets on Health Care Reform

also how many are committed to researching health care reform further by checking out the information at the URLs where the attached bit.ly forms lead them. This sort of reaction by the Obama Long Tail of tweet followers corresponds to Track 3 of a tweet life cycle. As shown in Figure 5.3, two major peaks indicate the occurrence of such reactions—one on June 23 with well over 40,000 click-throughs and on July 17 with a bit less than 70,000.

Obama followers reacted most intensely to his calls to check out the June 23 Press Conference and his speech on July 17: "Press conference at 12:30 on energy legislation, Iran, health care and the economy. Watch it live: http:// bit.ly/duw9t (6/23/2009)" and "[s]peaking on health care reform. Watch live at http://bit.ly/GOZOt #healthcare09 (7/17/2009)." In order to find out why these two tweets were so enthusiastically received by followers, it is important to examine the tweets that preceded and followed these two tweets—all of which contained official/factual information.

Figure 5.4 also shows how many followers of Obama's personal tweets actually looked up the URLs included in his tweet on the nomination of Sotomayor. These four tweets also belong to the "Third track" of tweet actions. Obama's choice of Sotomayor also generated a substantial amount of attention—almost as much as the HCR issue—especially due to the controversy surrounding the question of whether she was qualified to be a Supreme Court Justice. As the first Hispanic female nominee, her remark comparing the qualifications of white males to those of Hispanic females were controversial enough to divide the public, as well as the senators in charge of the confirmation hearings, evenly. On October 26, 2001, during a speech at the University of California, Berkeley, Judge Sotomayor had said, "I would hope that a wise Latina woman, with the richness of her experiences, would more often than not reach a better conclusion than a white male who hasn't lived that life," according to the CNN report. Due to the controversial nature of her statement, this historic nomination needed political support in order to secure votes from Democratic Senators and compete against Republican Senators on the Judiciary Committee. Even though Obama's tweets on the topic of Sotomayor were far fewer than those on health care reform, the actual number of click-throughs on the URLs that led to more detailed information about Sotomayor was almost as high as the amount of click-throughs in Obama's tweets on health care reform.

Between the start of the Senate hearings on July 13 and Sotomayor's confirmation on August 6, 2009, the crucial turning points in this case were, first, her official nomination on May 26; and second, when she fractured her ankle on June 10, according to Twitter data. Obama's tweet on May 26 read: "President Obama announces his Supreme Court nominee: http://bit .ly/1UUPj9 (5/26/2009)," and his June 10 tweet read "On Monday Supreme

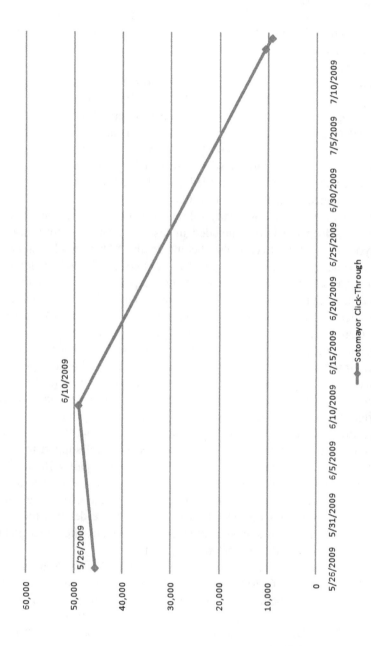

Figure 5.4   Number of Click-throughs on URLs in Obama's Tweet on Nomination of Sotomayor

Court Nominee Judge Sotomayor fractured her ankle. Sign her virtual cast: http://bit.ly/nBsg0 (6/10/2009)," clearly representing personal and emotional bonding between Sotomayor and Obama followers.

Out of a total of 384 tweets sent out by the White House from May 1 to August 7, 2009—much more than the 54 sent out personally by Obama—82 were on health care reform, 26 of which had shortened bit.ly forms of URLs attached for further information on healthcare issues. As marked in Figure 5.5, the tweet that created the most click-throughs was on July 21, which this study finds very interesting since that tweet was the same one that President Obama sent through his personal Twitter account on July 17, as shown in Figure 5.3. The July 21 tweet in Figure 5.5 and Obama's personal tweet on July 17 share the address "http://bit.ly/GOZOt," as shown in the following tweet message: "Streaming momentarily: Obama keeps fighting on health reform, watch live http://bit.ly/GOZOt (7/21/2009)." This fact provides significant insight into the current nature of Twitter—that the most active reactions in Twitter are generally caused by personally and emotionally oriented messages, as in the case of Obama followers. President Obama's personal charisma strongly and effectively reverberated through Twitter, which actively engages his NNIT-galvanized followers, as well as individuals who comprise his Long Tail, and incited them to interact with each other.

Figure 5.5 provides further evidence of this finding. In this figure that includes data from almost 50,000 click-throughs, another peak was on July 29 when the Council of Economic Advisors (CEA), Chair Romer, answered questions from small business owners. According to the White House blog, President Obama, in his July 25th Weekly Address, asked small business professionals to read the CEA report on how health insurance reform would affect small businesses, and encouraged them to come forward with questions. Thousands of them did, including 1,500 through the LinkedIn network alone. Clearly, in the case of July 21, it was President Obama's request to his followers to check out the CEA Chair's interview session that generated the most click-throughs in the White House tweet activities.

Among those 384 tweets sent out by the White House, fifteen were related to the nomination and controversy of Sotomayor, five of which had URLs attached for further references to the issue. From May to mid-July, the amount of those who clicked-through to read suggested information about this issue was just over 20,000; however, starting on July 20 (Fig. 5.6), there was a sudden and explosive increase in traffic checking out additional information delivered through various URLs reflecting the major political events: the Senate confirmation hearings started on July 13, and the confirmation of Sotomayor on August 6, 2009. The opposition reached its high mark on July 21, when a Senate panel decided to delay the vote on Sotomayor's

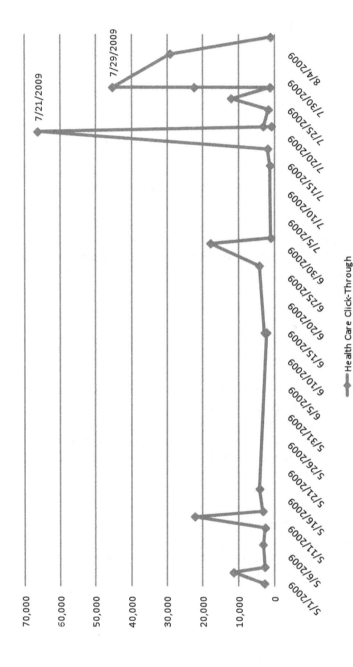

Figure 5.5 Number of Click-throughs on URLs Included in the White House's Tweet on HCR

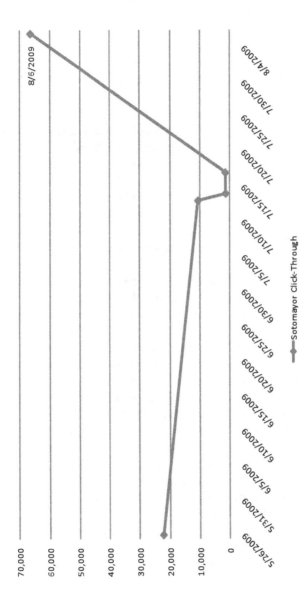

Figure 5.6   Number of Click-throughs on URLs Included in the White House's Tweet on Sotomayor's Nomination to the Supreme Court

nomination and two key Republican Senators made clear their opposition against Obama's choice of Supreme Judge nominee. This explosive trend in followers' click-through activity as they searched for supplementary information seems to correlate directly with the Republican opposition and the needs of the White House to mobilize Obama's Long Tail.

In comparison to President Obama's personal Twitter account, the White House's tweets, as well as the reactions from their followers, provide interesting observations. The second highest click-through occurred on May 26 with the following tweet, "BTW, we will livestream the President's announcement about his Supreme Court nominee here: http://bit.ly/12nxRn (5/26/2009)," which may serve as an indication of the popularity and influence of President Obama. On July 13, Judge Sotomayor made an opening statement at the Senate hearing, as announced in the following tweet: "Judge Sotomayor's opening statement at 1:30. Tune in to any cable news network or watch it streamed: http://bit.ly/fhfXx (7/13/2009)." Followers reacted explosively to the news of the Senate confirmation of the first Hispanic woman as Supreme Judge, as represented in the following tweet: "History: Judge Sotomayor confirmed 68–31. Watch Obama's response live around 3:30 http://bit.ly/GOZOt (8/6/2009)."

In order to gauge the popularity and influence of both President Obama's tweets and those of the Obama-influenced White House within the context of the total number of click-throughs, we need to also examine other prominent media institutions, such as CNN, and other influential politicians, such as Nobel Peace Laureate and former Vice President Al Gore and Senator John McCain, to see how many click-throughs their tweets had received from May 1 to August 10, 2009. In CNN's tweets, the most highly clicked URL (44,474 click-throughs) was "http://bit.ly/16BNY2," which was included in the tweet about Michael Jackson's death on June 25, 2009. Compared to the most highly clicked URLs in both President Obama's, even CNN's most highly clicked URL falls short by 25,000. Also, in the tweets sent out by Al Gore and John McCain, there was only one URL with more than 10,000 click-throughs. Table 5.3 below clearly demonstrates that the amounts of click-throughs obtained by both President Obama and the White House are far higher than the highest obtained by CNN, Gore or McCain.

Table 5.4 below presents a complete picture of the popularity and influence of both President Obama's and the White House's tweets compared to that of one of the most influential news media, CNN, and other top politicians in U.S. politics.

This study also found this data by searching for the unique URLs included in one particular tweet from the White House that produced the largest re-tweet volume—on August 4, the White House tweeted the following

Table 5.3. **Number of Click-throughs in Tweets that Included Shortened URLs from CNN, Al Gore and Senator John McCain**

	Date	URL	Click-throughs	Tweet
CNN	6/25	http://bit.ly/16BNY2	44,474	Pop icon Michael Jackson is in a coma, sources say.
	6/25	http://bit.ly/AG0F3	44,419	"King of Pop" Michael Jackson has died, according to multiple reports.
	8/6	http://bit.ly/1WNEXM	43,344	Ashton Kutcher #aplusk & Demi Moore tweet following emergency landing at Las Vegas airport.
	6/23	http://bit.ly/q3O40	40,192	Rush-hour collision between two D.C. Metro trains killed at least six people, Mayor Adrian Fenty said.
	7/2	http://bit.ly/Vdwdr	33,078	Video of Michael Jackson's rehearsal now posted on CNN.com
Al Gore	6/22	http://bit.ly/WYLaC	14,039	Last chance to join me for an urgent briefing.
	6/26	http://bit.ly/VfAt1	8,615	Climate debate happening on the House floor right now. Call your member of Congress.
	8/4	http://bit.ly/MgvKf	6,750	We are overjoyed by Laura and Euna's safe return.
	8/4	http://bit.ly/7CmmV	6,028	Warmest seas on record.
	7/3	http://bit.ly/CCQvC	3,855	Bi-partisan leadership and the climate crisis:
Sen. John McCain	7/10	http://bit.ly/8rJRy	6,914	A good perspective on media bias:
	5/21	http://bit.ly/gqEYS	4,551	worth the click: http://bit.ly/gqEYS - All about the pork!
	6/16	http://bit.ly/8NsjF	3,641	Stars & Stripes:
	5/14	http://bit.ly/16K4lh	3,536	And my mom Roberta was on The Tonight Show with Jay Leno last night!
	7/17	http://bit.ly/vdmVw	2,843	In total agreement with Secretary Gates on the F-22:

*Source: http://bit.ly/info/ and the Twitter accounts of CNN (twitter.com/cnnbrk), Al Gore (twitter.com/algore) and John McCain (twitter.com/SenJohnMcCain), all from May 1 to August 10, 2009.

Table 5.4. Average Click-throughs for President Obama, White House, CNN, Al Gore and Senator McCain

	Barack Obama	White House	CNN	Al Gore	John McCain
Average Click-through of Top 5 URLs	48,835.6	50,518.8	41,101.4	7,857.4	4,297.0

* *Source:* http://bit.ly/info/ and the Twitter accounts of Barack Obama (twitter.com/ barackobama), the White House (twitter.com/whitehouse), CNN (twitter.com/cnnbrk), Al Gore (twitter.com/algore) and John McCain (twitter.com/SenJohnMcCain)

message to its followers, "Don't believe everything you see on the Web about health insurance reform. Pls share: http://bit.ly/maVkF #healthreform #hc09." This tweet was re-tweeted (RT) 432 times over three days. As Figure 5.7 illustrates, the initial RT was delivered to about 160 followers, which is the most out of any RT. The number of RT deliveries then reduced dramatically over three days, with the exception of the seventh hour when levels spiked presumably from online activity during lunch hour. Several interpretations of this finding are plausible. The first is that re-tweeting is effective for the initial stage of the first group of specific tweet followers. Immediate Obama followers constituted the major distribution channels in the tweet's overall life cycle, whereas other second loops of followers were not actively engaged in redistributing the tweets. Related to this point, the second finding implies that, as a medium, MC-OSNs are ill-suited for long-term dissemination of information because the information distribution structure remains shallow and incapable of extending beyond the first loop of the follower group.

Covering the three and half months from April 24 to August 7, Figure 5.8 illustrates the rise in Obama's amount of followers, the amount of their tweets on both health care reform and Sonia Sotomayor, and the causes of the most substantial amounts of tweet activity. In comparison to the straight line, which represents the average, the top blue line (i.e., the amount of Obama followers) showed a modest increase from April 24 to May 29, a modest decrease until June 26, and then a continuing increase. Thus, June 26 becomes an important watershed in the overall increase in the amount of Obama followers. So, what triggered these changes? On June 24, the White House hosted a Town Hall meeting on health care reform that was broadcasted that night by ABC. On June 27, many followers were encouraged to hold various HCR events in each region. This trend corresponded with the overall increase in the number of total tweets, with the tweets on health care to a lesser degree, and with the tweets on Sotomayor to an even lesser degree.

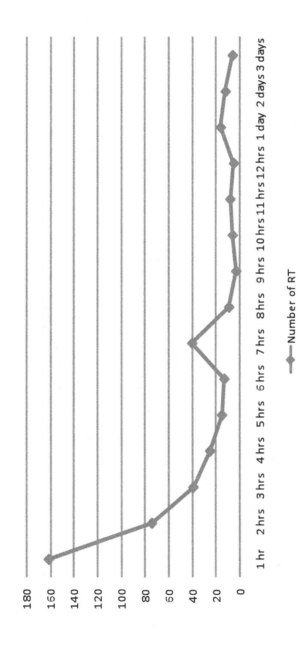

Figure 5.7   Trends in the Distribution of Re-tweeted Messages

In regard to the HCR agenda, July 17 served as the most critical moment, suddenly boosting the number of tweets. Obama's HCR effort became the subject of both the usual Republican opposition and the Blue Dog democrats' rebellion. Released on July 20, a poll conducted by *The Washington Post* and ABC revealed that opposition force was gaining influence upon the constituency. The approval rating for Obama's HCR policy dropped from 57 percent to 49 percent, and the disapproval rating increased dramatically from 29 percent to 44 percent. Partisan politics were clearly reflected in this change. Three-fourths of Democrats favored the reform policy, while the same ratio of Republicans opposed it. In addition, President Obama's White House meeting with representatives of the Blue Dog democrats on July 21, 2009 achieved no concrete outcome. All of these significant events are well reflected in Diagram 5.1, including the special news conference that President Obama delivered from the White House on the status of HCR policy on July 22. Ultimately, on July 30, 2009, Speaker of the House Nancy Pelosi declared war against the health care industry and excoriated the Blue Dog democrats. The need to defend the passage of universal health care legislation in Congress motivated President Obama, the White House, and the Democratic leadership in the Congress to rally their supporters, to pressure the opposition, and to mount a massive campaign during the season of Town Hall meetings as Congress entered recess on August 6. This is what happened two months after President Obama officially proclaimed the beginning of HCR policy at the National Archive building on May 21, 2009.

Figure 5.8 clearly illustrates that health care reform is a much more important agenda for Obama followers than the nomination and confirmation of Supreme Court Justice Sonia Sotomayor. The followers of HCR issues demonstrate a linear increase almost parallel with that of the average, except in the time before and after June 25. In particular, the tweets on health care around this time increased dramatically. The sudden increase around June 25 reflects the Town Hall meeting on health care at the White House, which was broadcasted by ABC.

In Figure 5.8, the White House's Twitter account discloses a similar pattern to that witnessed in Obama's personal tweet account—a major hike in tweets for health care reform around July 20. Since the opening of the White House Twitter account on May 1, as Figure 5.8 shows, there was a dramatic and linear increase in both the number of White House followers and the total number of tweets about topics on the White House agenda. This also confirms that health care reform was much more important to the followers than the nomination of Sonia Sotomayor. On July 28, 2009, the White House sent the following tweets: "Obama AARP tele-town hall on health care reform around 1:30, watch & chat through Facebook http://bit.ly/tCHXt ," "On tap: AARP

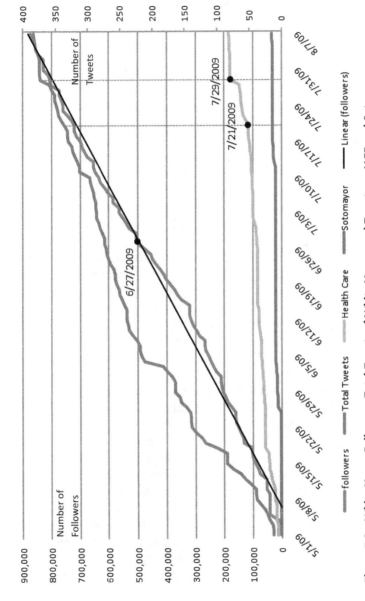

Figure 5.8 White House Followers, Total Tweets of White House, and Tweets on HCR and Sotomayor

tele-town hall on health care reform 1:30 (7/28/2009)." White House followers replied back to the White House, and the White House re-tweeted the next
day (July 29). This re-tweet process clearly indicates that a cycle of feedback
had been completed between Obama and his followers through the re-tweet
process on health care reform.

TWITTER AS AN OPEN DATA MINE

Research on Twitter contributes significantly to the scholarly attention
on how new networked information technologies, such as OSNs and
MC-OSNs, affect political discourse and election campaigns because the
data itself reveals the content of the communications that are taking place
through these mediums, whereas data in other mediums, such as mobile
phone records or SNS data, do not generally disclose the content of the
conversations. For example, my research (Han 2007) on the correlation
between the election of candidate Roh Moo-hyun in the 2002 Korean
Presidential election and the increased volume of mobile phone use on
Election Day found the data incapable of indicating that the increased volume was directly due to the activity of those in support of electing Roh in
particular; it merely serves as an implication of voting activity in general.
Tweets, however, disclose their contents and, due to the nature of Twitter's rules and architecture, can be tracked through replies, re-tweets and
click-throughs. Therefore, more research on MC-OSNs will provide greater
insight into the impacts of NNITs upon general political discourse, politics
and electoral politics.

Also, in this research, as in my previous studies (Han 2007, 2009) on the
relationship between NNITs and electoral politics, recent increases in the use
of MC-OSNs are found to be closely related with the users of conventional
OSNs, such as Facebook, MySpace, YouTube and LinkedIn, which supports
this study's claim that the NNIT-galvanized young generation of Obama
supporters—the Long Tail that Senator Obama successfully cultivated and
tapped into during the 2008 presidential election–continued their participation in public discourse on the major agendas of the Obama administration's
first seven months. Also, due to Twitter's filtering process whereby each
individual follows certain tweets and often re-tweets these messages to followers of their own, the Twitter community appears to have a high level of
trust in the reliability of the information they share. By filtering a tremendous
amount of tweets through an individual subscribing process, Twitter users
seek specific and trustworthy information and are deeply involved in the
political process.

Despite a big difference between the total number of tweets and the amount of followers on both HCR and Sotomayor nomination issues, an average of more than 1.5 million followers of President Obama's account and around 450,000 followers of the White House account clearly shows a strong engagement in the Twitter network. When tweeters reacted actively, they did so on the same issues, around June 20 and July 20, when the HCR issue was at an important turning point. The difference between followers' reactions to President Obama's personal tweets and those sent from the White House clearly indicates that Twitter still relies significantly on personal charisma and popularity.

Nonetheless, Twitter has a long way to go before it can be considered a serious public sphere—there must be several loops of re-tweeting after the initial re-tweet, and a consistent level of re-tweets must be maintained. In other words, the volatility and the personalization of the tweet life cycle must be overcome. Due to the enormous amount of tweet contents on these two major issues, this study did not make a comprehensive attempt to analyze the actual contents of the tweets.

NOTES

1. Regarding the notions of "Blue Ocean" and "Long Tail," refer to chapter 4.

2. On November 11, 2008, the total number of Twitter users was 3,183,544; Twitter's average daily amount of messages was 225,000; and the number of messages from Barack Obama followers ranged from 6,367 to 7,959 per day, 265 to 332 per hour, and 4.4 to 5.5 per minute. See twitterfacts.blogspot.com/.

Chapter 6

Conclusion

Making Sense of the New Experimentation

Political experimentation in human society often comes with extreme risks since rapid and radical changes in political ideologies, institutions and ways of life tend to produce victims. In the political experimentation of China's Cultural Revolution, for example, Mao Zedong forced the Chinese people to leave behind the legacies of the Ancient Regime's Confucian idea of politics, culture, customs, and traditions. This experimentation left deep wounds in the minds of many Chinese and has limited the old Chinese way of Confucian thinking. Although it can be said that the gender inequality and repressive social hierarchy of the Confucian system were eradicated, many were forced to accept Communist ideology, were separated from their families, and were killed. Numerous are the examples of the losses endured due to political experiments—millions were persecuted, purged and killed in political experimentation during the French Revolution in 1789, the Paris Commune in 1871, the Great Purge by Joseph Stalin from 1936 to 1938, the Cultural Revolution by Mao Zedong from 1966 to 1976 and the Khmer Rouge's massacre from 1975 to 1979. In most of these cases, radical republicans, anarchists, socialists and communists designed political experiments with the intent to create an entire society according to their ideals.

Applying the notion of NNIT-induced new experimentation in political realms, this book attempts to conceptualize the changes that arose from the extensive and intensive use of NNITs in political discourse, electoral politics and democracy. In this book, however, this concept of political experimentation is applied in such a way as to focus on the spontaneous processes and outcomes of the interplay between NNITs and the central players of the new cybersphere. This is in stark contrast to the political experimentations mentioned above, which were dogmatic, ideological, and driven by ideals

179

to rectify the whole society. The current NNIT-based changes that have emerged in recent politics and elections are conceptualized here as a new ongoing experimentation markedly different from the old experimentation of nineteenth-century America, when face-to-face, voluntary interaction in local communities was the primary source of social capital.

The core elements of the new experimentation are the emergence of a new cyberspace for human interaction, which has given rise to a networked public sphere and new central actors within this newly created space. The rules to these new power games of human interaction in cyberspace significantly challenge the conventional power structure and dynamics of Industrial Age mass media in the public sphere and electoral politics. As an immediate outcome, this experimentation has resulted in the emergence of new players who are socially active in virtual space—the youth. They not only indulge in online games, download music and upload their own digital content, they also share their own individual profiles through new OSN sites and engage in political discourse, which has resulted in the electoral mobilization of the youth at large.

This new experimentation with NNITs is providing a new environment in electoral politics, represented here by the concepts of the Blue Ocean and the Long Tail, which together describe an emerging electoral market of an increasingly cohesive and politically involved young constituency. The major source of the change lies in the way people interact with each other and build community; however, virtual interactions differ from their conventional face-to-face counterpart in that the former can be achieved without physical interaction. The main challenge encountered by this new experimentation with regards to the formation of social capital and democracy is exactly how cyber (i.e., virtual) interactions will affect social capital and trust among masses. Utilizing a comparative design, this book examined a presidential election and a major political event in two countries—the United States and the Republic of Korea—in order to argue that the use of NNITs by these younger generations in particular has attracted their interest in pubic agendas and elections, and has increased their participation in the presidential elections and major political agendas of the current administrations.

To examine the nature of the changes that this new experimentation is bringing forth, this book raises three important theoretical questions: the first examines how these previously apolitical and disparate generations first began to take interest in public agendas and electoral politics; the second examines the impact of NNITs on the nature of political community; and the third discusses the intrinsic nature of political community and the cyber interactions that are becoming increasingly popular as a means of political participation. To explain the process by which younger apolitical generations were induced to participate in political agendas and elections through their use of NNITs, chapter 2 investigated how the Winter Olympics in Utah and the World Cup Soccer Games in May 2002 opened the eyes of Korea's 2030 Generation to their potential power (through demonstration effects), and how the death of two school girls by American military vehicles impelled the young generations of Korea to initiate anti-American candlelight demonstrations. All of these events, which energized the youth in cyberspace and subsequently led to offline test-run mobilizations and demonstrations, ultimately resulted in the increase of young votes for liberal candidate Roh Moo-hyun in the 2002 presidential election in Korea. Thus, even before Senator Obama had successfully tapped into the recently activated American youth, candidate Ro Moo-hyun attracted a Blue Ocean of young Korean voters newly interested in politics. As the culmination of these events, in Korea's 2002 presidential election, the young generations became a deciding factor in electing President Roh Moo-hyun. The Korean experience in 2002 suggests that, despite the fact that turnout had declined among all generational groups, NNITs can play a decisive role in shaping the political cohesiveness and voting patterns of younger generational groups in electoral politics. In the case of the Korean presidential election, a causal relationship between NNITs, *voter cohesion* and electoral outcomes was found to be more plausible than one between NNITs, *increased voter turnout* and electoral outcomes; while the 2008 presidential election in the United States indicates both voter gravitation toward the Democratic party and overall increase in the votes of young generations, as examined in chapter 4.

In order to confirm whether any link exists between the increase in voting rates and the use of NNITs by the young constituency and candidates more empirical studies will be needed in the United States and Korea based on rigorous election data over the next two decades and several presidential elections. In fact, President Roh (Yoo 2010, 202) himself pointed out that "his victory was unexpected and an outcome of complicated combinations of conditions that occurred during the campaign period in 2002." Another important point is that this new experimentation is not fixed to a certain segment of the political spectrum. For example, in these presidential elections, although there was a strong gravitation towards Democrats in the United States and towards liberal candidates in Korea, that trend may be overturned in future elections depending on the characteristics of election candidates and the political situation at the time.

Regarding the impact of NNITs upon social capital, this book analyzes two opposite schools of thought—dystopian and utopian perspectives. As more research becomes available on how interactions in cyberspace increase follow-up offline face-to-face interactions, the dystopian claim that NNIT use weakens social capital seems too simplistic to explain the complex reality of the "six degrees of separation" that cyber interactions constantly create. To support the argument that new experimentation will actually strengthen social capital and contribute to the activation of youth involvement in the political context, however, more research on the causal links between the use of NNITs and political participation will be necessary. Until that research has been conducted, it would be premature to generalize the increasing trend in the youth's voting and participation in major national political discourse and agendas. To fully authenticate the concept of the Blue Ocean of the Long Tail, more quantitative empirical studies are needed; however, this book contributes to that literature by identifying the countries with the highest level of IT infrastructure and strong civil society.

The overarching issue that this seeks to explicate raises questions regarding the intrinsic nature of political community in general. As Anderson (1991) argues, all political communities larger than small villages are imagined; no political community is built on 100 percent genuine and real acquaintanceships among its members. Thus, from the beginning, the essential nature of a political community is virtual, based on the projection of imagined loyalty and togetherness towards the symbolic center. Since cyberspace is created by a suite of cyber codes (i.e., software, hardware and protocols such as TCP/IP) and human interaction in the networked public sphere—and since, as a Blue Ocean, cyberspace brings new rules to the game—NNITs can even be seen as strengthening the process of imagining community and thereby consolidating the process of projecting loyalty and enhancing the symbolic meaning of sovereignty and nation-ness. By supporting the effect of bridging the social capital, interactions based on the use of NNITs across the conventional boundaries of age, culture, gender, organizations, spatial and temporal limitations can expand the scope of social capital and bring together more people who would have otherwise been unavailable for such interactions.

The focal point of the proposed concept of a new experimentation is its power to transcend the conventional boundaries of Industrial Age institutions in every aspect of our lives. The notion of the Long Tail helps conceptualize the increased level of participation by the NNIT-activated younger generations, and the notion of the Blue Ocean helps conceptualize the new market of younger voters for politicians, although more empirical data is needed to generalize the causal effect of the power of NNITs upon the young constituency.

More specifically, though, what pre-conditions are needed in order for this new experimentation to be realized? In the case of Korea, this study finds that the following three conditions were met: (1) rapid and broad deployment of NNITs with the highest concentration among the younger generations of eligible voters; (2) a series of test-run mobilizations around non-political, social events salient to younger generations; and (3) the building up of a generational consciousness and sense of a community. The actual usage of NNITs in society is a necessary pre-condition for the success of a new experimentation, as we observed in the cases of America and South Korea. Another important point to be considered in understanding the success of this new experimentation relates to the level of the maturity of civil society. Korea's new experimentation was achieved through the extensive deployment of NNIT infrastructure and actual usage of NNITs combined with the explosive growth of civic organizations and activism. The civic movements in the United States reached a peak in the 1960s and '70s, which means that American civic activism had been institutionalized long before the advent of NNITs; but it was the national crisis caused by the 9/11 terrorist attack and the Iraq War that co-opted young generations' attention, followed by the campaign mobilizations by Democratic candidate Howard Dean in the 2004 presidential election, 2006 mid-term election, and the primaries and caucuses of the 2008 presidential election.

VARIATIONS OF THE NEW EXPERIMENTATION IN ASIA: CHINA AND JAPAN

Demonstration effects can be accomplished in different contexts in different countries. For example, in the Hainan Island incident, when an American Navy surveillance EP-3E aircraft collided with a Chinese J-811 interceptor fighter and became a major military conflict on April 1, 2001, a Chinese Netizen called *Qiangguo* (Strong Nation, www.qglt.com), heavily involved in cyberspace and sponsored by the official newspaper of the Chinese Communist Party, the *People's Daily*, expressed patriotism in his condemnation of the United States and criticized the Chinese government for its weak reaction against the U.S. government (Li, et al. 2003, 147). Li et al. (2003) analyzed how such explosive reactions and the public discourse of this Chinese Netizen evolved from an Initial Period (April 2–4) to a Negotiating Period (April 5–11), and then a Letter of Regret (April 12) between the United States and China. Thus, the Chinese government might have taken advantage of patriotic movements among their own citizens; however, this Chinese Netizen experienced connectedness in cyberspace with other Chinese citizens and must have recognized their potential power to convince their government to take a more aggressive stance against America. In this case, NNITs appear to have helped consolidate the Chinese people through international military conflict to support the Chinese communist regime; however, this cohesiveness may also eventually work against the regime when the regime is seen as responsible for disastrous accidents or major policy failures because those who were awakened to their own potential in cyberspace and connected to each other can later deliberate and mobilize when occasions for action arise. For Korea, it was a series of international athletic games, but for China, it was international military confrontations that ignited and consolidated solidarity and a sense of connectedness in cyberspace; however, incidents such as the Nanjing food poisoning (Li, et al. 2003, 250) or the Jiangxi school explosion (253) could lead this cohesive group to use their potential against the government instead.

There are many authoritarian countries in Asia where young generations have been involved in anti-government democratic movements utilizing the power of the Internet, mobile phones, and other NNITs, as illustrated by the way in which Burma's diaspora community connected through cyberspace, using the website www.burmanet.org. In this way, the virtual dissidents of Burma's cybercommunity were able to engage in virtual collective actions and ultimately convince foreign governments to pressure business organizations to drop their business deals with Burmese governments (Oo 2004). For example, the network Free Burma's collective actions of cyber diaspora activists (Oo 2004, 532) resulted in a much-publicized Pepsi boycott at Harvard University dining services due to Pepsi's business deal with the authoritarian military regime of Burma. Similarly, Carlsberg and Heineken were forced by local Dutch activists to drop their investment in Burma (Oo, 2004, 533). The catch phrase of the Burmese diaspora cybercommunity, "When spiders unite, they can tie down a lion" (Oo 2004, 515) has worked to build international pressure against the Burmese authoritarian military junta. This serves as a perfect example of the power of a new experimentation on an international scale. New experimentations in countries under authoritarian regimes may strengthen their democratic forces—as vividly illustrated in the use of Twitter by anti-Ahmadinejad progressive protestors in the wake of Iran's contested 2009 presidential election—and contribute to the fall of authoritarian regimes.

Japan provides us with a very different story on how this new experimentation evolves. Japan's political culture and entrenched power structure is considered to be controlled by the iron grip of Liberal Democratic Party (LDP) in alliance with big industry (keiretsu) and invincible bureaucracy. Throughout its history, which spans over a half-century, Japan's LDP has drawn its support from almost exclusively from its rural constituency with only limited success in garnering support from urban populations or the youth. Such electoral dominance was turned on its head in 2009 with the victory of Democratic Party of Japan (DPJ) in the Lower House elections. But this victory and the change in power dynamics and record voter turnout associated with it cannot be attributed to the combined power of NNITs and younger generations as were the cases in the United States and Republic of Korea. Previous chapters have described how in each of these cases, the new experimentation of young voters equipped with NNITs have demonstrated their influence as well as how politicians have successfully cultivated the Blue Ocean of this Long Tail. In these examples, young voters have made their voices heard at the ballot box, and the emergence of networked information technology has revitalized the youth, who have pushed for reforms and demonstrated against unpopular figures. That has not been the case for Japan, where youth activism exists, but only to a minimal degree.

Emerging from the devastation of World War II, Japan quickly grew into the third largest economy (very recently surpassed by China) and institutionalized democracies in the world. Its citizens have traditionally higher voter turnout rates than Americans. In addition, Japan is one of the most advanced countries in terms of its NNIT infrastructure. Its mobile phone subscriptions increased from just below 57 million in 2000 to over 107 million in 2008. In the same period, cable Internet subscribers jumped from 216,000 to 3.87 million. Approximately 71 percent of the general population utilizes the Internet for anything from e-mail to dialogue with friends (Ministry of Internal Affairs & Communications).

Disaggregating these statistics by age is perhaps more telling. A 2008 report released by the World Internet Project shows that 74 percent of survey participants between the ages of 16 to 19 use both a PC and mobile phone. The percentage drops significantly for those 40 and above, slumping to 38 percent for those in their 50s and a nadir 3 percent for septuagenarians (World Internet Project, 2008).

In addition, 96.1 percent of 16–29 year olds use the Internet, along with 99.1 percent of those in their 30s. A great majority of people in their 20s use the Internet most for visiting websites and blogs hosted by others and posting to BBS (bulletin board services). However, only 11.4 percent of those surveyed, regardless of age, said they used the Internet to find political news. Television and newspapers are the major source for this information (WIP 2005, 2008). This does not necessarily mean that political awareness among the population does not exist. In fact, these data only show that Japan's younger generations expose themselves to communications devices daily and do not consult such devices for political news. These data also show that young people comprise the majority of those using this technology. This knowledge can be applied to interpret the degree of political interest based on Internet usage.

Therefore, the first condition for young generations' NNIT-activated participation in the political process is met. What about their voting records? Indeed, Japan and Korea have different political experiences that shaped the level of youth involvement in the last few decades. Generally, voter turnout among Korean youth has been much higher than that of Japanese youth. In the 2002 Korean presidential election, 56.55 percent of people in their 20s voted, compared to 35.62 percent of Japanese in this same age group for the 2003 Lower House election (Han 2007, 71). The numbers are even more skewed when looking back at the late 1990s. In Korea, then, the youth tended to be more involved in electoral politics and demonstrated that groups with a history of activism those can unite for a common cause.

Young Japanese have not always been politically passive. A long-term look at Lower House voting rates reveals that people in their 20s and 30s had historically higher turnout numbers, rivaling and sometimes even surpassing older generations. Data indicate from 1967 through the late 1980s, turnout was above 50 percent for the 20-year-old age group. All age groups displayed fairly consistent patterns in this same period. Those in their 50s and 60s maintained an impressive showing of above 80 percent for the entire duration. Total voter turnout remained stable from 1950 through the 1980s. Then, suddenly, the numbers plummeted following the 1990 Lower House election. Between 1990 and 1996, for example, turnout among 20-year-olds fell by more than 20 percent, and they were the most affected age group (Ministry of Internal Affairs and Communications). Since that precipitous drop, the younger voters have slowly increased their participation, while older voters have shown less variation in their political participation. Much of the same can be said for the Upper House (The Association for the Promotion of Fair Elections).

Nonetheless, from 1990 until now, youth political participation exhibits a general downward trend. We can impute several events for this. They include:

- The Public Offices Election Law (POEL), which strictly limits the use of text and images during campaign season both for candidates and voters;
- The LDP Recruit Scandal of 1989, when political misdealing significantly eroded public trust in government leadership;
- Japan's economic "bubble burst" and stagnation of the 1990s, leading to a break from the typical corporate past that has marginalized many young people;
- Older voters' domination of the political process, getting policies enacted to benefit them while leaving younger generations feeling excluded.

Each of these factors is partly responsible for the widespread social exclusion and disappointment that typifies young, eligible voters. The first factor, the issue of changes to elections laws, merits particular attention as it relates to

NIT deployment in the political realm. However, the others are significant in that they are reasons why young Japanese would likely eschew politics even in the absence of an election law and pressing security issues.

As much as social science appears to be the popular subject of study across Japanese universities, it does not seem to translate into participation in electoral politics (School Education). Actually, a large part of the answer lies in the archaic Public Offices Election Law. Originally passed in 1950 for printed material, the POEL bars candidates from distributing information in certain formats, such as posters, electronic lighting, and billboards. Restrictions are in place during the sanctioned 7- to 20-day campaign period prior to Election Day and are as particular as keeping a candidate's name on a lantern no larger than 85 by 45 centimeters. Door-to-door campaigning is illegal as well. Candidates are not permitted to update their websites or blogs, nor can voters write online in blatant support of a candidate (Wallace 2005). The rationale behind the law at its inception was that all candidates would have a better chance to represent themselves by keeping costs low, but the cyber era has made this a paradox because political hopefuls can cheaply reach their voters via blogs and e-mail messages.

In an effort to change the law, in 1997 the DPJ hosted a study group with the LDP and Shinshinto party that proposed allowing the Internet to be used for campaign purposes. Unfortunately, the idea was never taken up. Later, in 1999, the issue resurfaced, but the LDP refused to support such as measure because it said it worried about "anonymous defamation" and argued that only a small percentage of Japanese used the Internet anyway. Some scholars contend that LDP politicians, many of whom are older, do not know how to interact with users in cyberspace and fear that they would lose their seats to more technologically-savant opposition candidates. Actually, the LDP has historically held the smallest percentage of Diet members who maintain websites. The DPJ boasts higher percentages, and in 2000, now-Prime Minister Yukio Hatoyama supported the use of the Internet in politics, citing the need for better communication between voters and government officials. But no formal action has been taken since then, allowing the POEL to keep online users separated from policymakers and potential Diet members (Tkach-Kawasaki, 2003: 112–114).

Not only do such restrictions make it harder for citizens to learn about a candidate's specific policies, it also fails to promote the buildup of social capital in a community in the Information Age. Since its nascent years, the Internet has always held the potential to be a utopian force. In the case of Japan, the POEL has constrained potential the Internet might have to work in a utopian manner during the crucial time just before an election. An astounding example of the state's powers of limitation here involves the actions of several activist groups during the June 2000 election that reflects many of the defining characteristics of the Korean example. These groups collectively blacklisted candidates online who they believed were unsuitable for public office. At least one such group, the Alliance to Defeat Unqualified Parliamentarians, stationed in Osaka, voluntarily removed its list from the web, fearing punishment from the Ministry of Home Affairs for partaking in illegal activities (Schwartz & Pharr, 2003: 253–254). Most recently, in the August 2009 Lower House election, page views for both the LDP and DPJ websites plunged in the days and weeks leading up to the election. Interestingly, page views remained high in June and July and picked up again in early September (Alexa.com). Such evidence points directly to the injurious effects of this law on sparking voter interest. If 20 year olds comprise the greatest number of people who use the Internet but cannot go to reliable websites to find information during crucial political periods, how can we expect them to be informed, let alone actually vote?

Such a tight legal framework to regulate the use of NNITs in the election campaign was clearly reflected in Japanese version of the "defeat movement," an idea imported from the successful Korean defeat movement in 2000 General Assembly election. In June, 2000, about two months after the defeat movement in the General Election in April 2000 in Korea demonstrated the unprecedented success of NNIT-oriented civil disobedience by civic organizations, similar groups in Japan adopted a comparable approach with their "*Rakusen* (defeat) *Undou* (movement)" in the Diet election (*Mainichi Shinbun*, June 26, 2000). The access of the homepage of the Joint Civil Organization—Wave 21 (*shimin rentai—ha* 21)[1], which initiated this movement, went over 160,000 within less than two months.

The members of this organization, formed in April 2000 included lawyers and other civil activists. The criteria for selecting which candidates to defeat focused on their involvement in either crime, dishonesty, corruption scandals, violations of the Public Office Election Law, violations of the Political Funds Regulation Control Law, disparaging remarks regarding civil rights, broken promises, and the list goes on. The organization received information by 70 faxed letters and 4,000 email letters, as well as from newspaper databases. The one who selected and collected these data were those who could judge the necessary information objectively. But because the distribution of such documents, including specific names, might have conflicted with the Public Offices Election Law, as of June of 2000, the list was not to be published during the election.

Learning from the Korean success, alliances of civic organizations in Japan hoped for changes of Liberal Democratic Party's half-century dominance and rigid traditions of politics and elections based on personal relationships and a personal support-group, *koenkai*. The outcome was a total failure as only five candidates from the list of *Rakusen Undou* in Osaka were defeated. In other words, most of the politicians in Osaka listed as unfit and corrupt by civic organizations, including Prime Minister Mori and 27 others, survived the first collective action organized with NNITs. This is not just the result of the dominance of traditional political power of the Liberal Democratic Party (LDP) but also the support of a constituency who has supported LDP from the mid-twentieth century via traditional campaign methods. *Yoneko Matuura*, a representative of this defeat movement, said "[t]here were some effects on this election," but "many politicians from the list won this election. In the rural area, as opposed to the city, people who carried a sign or billboard, knowing the risk of scandals, they wanted those politicians to win. This was a traditional way of the election, and I realized the difficulty (wall) of this movement." Regarding the continuation of Prime Minister Mori's cabinet, she said "even though many made the improper remarks of Prime Minister Mori, the number of Government Part's seat in the diet did not decrease. Liberal Democratic Party and Democratic Party did not mention the critical issue in the election, and as a result there were no focal point (the point at issue) in this election."

On the other hand, as the result of *the Rakusen Undou* in Tokyo, six people out of thirty from the list were rejected. While this outcome is similar to that of Osaka, it was heralded as a big success. Zensaku Sakurai said, "We thought it would be good if we could have three or four people rejected. This was an unexpected result." He goes on to say that "the opinion of the citizens has been changed, and Liberal Democratic Party's constitution up to the present and its ideology has been denied. This was probably the biggest success in the election. This was a small movement in the beginning, but this movement has been burst into the threshold of the 21st century politics." Such radically opposite interpretations seems to serve as evidence of how entrenched the traditional Japanese politics is in the Japanese society.

Finally, in the LDP was defeated in the 2009 Diet election, which established Japan's Democratic Party (JDP) as a the majority party with Hatoyama as the Prime Minister. Hatoyama proved to be a revolutionary politician and under his leadership the JDP did enact various reform measures which challenged the LDP monopoly. One of these new policies was to allow both constituents and candidates to expand the use of NNITs such as email and websites for campaigns and voter mobilization. However, such reform measures were faced with stark opposition from both politicians and voters who continued to favor a hierarchical and personally-oriented traditional political culture.

Outside the official campaigning period, the Internet's potential impact as far back as November 2000 showed great promise. At that time, LDP faction leader Kato Koichi tried to unseat his rival, Prime Minister Mori Yoshiro, by gaining popular support online. His attempt ultimately failed, but it was enough to convince LDP leaders that the Internet was a force to be reconed with (Tkach-Kawasaki, 2003: 116–117). By and large, the Internet is not the top news source in Japan, yet without the POEL in place, it is possible it could surpass television's dominance.

In any case, the institutional arrangement around which politics operates has not yet granted the cyber world its proper role. Before the DPJ took the Lower House, the minority parties usually pushed most for change. No longer a minority, the DPJ may reevaluate the law and take action on it, giving citizens newfound hope. The Japanese case clearly serves an example of why pre-existing social capital and the conventional political culture are critical elements in the concept of the new experimentation proposed in this book.

Compared to Japan, the Korean and American case studies examining how NNITs have affected the regimes of President Lee Myung-bak and President Obama also demonstrate the transformational power of the new experimentation in the top domestic political agendas of both countries. On December, 19, 2007, President Lee was elected the seventeenth president of the Republic of Korea by the widest margin in Korea's presidential election history. And as discussed in chapter 3, it took little more than 100 days for Lee's early record-high popularity to plummet to the lowest of all Korean presidents with so few days in office. The cause of this nosedive was more than simply Lee's misguided policies and staffing decisions—it was also the presence of a highly "wired" young generation, which quickly produced anti-Lee discourse that has escalated into massive, continuing street protests by a large cross-section of the population. In light of such an unprecedented phenomenon, it is important to gain insight into the exact mechanisms by which NNITs influence political discourse and contribute to the evolution of a political crisis and find out who are the most critical players in NNIT-induced politics. By applying Situational Crisis Communication Theory, the concepts underlying Heinrich's law, and the four stages of crisis evolution to the first question, and by invoking Giddens' theory of "life politics" in answering the second, we gained insight into how quickly a regular protest can escalate into a political crisis in the Information Age. In this way, the new experimentation may contribute to the fall of military dictatorships or authoritarian regimes; however, by dramatically shortening the cycles of crisis evolution and causing chain reactions of crises, the new experimentation can also pose a serious threat to the foundations of democracy. The predictability of a small accident rapidly evolving into a major crisis is examined through the lens of Situational Crisis Communication Theory, which implies that regimes in power have become more capable of dealing with the evolutionary stages of major crises, while at the same time political manipulation has become even more possible. The ubiquitousness of NNITs helps to establish a seamless matrix of human networks where seemingly negligible political mistakes or policy failures can be identified and escalated, as in the case of Korea's beef crisis.

THE 2007 PRESIDENTIAL ELECTION: A REAL INVERSE OF THE 2002 PRESIDENTIAL ELECTION?

A very recent survey poll by the RealMeter (http://www.realmeter.net/) on May 18–19, 2011 on the popularity of the deceased President Roh Moo-hyun and the current president Lee Myung-bak seems to confirm that following their use of NNITs during the 2002 Presidential election, the younger generation continues to engage in political and demonstrate their connectedness (Eom, 2011). According to RealMeter, which conducted polling on the perceived success of presidents Roh and Lee revealed that 65.5 percent consider Roh to be a successful president while 26.4 percent approved President Lee's job performance as a president. Surprisingly, among 83.4 percent of citizens in their 20s, 77.4 percent in their 30s, 61.3 percent in their 40s, and 49.0 percent in their 50s were among those who considered Roh a successful president. The disapproval rate of President Lee was 59.7 percent, which seems to prove that his largest margin of victory in the 2007 presidential election and his unprecedented popularity in the beginning of his administration before the beef crisis were temporary phenomena and due to other issues such as his constituency's high expectations regarding his ability to address Korea's ailing economy due to his CEO background and the strong return of conservative right-wing political forces that claimed Roh had been too supportive of North Korea. It is for these reasons that those in their 20s and 30s favored Lee Myung-bak during the 2007 presidential campaign, according to the Hyundai Research survey conducted from November 12 to 13, 2007, about a month before the election. In this survey, 60.0 percent of voters from their 20s to their 40s identified themselves as conservatives while 37.6 percent considered themselves liberal progressives (Jeong, 2007). Their online campaign activities were significantly curbed because of the new regulatory legislation on online campaigns, the Public Official Election Act in 2004 as explained in the chapter 3. In addition, the consistent lead by conservative candidate Lee from the early stage of the presidential race also seems to work as a factor that stifled the new experimentation which was successful in the 2002 election.

In this context, it is worth to raise a question whether the 2007 presidential election was a real inverse of the 2002 presidential election? In the 2007 presidential election, Korean voters elected the former Hyun Dai construction company CEO Lee, Myung-bak, the candidate of the opposition Grand National Party (GNP) with the biggest margin of victory in the history of presidential election and the lowest voter turnout since 1987 with 63 percent compared to that of 70.8 percent in 2002 and 80.7 percent in 1997. It was regarded as the return the GNP to power after 10 years of liberal rule during the reigns of President Kim Dae-jung (1998–2003) and President Roh Moo-hyun (2003–2008). This 2007 election was mostly framed from the beginning as a return to conservative power due to alleged failure of President Roh's reform initiatives to shake the foundation of conservative policy, which was represented by his positive engagement stance, his uneasy relationship with the Bush administration, the poor performance of his economic policy, and his uneasy relations with established and politically influential organizations and institutions such as conservative news and media, and the Public Prosecutor's Office. Even ardent NNIT-activated supporters who contributed to the election of President Roh in the 2002 election were defenseless in the wake of Roh's unsuccessful 5 year term. A Korean citizen, Kim Sung-ki's comment on the reason for his vote for President Lee explains the level of frustration on ailing economy: "I've always voted for liberals, but this time the economy became such a huge issue" (Onishi, 2007). It wasn't only Korea but most of countries were suffering from a stagnant economy and voters favored right-wing conservative former CEO candidates, as evidenced in elections such as France's Nicolas Sarkozy against Socialist Party candidate Segolene Royal in 2007.

There are other reasons for Lee's landslide victory. For example, there were no other viable contenders despite voters' skepticism about Lee's past records on ethics as a public official such as tax evasions using his children as proxy, false residential registration for better school districts for his children, and suspicion on his involvement in a stock manipulation case at a company called BBK. Even experts expected that Lee's experience as a successful businessman and pragmatic politician would fix the economic malaise and foreign policy issues with North Korea and the United States, as clearly shown in Gallup Korea analysis based on exit polling in 2007 (Baek, 2008). However, as of summer 2011, with one and half years to finish his one term presidency, this initial anticipation has been unfulfilled as his government seems to be unable to end the stalemate with North Korea and or improve the economy, to say nothing of the many other social and political problems. Dissatisfaction with Lee's administration was clearly reflected in the outcome of April 27, 2011 re-election of the National Assembly and local governments.

Going back to the main question raised in the chapter 1 on the enduring impact of NNIT-activated participation and support for the liberal candidate Roh Moo-hyun by young generations over the next presidential election in

2007, there seems to be an agreement that the 2007 election was "an intriguing inverse" (Lee, 2009: 317) of the 2002 election in that the NNITs were not activated in the election campaign and even young voters favored conservative candidate Lee. However, the former point seems to confuse the main argument on the new experimentation. The use of NNITs by young generations can support both liberal and conservative candidates. In other words, NNIT-activated young generations and their political decision run across the political spectrum of being liberal left-wing to conservative right-wing politics. Even though the 2002 Korean and 2008 American presidential elections proved otherwise, that does not mean that NNIT-led participation of young generations always support one side of the political spectrum over the other. As clearly pointed out in the chapter 1, such phenomena depend upon the characters of each election and candidates. In fact, various statistical information about the outcomes of the 2007 election proves an overall argument on the differences compared to 2002 one. As clearly shown in Table 6.1 below, the most salient feature in the 2007 presidential election as well as in the National Assembly election is that there was overall decrease of voter turnout in all age groups.

With regards to the young generations' voting records, voters in their early 30s recorded the biggest decrease with 13.0 percent while voters in their early 20s showed stronger turnout than those in their late 20s. Due to overall decreases in every age group, the relationship between the use of NNITs and young generations in the election campaign is difficult to decipher. A factor that clearly affected overall use of NNITs in the election can be found in new regulatory legislation, the Public Official Election Act passed on March 12, 2004. This legislation dramatically reduced the levels of NNIT-oriented campaign activities by prohibiting unlawful distribution or posting of documents and pictures containing support for or opposition to a political party or candidate within 180 days before the election day (Hur, 2008). As a direct outcome, election campaigns using NNITs of the new experimentation was discouraged. Also, the young generations favored by a significant margin the GNP candidate Lee over the ruling party candidate Jeong Dong-young.

Table 6.1. **Voting Rates by Age Groups in the Recent Elections**

Elections	19	20–24	25–29	30–34	35–39	40s	50s	Over 60s
17th PE	54.2	51.1	42.9	51.3	58.5	66.3	76.6	76.3
16th PE	—	57.9	55.2	64.3	70.8	76.3	83.7	78.7
17th NE	—	46.0	43.3	53.2	59.8	66.0	74.8	71.5
16th NE	—	39.9	34.2	45.1	56.5	66.8	77.6	75.2

Source: The National Election Commission (PE: Presidential Election, NE: National Assembly Election).

The most recent election on April 27, 2011 for the National Assembly and local governments, however, illustrated the enduring impact of NNIT in election campaigns with the last minute mobilization for voter turnout as well as the anti-President Lee movement. This election was expected to have the highest voting turnouts in the recent re-election history mainly because voters in all age groups were disappointed by the poor performance of the Lee administration's economic approach and other policy failures. The most competitive rivalry in this re-election was between GNP candidate Kang Jae-seop and the opposition party candidate Sohn Hak-kyu in the district of *Boondang Eul*. If Sohn were to be elected, this would have marked President Lee as a lame duck. Overall, the average voting turnouts in the 38 districts in this re-election was 39.4 percent, which is far higher than the average of 6 elections that occurred during the Lee administration and 6.6 percent higher than any re-election occurred since 2000. The highest voting turnout was recorded in the *Boondang Eul* district with 49.1 percent, which was far higher than that of 2008 General Election with 45.2 percent, which was evidence of overly heated judgment-call election against the President Lee and his policy.

What were the decisive factors in the landslide victory for anti-Lee forces? Experts and scholars agree on the following two points: the return of those young voters of the 386 Generation and the 2030 Generation and their use of online social media. The Time-Stamped Exit Poll on Voting Patterns in this election by YTN and the amount of Tweets showed a strong co-relationship between the increases in the use of Twitter and the increases in the votes the opposition candidate Kang secured. There two time periods when voters in their 30s and 40s (mostly the 2030 Generation and the 386 Generation) flocked to the voting both were around 9 am and 8 pm on their way to work place and back to home in the *Boondang Eul* district. For example, the voting rate at 7 SP was 1.8 percent, which is very low. However, as these Twitter-activated salary men went en mase into the voting booth on their way from their work places, the voting rate jumped to 10.7 percent which doubled the 5.4 percent voting rate during the same time period in the 18th General Election. The same effect is demonstrated in the *Boondang Eul* district with the 42.8 percent rate at 7 SP that jumped to 49.1 percent at 8 SP , to the result of the lopsided votes for candidate Kang by the 2030 and 386 Generations on their way back to home (Kang, 2011). Figure 6.1 confirms the lead by candidate Kang when the overall use of tweet messages and retweets recorded sharp increases.

The number of two candidates' Twitter followers provides clear evidence on this co-relationship as clearly illustrated in Figure 6.1. The opposition party candidate Sohn and the ruling party candidate Kang began to use Twitter in August of 2010. However, Kang has maintained far more followers than his rival: 18,000 vs. 3,000. It was also the case for other competitive

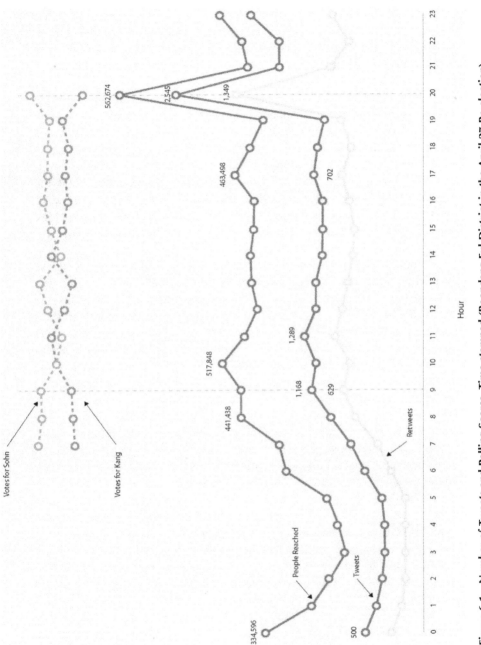

Figure 6.1 Number of Tweets and Polling Scores, Time-stamped (Boondang Eul District in the April 27 Re-election)

district, Kangwon Province where the opposition party candidate Choi Moon-soon won the landslide victory against the ruling party candidate Eom Ki-young. The former maintained 40,000 followers since his use of twitter in June of 2009 while his opponent had about 8,000 followers since his use of Twitter in January of 2011.

In conclusion, the argument that the 2007 presidential election was an inverse of the 2002 presidential election may have a limited relevancy on the reduced levels of online election campaign. However, it is difficult to line that with the decreased level of participation from young generations because of the overall decreases in voting turnouts across the all age groups as well as newly passed Public Official Election Act, which significantly shrank the online election campaign activities. Rather, the election on April 27 of 2011 seems to provide more evidence on the main argument of this book that the use of NNITs by young generations may have an enduring effect upon electoral politics and election campaigns.

The power of the networked public sphere is reinforced by the growing use of micro-content online social networking sites such as Twitter, which was used in the Obama administration's most important political agenda—the legislative battle for health care reform. Spontaneous communication of short messages provides a rare opportunity for social scientists to analyze what kind of contents were actually exchanged on specific political issues, whereas other NNITs, like mobile phones, reveal none of the actual content of the conversations exchanged. Of course, researchers could conduct subsequent interview surveys, but that would raise the possibility of inaccuracy due to interviewee bias. MC-OSN tools, however, reveal the contents and distribution patterns of information and thereby enable researchers to track information flow. These features of microblogging tools provide an unprecedented opportunity to examine the linkage between constituency opinions and Congressional behavior, which has been one of the major questions that political scientists have long hoped to answer. With Natural Language Processing (NLP) techniques, opinion analysts can decipher millions of tweets systematically with a high level of accuracy, examining the actual messages exchanged and measuring their effectiveness in building political pressure among politicians. For example, opinion analysis can categorize all of the tweet messages used in the HCR legislation process into three groups—"for," "against" and "neutral."

The new experimentation has just begun and, by changing the relationship among social actors and institutions, it has dramatically affected the conventional power structure and the way in which people interact and build political community. In order to monitor the impact of this new experimentation on public discourse, electoral politics and democracy, researchers should focus on any changes in the social capital, levels of participation, and generational cohesiveness of the young generations, for it is these youths who are the major players in this new experimentation.

NOTES

1. The URL for this movement was nvc.halsnet.net/jhattori/rakusen. However, this is not available now.

References

Abroms, L. C., and C. Lefebvre. 2009. "Obama's Wired Campaign: Lessons for Public Health Communication." *Journal of Health Communication* 14: 415–23.

Altschuler, G., and R. Spitzer. 2007. "Tactics, Turnout, and Timing in the Elections of 2004." *American Literary History* 19 (1): 108–119.

Anderson, Benedict. 1983. *Imagined Communities*. New York: Verso.

Anderson, Chris. 2004. "The Long Tail." *Wired, October*. www.wired.com/wired/archive/12.10/tail.html.

Backstrom, L., D. Huttenlocher, J. Kleinberg, and X. Lan. 2006. "Group Formation in Large Social Networks: Membership, Growth, and Evolution." Paper presented at the 12th ACM SIGKDD International Conference.

Baek, S. G. 2008. Gallup Korea 2007 "Presidential Election Voter Analysis." *Monthly Chosun*, February.

Baron, S., J. Field, and T. Schuller. 2000. *Social Capital: Critical Perspectives*. Oxford, England: Oxford University Press.

Benkler, Yochai. 2006. *The Wealth of Networks: How Social Production Transforms Markets and Freedom*. New Haven, Connecticut: Yale University Press.

Bimber, B. 2000. "The Study of Information Technology and Civic Engagement." *Political Communication* 17: 329–35.

Boatright, R. G. 2009. *Campaign Finance in the 2008 Election*. New York: Rowman & Littlefield.

Bourdieu, P. 1986. "The Forms of Capital." In *Handbook of Theory and Research for the Sociology of Education*, edited by J. Richardson. New York: Greenwood.

Box-Steffensmeier, J. M., and S. E. Schier. 2009. *The American Elections of 2008*. New York: Rowman & Littlefield.

Boyd, Danah, and Nicole Ellison. 2007. "Social Network Sites: Definition, History, and Scholarship." *Journal of Computer-Mediated Communication* 13 (1): article 11.

Brynjolfsson, Erik, Yu Jeffrey Hu, and Michael D. Smith. 2006. "Consumer Surplus in the Digital Economy: Estimating the Value of Increased Product Variety at Online Booksellers." *Management Science* 49 (11): 1580–1596.

Burchell, Graham. 1993. "Liberal Government and Techniques of the Self." *Economy and Societ* 22 (3): 267–282.

Burchell, Graham, Colin Gordon, and Peter Miller, eds. 1991. *The Foucault Effect*, London: Harvester Wheatsheaf.

Carr, Brendon. "Citizens Reject Charity for Namdaemun Restoration, Demand Government Money." www.korealawblog.com/entry/citizens_reject_charity_for_ namdaemun_restoration_demand_government_money.

Castells, M. 1996. *The Rise of the Network Society*. Malden, Massachusetts: Blackwell.

Castells, Manuel. 1997. *The Power of Identity*. Malden, Massachusetts: Blackwell.

Catone, Josh. 2008. "Another Way to Measure Electoral Clout: Watch the Widgets." *Read Write Web*, May 21. www.readwriteweb.com/archives/widget_politics_ obama_clinton_mccain.php.

Catone, Josh. 2008. "The Birth of the Political Long Tail." *ReadWriteWeb*, February 18. www.readwriteweb.com/archives/the_birth_of_the_political_long_tail.php.

Catone, Josh. 2008. "How the Barack Obama Campaign Uses Wikis to Organize Volunteers." *ReadWriteWeb*, March 4. www.readwriteweb.com/archives/barack_ obama_campaign_central_desktop.php.

Catone, Josh. 2007. "The Web 2.0 Election: Does the Internet Matter in Election Politics?" *ReadWriteWeb*, August 23. www.readwriteweb.com/archives/web_20_ election.php.

Center for Information & Research on Civic Learning & Engagement (CIRCLE). "A Voter Turnout Time Series for 1972–2004, the Hyperlink for Excel Spreadsheet." www.civicyouth.org/?page_id=241.

Center for Information & Research on Civic Learning & Engagement (CIRCLE). "Young Voter Mobilization Tactics." www.civicyouth.org/PopUps/Young_ Voters_Guide.pdf.

Center for Information & Research on Civic Learning & Engagement (CIRCLE). "Young Voters in the 2008 Presidential Election." www.civicyouth.org/quick-facts/youth-voting/.

Center for Information & Research on Civic Learning & Engagement (CIRCLE). "Youth Turnout up Sharply in 2004." www.civicyouth.org/PopUps/Release_ Turnout2004.pdf.

Center for Information & Research on Civic Learning & Engagement (CIRCLE)."Youth Turnout Rate Rises to at Least 52%." www.civicyouth.org/?p=323.

Chang, W. Y. 2006. "Jeongchijeok Kihoikoojowa Sahoiwoondong: Chongseong-yundaewa Nosamoeui Cyberactivism (Structure of Political Opportunities and Social Movement: Cyber Activism of Defeat Movement and No Sa Mo)." *Jeongbohwa Jeongchaek* 13 (3): 49–68.

Choe, Sang-Hun. 2008. "Protests in South Korea Imperil Government." mikemcstay .blogspot.com/2008/06/protests-in-south-korea-imperil.html.

Choo, Kwan-kyu. "Portal Site Daetongryung Tanhaek Seomyung 15man Neomeo (over 150,000 Signatures for the Impeachment of President in a Portal Site)."

Choo, S., and J. Nam. 2001. *Korea Ngo Report, 2001.* Seoul, Korea: Hanyang University Press.

Chosun.com. 2000. "Parties Considering Black List in Picking Candidates."

Chung, Jin-hong. 2002. "The Wellspring of National Pride." *JoongAngIlbo,* July 1.

Chung, S. H. 2002. "Sede Jeongchi: 4.19, 68, Keurigo 386 (Politics of Generation: 4.19, 68, and 386)." In *Yoo Que Han Jeongchi Banran No Sa Mo [Exciting Political Rebellion, No Sa Mo],* edited by H. K. Roh. Seoul, Korea: Gae Ma Ko Won.

Chung, Sungwoo. "South Korea's Top National Treasure Was Burnt Down." *NowPublic,* February 10. www.nowpublic.com/world/south-koreas-top-national-treasure-was-burnt-down.

CNN Sports Illustrated. 2002. "Thrown Out: Skating Union Rejects Protest of South Korean's Dq." *CNN Sports Illustrated,* February 21. sportsillustrated.cnn.com/olympics/2002/speed_skating/news/2002/02/21/south_korea_lawsuit_ap/.

Cleveland, Harlan. 1985. "The Twilight of Hierarchy." In *Information Technologies and Social Transformation* edited by Guile, Bruce. Washington, D.C.: National Academy Press.

Coates, Ta-Nehisi. 2009. "WoW, the Virtual and the Real." *The Atlantic.* June 25. www.theatlantic.com/culture/archive/2009/12/wow-the-virtual-and-the-real/32141/.

Cohen, Roger. 2008. "The Obama Connection." *The New York Times,* May 26. www.nytimes.com/2008/05/26/opinion/26cohen.html?_r=1&hp&oref=slogin.

Coleman, J. S. 1988. "Social Capital in the Creation of Human Capital." *American Journal of Sociology* 94/Supplement: S95-S120.

Coombs, W. Timothy. 2004. "Impact of Past Crises on Current Crisis Communication: Insights from Situational Crisis Communication Theory." *Journal of Business Communication* 41 (3): 265–89.

Coombs, W. Timothy. 1999. *Ongoing Crisis Communication: Planning Managing, and Responding.* Thousand Oaks,: SAGE Publications.

Cornell, C., and S. Cohn. 1995. "Learning from Other People's Action: Environmental Variation and Diffusion in French Coal Mining Strikes, 1980–1953." *American Journal of Sociology* 101: 366–403.

Cover, Albert D., and Bruce C. Brumberg. 1982. "Baby Books and Ballots: The Impact of Congressional Mail on Constituent Opinion." *The American Political Science Review* 76 (2): 347–59.

Crowley, David, and Paul Heyer. 1999. *Communication in History: Technology, Culture, Society (Third Edition).* New York: Addison Wesley Longman.

Cummings, J., B. Butler, and R. Kraut. 2002. "The Quality of Online Social Relationships." *Communications of the ACM* 45.

Czempiel, Ernst-Otto. 1992. "Governance and Democratization." In *Governance Without Government: Order and Change in World Politics,* edited by James N. Rosenau and Ernst-Otto Czempiel. Cambridge: Cambridge University Press.

Dahlgren, P. 2000. "The Internet and the Democratization of Civic Culture." *Political Communication* 17: 335–40.

Dale, Allison, and Aaron Strauss. "Mobilizing the Mobiles: How Text Messaging Can Boost Youth Voter Turnout." www.newvotersproject.org/uploads/vR/2v/vR2vTV3whpkhL5XVBlkBrQ/Youth-Vote-and-Text-Messaging.pdf.

Danitz, T., and W.P. Strobel. 1999. "Networking Dissent: Cyber Activists Use the Internet to Promote Democracy in Burma." In *Networks and Netwars: The Future of Terror, Crime, and Militancy*, edited by J. Arquilla and D. Ronfeldt. Santa Monica, CA: Rand Corporation.

Dator, Jim, and Yongseok Seo. 2004. "Korea as the Wave of a Future: The Emerging Dream Society of Icons and Aesthetic Experience." *Journal of Future Studies* 9 (1): 31–44.

Delli Carpini, M. X. 2000. "Gen.Com: Youth, Civic Engagement, and the New Information Environment." *Political Communication* 17: 341–50.

Diani, Mario. 1997. "Social Movements and Social Capital: A Network Perspective on Movement Outcomes." *Mobilization* 2 (2).

Diani, Mario. 2001. "Social Capital as Social Movement Outcome." In *Beyond Tocqueville: Civil Society and the Social Capital Debate in Comparative Perspective*, edited by Bob Edwards, Michael Foley and Mario Diani. Hanover: University Press of New England.

Dizard, W. P. 1982. *The Coming Information Age*. New York: Longman.

Dutta-Bergman, Mohan J. 2006. "Community Participation and Internet Use after September 11: Complementarity in Channel Consumption." *Journal of Computer-Mediated Communication* 11 (2): 469–84.

Edwards, Bob, Michael W. Foley, and Mario Diani. 2001. *Beyond Tocqueville: Civil Society and the Social Capital Debate in Comparative Perspective*. Medford, Massachusetts: Tufts University Press.

Ehrenberg, J. 1999. *Civil Society: The Critical History of an Idea*. New York: New York University Press.

Ellison, Nicole B., Charles Steinfield, and Cliff Lampe. 2007. "The Benefits of Facebook "Friends": Social Capital and College Students' Use of Online Social Network Sites." *Journal of Computer-Mediated Communication* 12 (4): 1143–68.

Eom, Soo-ah. 2011. "65.5 % Roh was a successful president, MB's popularity 26.4 %." *ViewsandNews*. Accessed on June 11, 2011. www.viewsnnews.com/article/print.jsp?seq=75654.

Erickson, B. H., and T.A. Nosanchuk. 1990. "How an Apolitical Association Politicizes." *Canadian Review of Sociology & Anthropology* 27, (2): 206–219.

Faughnan, Brian. 2008. "Superdelegates: Make It out to Cash." *The Weekly Standard*, March 31, www.weeklystandard.com/weblogs/TWSFP/2008/03/do_superdelegates_respond_to_c.asp.

Ferguson, H. 2001. "Social Work, Individualization and Life Politics." *British Journal of Social Work*, 31: 41–55.

Fink, S. 1986. *Crisis Management: Planning for the Inevitable*. New York: AMACOM.

Fleschner, D. "Apolo Vs. South Korea: How a Short-Track Race Triggered a Long-Distance Rivalry." www.nbcolympics.com/shorttrack/5070418/detail.html.

Flinter, Michael, and Volker Heins. 2002. "Modernity and Life Politics: Conceptualizing the Biodiversity Crisis." *Political Geography* 21: 319–40.

Forester, T. 1985 *The Information Technology Revolution*. Oxford: Blackwell.

Foucault, Michael. 1991. "On Governmentality." In *The Foucault Effect* edited by Graham Burchell, Colin Gordon, and Peter Miller. London: Harvester Wheatsheaf.

Fraser, Matthew, and Soumitra Dutta. 2008. "Obama's Win Means Future Elections Must Be Fought Online." *The Guardian*, November 7. www.guardian.co.uk/technology/2008/nov/07/barackobama-uselections2008.

Freedman, Warren. 1987. *The Right of Privacy in the Computer Age*. New York, Westport, Connecticut: Quorum Books.

Frommer, Dan. 2009. "Celebrities Take over Twitter, Kick Geeks Aside." *Business Insider*, April 17. www.businessinsider.com/celebrities-take-over-twitter-kick-geeks-aside-2009–4.

Fukuyama, Francis. 1999. *The Great Disruption: Human Nature and the Reconstitution of Social Order*. New York: Simon & Schuster.

Fukuyama, Francis. 1995. *Trust: The Social Virtues and the Creation of Prosperity*. New York: Free Press.

Gallup Korea. 1998. *Trial-Heats of the 1997 Presidential Election*. Seoul, Korea: Han Yang Jeong Pan Sa.

Gallup Korea. 2003. *Trial-Heats of the 2002 Presidential Election*. Seoul, Korea: A-Ram Publishing.

Gan, S., J. Gomez, and U. Johannen. 2004. *Asian Cyberactivism: Freedom of Expression & Media Censorship*. Thailand: Friedrich Naumann Foundation.

General Election Citizen Alliance. "General Election Citizen Alliance." www.ngokorea.org/main.htm.

Gerstein, Josh. 2008. "Secret Money Floods Campaigns: Big Count of Small Gifts Is Opaque to the Public." *The New York Sun*, February 12. www.nysun.com/national/secret-money-floods-campaigns/71113/

Giddens, Anthony. 1994. *Beyond Left and Right: The Future of Radical Politics*. Cambridge: Polity Press.

Giddens, Anthony. 1998. *The Third Way: The Renewal of Social Democracy*. Cambridge, UK: Polity Press.

Gonzalez, Justo. 1996. *Church History*. Nashville: Abingdon Press.

Green, Joshua. 2008. "The Amazing Money Machine." *The Atlantic*, June. www.theatlantic.com/doc/200806/obama-finance.

Guile, B. 1985. *Information Technologies and Social Transformation*. Washington D.C.: National Academy of Engineering, National Academy Press.

Habermas, Jurgen. 1992. *The Structural Transformation of the Public Sphere: An Inquiry into a Category of Bourgeois Society*. Cambridge, Massachusetts: The MIT Press.

Halpin, D. P. 2001 "South Korea and Regime Change in North Korea: Be Not Afraid." In *North Korea Human Rights Conference*, edited by John Paul II.

Han, Jongwoo. 2007. "From Indifference to Making a Difference: New Networked Information Technologies (NITs) and Patterns of Political Participation among Korea's Younger Generations." *Journal of Information Technology and Politics* 4 (1): 57–76.

Han, Jongwoo. 2010. "Microblogging and Health Care Reform: Young Generations, Social Capital, Politics and Democracy in the Information Age." Grant proposal submitted to National Science Foundation.

Han, Jongwoo. 2009. "The Obama Presidential Campaign: How a "Long Tail" of American Young Voters Becomes a "Blue Ocean" That Is Transforming American Electoral Politics."

Han, Jongwoo. 1997. "On the Origins of the Developmental State in Korea: Reading the Capital City." Syracuse University.

Han, Jongwoo, and Youngseek Kim. 2009. "Obama Tweeting and Tweeted." Paper presented at the annual meeting of the American Political Science Association, Toronto.

Han, Jongwoo, and L. H. M. Ling. 1998. "Authoritarianism in the Hypermasculinized State: Hybridity, Patriarchy, and Capitalism." *International Studies Quarterly* 42: 53–78.

Han, Marie-France, and So-eui Rhee. 2008. "Korea Protests a Proving Ground for Gadgets, Geeks." *Reuters*, June 12. www.reuters.com/article/technologyNews/idUSN0534545220080612.

Han, Xiaoqiang. 2010. "A Butterfly Dream in a Brian in a Vat." *Philosophia* 38 (1): 157–167.

Harden, Blaine. 2008. "S. Korea President Backs Away from Beef Deal with U.S." *The Washington Post*, June 4. www.washingtonpost.com/wp-dyn/content/article/2008/06/03/AR2008060301714_pf.html.

Harrison, Janelle L. 2009. "A Virtual Society." *Rocky Mountain Communication Review* 6 (1): 5–7.

Harvard Institute of Politics. 2005. *Harvard Institute of Politics' Survey of Student Attitudes: The Global Generation*. Cambridge, MA: Harvard University Press.

Heinrich, H. W. 1980. *Industrial Accident Prevention: A Safety Management Approach*. McGraw-Hill.

Heinrich, Herbert William. 1941. *Industrial Accident Prevention: A Scientific Research*. New York: McGraw-Hill Book Company.

Korea Herald, 2000. "Civic Groups, Political Circle Set to Clash over Rejection Drive." January 13.

Korea Herald. 2002. "Police Chief Thanks Devils." July.

Hiltz, Starr R., and Murray Turoff. 1978. *The Network Nation: Human Communication Via Computer*. Reading, Massachusetts: Addison-Wesley.

Hindess, Barry. 1997. "Politics and Governmentality," *Economy and Society* 26 (2): May.

Hirst, Paul & Thompson, Grahame. 1996. *Globalization in Question*. Malden, MA: Blackwell.

Huh, I. H. 2003. *Role of the Internet in the R.O.K. Presidential Election in 2002.* Honolulu, Hawaii: Asia-Pacific Center for Security Studies.

Hur, A. 2008. "The 2007 Korean Presidential Election and Internet Censorship," Berkman Center for Internet & Society at Harvard University Blog, January 16. Accessed on June 14, 2011. blogs.law.harvard.edu/idblog/2008/01/16/the-2007-korean-presidential-elections-and-internet-censorship/.

Huysman, M., and Volker Wulf. 2004. *Social Capital and Information Technology.* Cambridge, Massachusetts: The MIT Press.

International Telecommunication Union (ITU). 2009. "Information Society Statistical Profiles, 2009: Asia and the Pacific."

International Telecommunication Union (ITU). 2009. "Information Society Statistical Profiles, 2009: Asia and the Pacific."

International Telecommunication Union (ITU). "World Telecommunication/ICT Development Report, 2010: Monitoring the World Summit on Information Society Targets (a Mid-Term Review). The 9th Edition.," 2010.

International Telecommunication Union (ITU). "World Telecommunication/ICT Indicators Database Online." 2009.

Itzigsohn, Jose. 2000. "Immigration and the Boundaries of Citizenship: The Institutions of Immigrants' Political Transnationalism." *International Migration Review,* 34 (4): 1126–1154.

Jameson, Fredric. and Masao Miyoshi. 1998. *The Cultures of Globalization,* Durham: Duke University Press.

Java, A., X. Song, T. Finin, and B. Tseng. 2007. "Why We Twitter: Understanding Microblogging Usage and Communities." Paper presented at the The 9th WebKDD and 1st SNA-KDD 2007 workshop on Web Mining and Social Network Analysis, San Jose, California.

Jeong, Y. J. 2007. "Lee Myung-bak 36.2% Lee Hoi-chang 14.9 % Jeong Dong-young 13 %," *Weekly Kyunghyang,* November 25. Accessed on June 14, 2011. weekly. khan.co.kr/khnm.html?mode=view&artid=16109&code=113.

Jin, S. H. 2002. "New Generation Powers Rho to Victory." *The Chosun Ilbo,* December 20.

Jones, Sydney, and Susannah Fox. 2009. "Generations Online in 2009." Pew Internet and American Life Project. pewresearch.org/pubs/1093/generations-online.

JoongAng Ilbo. 2000. "Civil Organization Releases Political Blacklist." January 10.

Jordan, Tim. 1999. *Cyberpower: The Culture and Politics of Cyberspace and the Internet.* New York: Routledge.

Kang, BH. 2011. "Mooseowun toikeuntoopyo (Fearful Votes on the Way Back Home)." *Kyunghyang Shinmoon.* Accessed on June 01, 2011. news.khan.co.kr/kh_news/khan_art_view.html?artid=201104272305145&code=910110.

Kang, Young-jin. 2008. "Lee Myung-Bak Jeongbooneun Rubicon Gang Geonneotda (Lee Administration Crossed the Rubicon)." *Pressian,* June 25, www.pressian.com/Scripts/section/article.asp?article_num=60080625204417.

Katz, J. E., and R. E. Rice. 2002. *Social Consequences of Internet Use.* Cambridge, MA: The MIT Press.

Kavanaugh, A. L., and S. J. Patterson. 2002. "The Internet in Everyday Life." In *The Impact of Community Computer Networks on Social Capital and Community Involvement in Blacksburg*, edited by B. Wellman and C. Haythornthwaite, Malden, MA: Blackwell.

Keeter, Scott, Juliana Horowitz, and Alec Tyson. 2008. "Young Voters in the 2008 Election." Pew Research Center for People and the Press, November 12. pewresearch.org/pubs/1031/young-voters-in-the-2008-election.

Kelly, J. A. 2004. "Bush Administration's East Asia Policy Successful." Paper presented at the Woodrow Wilson Center Confreence on George W. Bush and Asia, November 9.

Kim, H. J. 2003. "2002 Nyun Daeseon Pyungawa Chaki Haengjeongbooeui Kwaje [Evaluation of 2002 Presidential Election and the Task for a New Government]." Annual Conference of The Korean Political Science Association: National Assembly.

Kim, Hyun-chul. 2002. "R-generation Born of Soccer." *JoongAngIlbo*, July 1.

Kim, K. T. 2002. "Roh's Young Army Used Internet to Win." *The Korea Times*, December 2.

Kim, S. K. 2003. "Initiator Is the Reporter at Ohmynews." *Donga.com*, January 8.

Kim, T. H. 1997. "The 15th Presidential Election Process, the Result Analysis, and the Presidential Agenda for the Nation." *Sa-Hoi-Kwa-Hak Yeon-Goo*, 7.

Kim, W. Chan, and Renee Mauborgne. 2005. *Blue Ocean Strategy: How to Create Unconstested Market Space and Make Competition Irrelevant*. Boston: Harvard Business Review.

King, Alexander and Schneider, Bertrand. 1991. *The First Global Revolution: A Report by the Council of the Club of Rome*. New York: Pantheon Books.

King, Cheryl Simrell. 1998. "Images of Citizenship: Citizen/Government Connections." Paper presented at the 1998 Annual Meeting of the American Political Science Association, Boston, September 3–6.

Kirby, E. H., K. B. Marcelo, and J. Gillerman. 2008. *The Youth Vote in the 2008 Primaries and Caucuses*. The Center for Information & Research on Civic Learning & Engagement.

Kleinberg, Jon. 2008. "The Convergence of Social and Technological Networks." *Communications of the ACM* 51 (11): 66–72.

Kline, D., and D. Burstein. 2005. *Blog!: How the Newest Media Revolution Is Changing Politics, Business, and Culture*. New York: CDS Books.

Kluver, R. 2007. *The Internet and National Elections: A Comparative Study of Web Campaigning*. New York: Routledge.

Koehler, Robert. 2008 "National Treasure No. 1 Burns." February 10. www.rjkoehler .com/2008/02/10/national-treasure-no-1-burns/.

Kohut, Andrew and Lee Rainie. 2000. "Internet Election News Audience Seeks Convenience, Familiar Names." Pew Internet and American Life Project, December 3. www.pewinternet.org/Reports/2000/Internet-Election-News-Audience-Seeks-Convenience-Familiar-Names/Report.aspx.

Koo, Heejin. "Fire Destroys Sungnyemun, South Korea's Top Treasure (Update1)." *Bloomberg*, February 10. www.bloomberg.com/apps/news?pid=20601088&sid=a OvFgPKEKMps&refer=muse

Korea Herald, The. "Police Chief Thanks Devils . . .," July 2 2002.

Korea Research Center. 2003. *The Review of the 16th Presidential by Polls.* Seoul, Korea: Korea Research Center.

Kraut, R, and S Kiesler. 2003. "The Social Impact of Internet Use." *Psychological Science Agenda* 16 (2): 8–10.

Kraut, R., S. Kiesler, B. Boneva, J. Cummings, V. Hlegeson, and A. Crawford. 2001 "Internet Paradox Revisited." *Journal of Social Issues* 58 (1): 49–74.

Kuklinski, JH. 1979. "Representative-Constituency Linkages: A Review Article." *Legislative Studies Quarterly* 4 (1): 121–40.

Kushin, Matthew J. 2009. "How Young Adults and Social Media Are Challenging Traditional Perspectives of Civic Life." *Rocky Mountain Communication Review* 6 (1): 26–31.

Kwak, Young-sup. 2002. "Record Number of Cheering Fans Turn Korea Red," *The Korea Herald*, July 2.

Kwon, H. S., and J. Y. Lee. 2004 "NGO's Political Reform Movement Process Via Internet: Focusing on 'Election Defeat Movement' in Korea." *International Review of Public Administration* 8 (2).

Larson, James F. 2008. "Where's the Beef? Information Age Politics in Korea." May 29. koreainformationsociety.blogspot.com/2008/05/wheres-beef-information-age-politics-in.html.

Lasky, Ed. 2008. "Barack Obama's Goldmine." May 5. www.americanthinker .com/2008/05/barack_obamas_goldmine_1.html.

Lebkowsky, Jon. 2005. "Extreme Democracy, Blog-Style." In *Blog!: How the Newest Media Revolution Is Changing Politics, Business, and Culture*, edited by David Kline and Dan Burstein. New York: CDS Books.

Lee, B. J. 2006. "South Korea, Too Much Activism?: The Country's Idealistic '386 Generation' Helped Usher in Democracy, but Has Bungled Its Political Opportunity." *Newsweek International*, November 27.

Lee, K. Y., and Y. J. Moon. 1996. "Minjoohwa Wa Jeongdangchegye Mit Topyo Haengtaeeui Byunhwa [Democratization, Party System, and the Changes in Voting Behavior]." Seoul, Korea: Monograph submitted to Korea Legislative Studies Institute.

Lee, Min-a. 2008. "By-Elections Expected to Be Message to President." *Joongang Ilbo Daily*, June 5.

Lee, Sook-Jong. 2006. "The Assertive Nationalism of South Korean Youth: Cultural Dynamism and Political Activism." *SAIS Review* 26, (2): 123–132.

Lee, T. H., and H. J. Choi. 2002. "IT Generation's Young Politics Won."

Lee, Y.O. 2009, "Internet Election 2.0? Culture, Institutions, and Technology in the Korean Presidential Elections of 2002 and 2007." *Journal of Informaiton Technology and Politics.* 6: 312–325.

Lenhart, Amanda. 2009. "Adults and Social Network Websites." *Pew Internet and American Life Project*, January 14. www.pewinternet.org/Reports/2009/Adults-and-Social-Network-Websites.aspx.

Lenhart, Amanda, and Susannah Fox. 2009. "Twitter and Status Updating." *Pew Internet and American Life Project*, February 12. www.pewinternet.org/Reports/2009/Twitter-and-status-updating.aspx.

Lerman, K, and R Ghosh. 2010. "Information Contagion: An Empirical Study of the Spread of News on Digg and Twitter Social Networks." Paper presented at the Fourth International AAAI Conference on Weblogs and Social Media (, Washington DC, May 23–26.

Leskovec, J, M McGlohon, C Faloutsos, N Glance, and M Hurst. 2007. "Cascading Behavior in Large Blog Graphs: Patterns and a Model." Paper presented at the Society of Applied and Industrial Mathematics, Data Mining.

Lessig, Lawrence. 1999. *Code and Other Laws of Cyberspace*. New York: Basic Books.

Lister, Ruth. 1995. "Dilemmas in Engendering Citizenship," *Economy and Society*. 24, (1): 1–40.

Li, X., Q. Xuan, and R. Kluver. 2003. "Who Is Setting the Chinese Agenda? The Impact of Online Chatrooms on Party Presses in China." In *Asia.Com: Asia Encounters the Internet*, edited by K.C. Ho, R. Kluver and K. Yang. London: RoutledgeCurzon.

Lim, Jang-kyk. 2008. "GNP Is Seeking Damage Control after Sharp Loss." *Joongang Daily*, June 6.

Lipset, S. M. 1996. *American Exceptionalism: A Double Edged Sword*. New York: W.W. Norton & Company.

Lopez, M. H., and E. Kirby. 2005. *Electoral Engagement among Minority Youth*: The Center for Information & Research on Civic Learning & Engagement (CIRCLE). www.civicyouth.org.

Lopez, Mark Hugo, Emily Kirby, Jared Sagoff, and Chris Herbst. 2005. "The Youth Vote 2004: With a Historical Look at Youth Voting Patterns, 1972–2004." The Pew Charitable Trusts, July 1. www.pewtrusts.org/our_work_report_detail.aspx?id=24184.

Ludden, M. 2004. "Poll: College Students Moving toward Kerry." *CNN*, October 21. www.cnn.com/2004/ALLPOLITICS/10/21/college.poll/.

Luo, Michael. 2008. "Small Online Contributions Add up to Huge Fund-Raising Edge for Obama." *The New York Times*, February 20. www.nytimes.com/2008/02/20/us/politics/20obama.html.

Lusoli, W. 2005. "A Second-Order Medium? The Internet as a Source of Electoral Information in 25 European Countries." *Information Polity* 10 (3): 247–265.

MacKinnon, R. 2005. "Making Global Voice Heard." In *Blog!: How the Newest Media Revolution Is Changing Politics, Business, and Culture*, edited by D. Kline and D. Burstein. New York: CDS Books.

Marcelo, Karlo Barrios, and Emily Hoban Kirby. 2008. "Quick Facts About U.S. Young Voters: The Presidential Election Year 2008." The Center for Information and Research on Civic Learning and Engagement, October. www.civicyouth.org/PopUps/FS_08_quick_facts_national.pdf.

Marx, Karl. 1977. *A Contribution to the Critique of Political Economy*. Moscow: Progress Publishers.

Melber, Ari. 2009. "Obama for America 2.0?" *The Nation*, January 12. www .thenation.com/article/obama-america-20.

Melber, Ari. 2008. "Obama's Race Speech on Youtube Tops Cable News Ratings." *The Nation*, March 26. www.alternet.org/blogs/election08/80568/obama%27s_ race_speech_on_youtube_tops_cable_news_ratings/.

Miller, W., and D. Stokes. 1963. "Constituency Influence in Congress." *The American Political Science Review* 57 (1): 45–56.

Min, B. O. 2004. "Electoral Change and Voting Behavior of Independent Voters in South Korea, 1992–2002: Are Independent Voters Rational in Voting Choice?" University of Glasgow.

Min, S. 2007. "Online Vs. Face-to-Face Deliberation: Effects on Civic Engagement." *Journal of Computer-Mediated Communication* 12 (4): article 11.

Ministry of Information and Communications. 2005. "White Paper 2004: Dynamic Digital Korea." Seoul, Korea.

Minkoff, D. C. 1997. "The Sequencing of Social Movements." *American Sociological Review* 62: 779–99.

Minkoff, Debra C. 2001. "Producing Social Capital: National Social Movements and Civil Society." In *Beyond Tocqueville: Civil Society and the Social Capital Debate in Comparative Perspective*, edited by Bob Edwards, Michael W. Foley and Mario Diani. Medford, Massachusetts: Tufts University Press.

Mitroff, I. I. 1994. "Crisis Management and Environmentalism: A Natural Fit." *California Management Review* 36 (2): 101–13.

Mouzelis, Nicos. 2001. "Reflexive Modernization and the Third Way: The Impasses of Giddens' Social-Democratic Politics." *The Sociological Review* 49 (3): 436–56.

Naff, Katherine C. and Crum, John. 1998. "Reinventing Government: The Reaction of the Federal Community," paper delivered at the 1998 Annual Meeting of the American Political Science Association, Boston, September 3–6, 1998.

National Computerization Agency. "National Internet White Paper." Seoul, Korea: National Computerization Agency, 2002.

National Information Society Agency (NIA). 2008. "Internet Iyong Mit Kiban (Internet Use and Infrastructure) Kookka Jeongbohwa Baekseo (National Informatization Whitepaper 2007)."

National Internet Development Agency of Korea (NIDA). 2004. *Korea Internet Statistics Yearbook*. Seoul, Korea: NIDA.

Ohmae, K. 1990. *The Borderless World*. New York: Collins.

Ong, Aihwa. 1999. *Flexible Citizenship: The Cultural Logics of Transnationality*. Durham: Duke University Press.

Onish, N. 2007. "Conservative Wins Vote in South Korea." *The New York Times*, December 20. www.nytimes.com/2007/12/20/world/asia/20korea.html.

Osborne, David and Ted Gaebler. 1992. *Reinventing Government*. MA: Addison-Wesley Publishing Company.

Nippo, S. "Korea in Crisis: The Rise of the 386 Generation." wpherald.com/articles/38/1/Korea-in-Crisis-The-rise-of-the-386generation/Activists-born-out-of-the-1980-democracy-movement.html.

Oo, Z. 2004. "Mobilising Online: The Burmese Diaspora's Cyber Strategy against the Junta." In *Asian Cyberactivism: Freedom of Expression and Media Censorship*, edited by S. Gan, J. Gomez and U. Johannen. Bangkok, Thailand: Friedrich Naumann Foundation.

Center for Responsive Politics. "Presidential Fundraising and Spending, 1976–2008." / www.opensecrets.org/pres08/totals.php?cycle=2008. .

Owen, D. 2009. "The Campaign and the Media." In *The American Elections of 2008*, edited by J. M. Box-Steffensmeier and S. E. Schier. New York: Rowman & Littlefield.

Pace, M. 2008. "Voters Flocked to Barackobama.Com Last Week as the Election Neared." *Compete.com* (Candidate Sites Traffic Comparison).

Patton, A. E., and O. Gressens. 1926. "A Study of Utility Financial Structures: Current Position." *The Journal of Land & Public Utility Economics* 2 (3): 309–26.

PBS. "Web Tools Help to Reshape '08 Campaign Trail. PBS News Interview by Judy Woodruff." www.pbs.org/newshour/bb/politics/janjune08/wiredpolitics_06–16.html.

The Pew Research Center. 2007. "A Portrait of 'Generation Next': How Young People View Their Lives, Futures and Politics." Pew Research Center for the People and the Press, January 9.

Pierre, Jon, ed. 2000. *Debating Governance*. Oxford: Oxford University Press.

Prell, C. 2003. "Community Networking and Social Capital: Early Investigations." *Journal of Computer-Mediated Communication* 8 (3).

Putnam, Robert D. 1995. "Bowling Alone: America's Declining Social Capital." *Journal of Democracy* 6 (1): 65–78.

Putnam, Robert D. 2000. *Bowling Alone*. New York: Simon & Schuster.

Putnam, Robert D. 2008. "The Rebirth of American Civic Life." *The Boston Globe*, March 2. www.boston.com/bostonglobe/editorial_opinion/oped/articles/2008/03/02/the_rebirth_of_american_civic_life/.

Putnam, Robert D., Lewis Feldstein, and Donald J. Cohen. 2003. *Better Together*. New York: Simon & Schuster.

Putnam, Robert. 1993. *Making Democracy Work*. Princeton: Princeton University Press.

Quan-Haase, A., B. Wellman, J. C. Witte, and K. N. Hampton. 2002. "Capitalizing on the Net: Social Contact, Civic Engagement, and Sense of Community." In *The Internet in Everyday Life*, edited by B. Wellman and C. Haythornthwaite. Malden, MA: Blackwell.

Rainie, L., M. Cornfield, and J. Horrigan. 2005. *The Internet and Campaign 2004*. Washington, DC: The Pew Research Center.

Raphals, Lisa. 2009. "Skeptical Strategies in the 'Zhuangzi' and 'Theaetetus.'" *Philosophy East and West* 44 (3): 501–26.

RapLeaf. "Rapleaf Study Reveals Gender and Age Data of Social Network Users." www.rapleaf.com/business/press_release/age.

Reuters. 2006. "For South Korea, Speedskating Revenge Is Sweet: Ohno's Stumble Leads to Gold for Ahn, Avenges Bitter 2002 Loss." *Reuters*, February 14.

Robbins, Sarah Intellagirl. 2009. "Defining Virtual Worlds: Using a Definition as a Platform for Communications Research." *Rocky Mountain Communication Review* 6 (1): 8–13.

Roh, H. K. 2002. *Yoo Que Han Jeongchi Banran No Sa Mo [Exciting Political Rebellion, No Sa Mo]*. Seoul, Korea: Gae Ma Ko Won.

Romero, DM, and J Kleinberg. 2010. "The Directed Closure Process in Hybrid Social-Information Networks, with an Analysis of Link Formation on Twitter." Paper presented at the The Fourth International AAAI Conference on Weblogs and Social Media (ICWSM 2010), Washington DC, May 23–26.

Rose, Nikolas. 1993. "Government, Authority and Expertise in Advanced Liberalism." *Economy and Society*. 22 (3): 283–299.

Rosell, Steven A. 1999. *Renewing Governance: Governing by Learning in the Information Age*. New York: Oxford University Press.

Rosenau, James N. and Czempiel, Ernst-Otto, eds. 1992. *Governance Without Government: Order and Change in World Politics*, Cambridge: Cambridge University Press.

Rove, Karl. 2008. "How the President-Elect Did It: The New Voters Changed the Game," *The Wall Street Journal*, November 6. online.wsj.com/article/SB122593304225103509.html.

Ruffini, P. 2008. "The Straight-Ticket Youth Vote." *The Next Right*, November 6. Accessed on November 7, 2008. www.thenextright.com/patrick-ruffini/the-straight-ticket-youth-vote.

Saxby, Stephen. 1990. *The Age of Information: The Past Development and Future Significance of Computing and Communications*. New York: New York University Press.

Scott, J. 1988. "Social Network Analysis." *Sociology* 22 (1): 109.

Self, Peter. 1993. *Government by the Market?* Boulder: Westview Press.

Self, Peter, 2000. Rolling Back the Market, New York: St. Martin's Press.

Sen, Amartya. "Democracy as a Universal Value." *Journal of Democracy* 10, no. 3 (1999): 3–17.

Seong, K. H., A.M Lee, and P.M. Roh. 2003. "No Title." *Weekly Donga*, January 2.

Shah, D. V., N. Kwak, and R. L. Holbert. 2001"'Connecting' and 'Disconnecting' with Civic Life: Patterns of Internet Use and the Production of Social Capital." *Political Communication* 18 (2): 141–62.

Shapiro, A. 1999. *The Control Revolution: How the Internet Is Putting Individuals in Charge and Changing the World We Know*. New York: Century Foundation.

Shklovski, I., R. Kraut, and Lee Rainie. 2004. "The Internet and Social Participation: Contrasting Cross-Sectional and Longitudinal Analyses." *Journal of Computer-Mediated Communication* 10 (1).

Sklair, L. 1991. *The Sociology of the Global System*. Baltimore, Maryland: The Johns Hopkins University Press.

Smith, Aaron, and Lee Rainie. 2008. "The Internet and the 2008 Election." *The Pew Internet and American Life Project*, June 15. www.pewinternet.org/Reports/2008/The-Internet-and-the-2008-Election.aspx.

Smith, J. 2001. "Global Civil Society: Transnational Social Movement Organizations and Social Capital." In *Beyond Tocqueville: Civil Society and the Social Capital Debate in Comparative Perspective*, edited by B. Edwards, M. W. Foley and M. Diani. Medford, Massachusetts: Tufts University Press.

Song, H. K. 2005. "Icheoninyun Sedeeui Tansaeng [the Birth of "2002 Generation"]." In *Hankook, Mooseun Ili Ileonagoitna: Sede, Keu Kaldeungkwa Jhwaeui Mihak*. Seoul, Korea: Sam Sung Institute of Economy.

Song, H. S. 2003. "King-Maker No Sa Mo Eodiro [Where Is King-Maker No Sa Mo Going?]." *Weekly Donga*, January 2.

Song, Sang-ho. 2008. "College Students Gather for Beef Protests." *The Korea Herald*, June 5.

Sutton, S. 2006. "The 'My' in Ohmynews: A Uses and Gratifications Investigation into the Motivations of Citizen Journalists in South Korea." University of Leeds, United Kingdom.

Steinhaur, J. 2008. "G.O.P. Drops in Voting Rolls in Many States." *The New York Times*, August 5. www.nytimes.com/2008/08/05/us/politics/05flip.html.

Tapscott, Don. 1996. *The Digital Economy*. New York: McGraw-Hill.

Tarrow, S. 1994. *Power in Movement: Social Movements, Collective Action and Politics*. New York: Cambridge University Press.

The Special Internet Campaign Headquarters of New Millennium Democratic Party (SICH-NMDP). 2003. *Rho Moo-Hyun and Internet Election*. Seoul, Korea: SICH-NMDP.

Trippi, Joe. 2004. *The Revolution Will Not Be Televised: Democracy, the Internet, and the Overthrow of Everything*. New York: ReganBooks.

Turoff, Murray. 1997. "Virtuality." *Communications of the ACM* 40 (9): 38–43.

Vaidyanathan, R. 2008. Top hits of the YouTube election, *BBC News*, October 30. Accessed on November 11, 2008.

news.bbc.co.uk/2/hi/americas/us_elections_2008/7699509.stm.

Viner, Jacob. 1929. "Mills' Behavior of Prices." *The Quarterly Journal of Economics* 43 (2): 337–52.

Waters, Johanna L. 2003 . "Flexible citizens? Transnationalism and Citizenship Amongst Aconomic Immigrants in Vancouver." *The Canadian Geographer* 47 (3): 219–234.

Watts, J. "World's First Internet President Logs On: Web Already Shaping Policy of New South Korean Leader." *The Guardian*, February 24. www.guardian.co.uk/print/0,,4611774–104490,00.html.

Watt, S. E., M. Lea, and R. Spears. 2002. "How Social Is Internet Communication?: A Reappraisal of Bandwidth and Anonymity Effects." In *Virtual Society?: Technology, Cyberbole, Reality*, edited by S. Woolgar. New York: Oxford University Press.

Webster, F. 1995. *Theories of the Information Society*. New York: Routledge.

Wellman, B., and C. Haythornthwaite. 2002. "The Internet in Everyday Life." *In The Internet in Everyday Life*, edited by B. Wellman and C. Haythornthwaite. Malden MA: Blackwell.

Westling, Mike. 2007. "Expanding the Public Sphere: The Impact of Facebook on Political Communication." University of Wisconsin-Madison.

Wetherell, C, Plakans, A., and Wellman, B. 1994. "Social Networks, Kinship, and Community in Eastern Europe. *Journal of Interdisciplinary History* 24 (4): 639–663.

Whitney, D. 2008. "CNN, MSNBC Web Sites Most Popular on Election Day." *TV Week, November 5*. Accessed on November 11, 2008. www.tvweek.com/news/2008/11/cnn_msnbc_web_sites_most_popul.php.

Whitaker, R. 1999. *The End of Privacy: How Total Surveillance Is Becoming a Reality*. New York: The New Press.

Williams, C. B., and G. J. Gulati. 2008. "What Is a Social Network Worth?: Facebook and Vote in the 2008 Presidential Primaries." In *2008 Annual Meeting of the American Political Science Association*. Boston, MA.

Williams, Dmitri. 2006. "On and Off the Net: Scales for Social Capital in an Online Era." *Journal of Comuter-Mediated Communication* 11 (2): 593–628.

Wohl, R. 1979. *The Generation of 1914*. Cambridge, MA: Harvard University Press.

Wolfson, A. 2006. "Red and Blue Nation? Causes, Consequences, and Correction of America's Polarized Politics." The Brookings Institution Issues in Government Studies, May. www.brookings.edu/views/papers/wolfson20060531.pdf.

Woolgar, S. 2002. *Virtual Society?: Technology, Cyberbole, Reality*. New York: Oxford University Press.

World Bank. 1994. *Governance: The World Bank's Experience*. Washington, D.C.: World Bank.

Yang, S. J. 2002. "Korea Drives World Cup Fever with Internet." *The Korea Herald*, July 1.

Yoo, C. M. 2002. "Red Devils' Cheerers Fascinate Globe with Soccer Zeal." *The Korea Herald*, July 2.

Yoo, Shi-min. 2010. *Woonmyungida (It's a Destiny: A Biography of President Roh Moo-Hyun Edited by Yoo, Shi-Min)*. Seoul: Dolbaege.

Yoon, Sung-yi. 2007. "Internet Seonkeowoondongeui Hyokwa (Effect of Internet Election Campaign)." In *Annual meetings of Election Studies Association, 2007*.

Zhao, Dejin, and Mary Beth Rosson. 2009. "How and Why People Twitter: The Role That Micro-Blogging Plays in Informal Communication at Work." Presented at Conference on Supporting Group Work, Sanibel Island, Florida.

Zhao, Shanyang. 2006. "Do Internet Users Have More Social Ties? A Call for Differentiated Analyses of Internet Use." *Journal of Computer-Mediated Communication* 11 (3): 844–62.

Zukin, C., S. Keeter, M. Andolina, K. Jenkins, and M. X. Delli Carpini. 2006. *A New Engagement? Political Participation, Civic Life and the Changing American Citizen*. London: Oxford University Press.

Index

An italic page number indicates a figure.

About the Author

Jongwoo Han (Ph.D., Syracuse University) is a faculty member in the Department of Political Science and Senior Associate at the Center for Information Technology and Policy of Syracuse University's Maxwell School of Citizenship and Public Affairs. His major research and teaching areas include information technology and politics, democratic governance in the information age, cyber-activism and democracy, Korean political economy and informatization, and U.S.-North Korean relations.

Since 2002, Dr. Han has led a historic research collaboration between North Korea's Kim Chaek University of Technology (KCUT) and Syracuse University in the general area of standards-based integrated information technology, which has produced the first digital library in North Korea. In addition, he is currently working on the Korean War Veteran Digital Memorial project funded by the Korean government to build a permanent digital clearing house for veterans' artifacts and their interviews.

Born in Seoul, Korea, Dr. Han graduated Yonsei University. He has published various academic articles on NNITs and politics, hosted a weekly talk radio program on the U.S. presidential election and politics, *New York Radio Korea* (call name: WWUR, 1660AM), and has regularly written columns for many newspapers in Korea. Dr. Han also serves as principal of the Central New York Korean School (www.cny.ks.org) in Syracuse.